Fun and Games

MARGARET E. MULAC

FUN AND

GAMES

Illustrated by JULIANNE

COLLIER BOOKS, New York, N.Y.

Collier–Macmillan Ltd., London

This Collier Books edition is published by arrangement with Harper & Row, Publishers.

Published simultaneously by Collier-Macmillan Limited, London

Collier Books is a division of The Crowell-Collier Publishing Company

First Collier Books Edition 1963

Affectionately dedicated to my favorite nieces and nephews: To Jeanie who will, I hope, find this book useful in her teaching career; to Paul James, Mike, Peter and Johnny who may find fun here for themselves and their friends; to Julie who grew up in time to employ her talents and skills in illustrating this book

and to

Marian S. Holmes

Friend, business partner and party leader par excellence

Contents

Acknowledgments

Contributions of games, tricks, stunts and puzzles came from many sources. Enthusiastic party committee members, recreation leaders, teachers and party guests who were willing guinea pigs have all been generous with their suggestions and ideas. Teachers have used their classrooms as testing and proving grounds. This book then is the product of many minds. To all who have made contributions, the author is deeply grateful.

Special recognition belongs to Julianne Gross, my niece and illustrator, Harriet Smith Harris, who did all the music and accompaniments, Robert T. Howell, Marian S. Holmes, Jeanne K. Mulac and Viola Stevens.

Introduction

Joy is a very necessary part of the good life. The framers of the Declaration of Independence understood the importance of happiness and declared "the pursuit of happiness" to be one of the inalienable rights along with life and liberty. Never is its importance more acutely felt than when it is conspicuous in its absence. There can be laughter despite poverty; there can be gaiety in illness, joy and courage in the face of hardships. Fun makes the poor richer; pain becomes more bearable and hardships a challenge rather than insurmountable obstacles.

No family need ever apologize for allotting a portion of its income for the fun aspects of living. And when a church, school board or municipality sets aside funds for recreation, it acts with understanding and wisdom.

Whether we call it fun, recreation or leisure-time pursuits, it is all one. Whether it takes the form of sports, arts and crafts, music, dancing or study groups—it is a necessary ingredient of the full and rich life.

With leisure becoming an increasingly larger part of our days and our lives, it becomes correspondingly important whether we employ this time wisely or spend it extravagantly. Any project in which we actively participate makes demands on mind and body. The compensation for this expenditure is the feeling of joy of accomplishment, release from tension and the satisfaction of the creative urge. We cannot expect to experience the same satisfaction from watching someone else play a game or by listening to someone else sing that we would if we were doing these things ourselves. Being a spectator has its place and merits but not as a full-time leisure-time pursuit. Watch someone else eat and see how much that appeases *your* hunger. It is the pouring out of yourself that fills your life with happiness.

Let none ridicule or make snide remarks about the fun activities of another. What may seem childish to one may be a source of challenge, release and satisfaction to another. A group engaged in a hilarious round of charades may appear ridiculous to another group which prefers to spend its energies screaming hysterically at a player who has just completed a ground-gaining pass or batted out a clutch single. If the activity is wholesome and fun-giving, the participating individuals are benefited. The means thus justifies the end.

So—whether we find our fun writing a poem for publication, cogitating over a chessboard or standing thigh-deep in cold water in pursuit of a cautious trout, the good feeling it gives us is important to our well-being.

In recreation as in many aspects of life, each must find his own way. But when opportunities for wholesome play are offered in the home, church, school and community, the individual has a better chance to develop his own particular life-giving, joy-abounding, fun-making recipe for the good life.

This book then is for the fun seekers, large and small, young and old, rich or poor, who recognize that life without fun is mere existence. We hope this book will prove a useful tool in their search for joy. We can offer only sympathy to those who think life must ever be grim and earnest.

Fun and Games

Chapter 1

The Party Leader and the Party Plan

A SUCCESSFUL PARTY is a planned party and the good party plan has only one objective—to make the party fun for everybody. Executing the plan is the party leader. Whether the leader be the host or hostess in a home or the trained professional, he must like people, enjoy working with them and be emphatic at all times. If he can assume the feelings of another, he will want always to do the things that bring happiness to that person. He will recognize that people have different tastes and abilities and will plan the party program accordingly.

The good leader will attempt to draw even the shyest person into the fold but he will do it with subtlety so that no one, least of all the person involved, will be aware of his attempts.

He will avoid the stunts and games that may cause embarrassment to anyone, knowing that embarrassment is more contagious than the measles. Let one be affected and the whole group suffers. To avoid this possibility he will organize his group into teams so that the responsibility for coming up with the right answer will be a shared one. Not only does this take the pressure off the individual but it serves as a stimulant to all involved.

The good leader believes in the need for people to have fun and plans his program to give the most enjoyment to the most people.

He uses only the games and stunts which he can present with conviction and enthusiasm. Without sincerity, success is impossible.

He understands the importance of timing. He knows when to stop one activity before it has gone beyond its point of highest interest and when to introduce another. He *draws* the party to a close. He does not let it die a boresome death; neither does he let it disintegrate into an uncontrolled mess.

He knows the role of the leader is to guide and control. He knows when to hold the reins loosely and when to jerk them up tight. The good party can have only one leader. More than one only confuses the guests and leads to the collapse of a carefully laid plan.

This does not imply that the leader must not be willing to change his plan if the need arises. Even the most carefully conceived plan sometimes goes awry and sudden changes must be made. It must, however, be the leader who makes the changes if he is to remain in control of the situation.

THE PARTY PROGRAM

Whether the party is held in the home or in the meeting room of a church or school, certain types of activities are essential to the good party plan:

1. Name tags are important if guests do not all know each other.

2. The party program begins at the beginning. There is something to do for the first guest who arrives. This tends to dispel any feelings of embarrassment or strangeness the guest may have. Puzzles and tricks serve as preparty activities. Later, as more guests assemble, mixer-type activities are introduced which help to get the guests acquainted.

3. A variety of games and activities is planned, appealing to the tastes and interests of all the guests.

4. Colorful decorations add to the eye appeal of a party but are not essential, nor are they a substitute for program.

5. Refreshments are more than taste appealing. They serve as socializers. Simple refreshments will serve the same purpose as expensive and elaborate ones. If good fellowship exists, what is served doesn't need to be a banquet to taste good.

6. The good program builds to a climax and then gently descends again before it draws to a conclusion so that the guests do not leave all keyed-up but in a happy, relaxed mood. A session over the coffee cups and a good community sing tend to create this mood better than anything else.

7. If the guests go home from a party feeling that something very special has just happened to them, there is evidence of a good party plan that has been successfully executed.

8. The good party program, like the balanced menu, includes:

a. Preparty activities. (See Chapter 17 for tricks and puzzles, Chapter 13 for autograph treasure hunts, Chapter 5 for skill games and Chapter 2 for mystery contests and treasure hunts.)

b. Mixers and get-acquainted games. (See Chapter 16 for dance mixers.)

c. Dramatic games and stunts. (See Chapter 9.)

d. Musical games and activities. (See Chapter 12.)

e. Paper-and-pencil and word games. (See Chapter 13 for paper-and-pencil games and Chapter 18 for word games.)

f. A community sing.

Chapter 2 gives suggestions for games and ideas for children's parties and parties for teenagers, adults and family groups. Some sample party programs are given but these are only suggested programs. Actually the leader must tailor each plan to fit a specific group. No one can make a party plan that will fit every group any more than a dressmaker can make a dress that will fit all women.

The party leader must know his group. How many guests are invited or expected? What is the age range? What is the sex of the group? If both sexes will be represented what will be the ratio of men to women? How will they be dressed? Will they come in formal, informal casual dress or in costume? Are they coming voluntarily or is their presence required?

The party leader must know the physical setup of the place of the party. How large is the space? Is the floor slippery? Is the play space adequate?

The occasion must be taken into consideration in the planning. Is the party the main event of the evening or does it follow another event such as a speech or banquet? In other words, where will the guests have been before the party program? Will they have been seated for a long period? Will they be tired or fresh when the party leader takes over?

It is only when the leader knows the full particulars that he can plan intelligently and effectively. The home party planner not only sets up the plan for the party but he makes the rules for the guests. The mother planning a child's birthday party sets the hours for the party, tells the guests to wear casual clothes if the games are to be active and strenuous and, with the child, makes up the guest list. Once this is done, the party planning begins. The action of the party may be restricted to certain rooms of the house and all activities planned to take place in these areas. Unless restrictions are made, the guests will be all over the house making control difficult.

At best, the suggestions given in the chapter on parties can only be used as examples. Each party is unique. The plan for it comes from no mold. It is created for a special day, a particular group, and by a certain leader. The same combination will never again be possible. With this in mind, more space has been devoted to games, stunts and activities than to the presentation of complete plans. We have tried to give you the ingredients and the recipes, but only you can put the party together for the group you have in mind and in the manner in which you would like to do it.

Chapter 2

Party Ideas for All Ages

PARTY SUGGESTIONS FOR YOUNG CHILDREN

MANY TIMES ADULTS plan parties for young children and select the activities and refreshments according to adult standards. They arrange fancy and over-rich refreshments and elaborate decorations, set beautiful tables and, if they get around to it, plan "clever" games. Children come dressed in their party clothes, looking every inch little ladies and miniature gentlemen. But, bored with the lack of or kind of activity, they often act like untrained little ruffians and sabotage the whole party—much to the distress of the hostess, who wanted it to be such a "nice party."

Children's parties can be wonderful experiences for both the hostess and the children. If we had to put all our advice regarding children's parties into one phrase, we'd say: "Keep it simple!" Children aren't impressed with expensive and fancy decorations; they'd rather have fun. Rich cake with too-thick icing, large dishes of ice cream, candy and other sweets in too much abundance give them stomach-aches which their mothers do not appreciate. The cartoonists would have us believe that children gauge the success of a party by how sick they are afterward or how many fights they participated in. One such party is guaranteed to cure any well-meaning mother of giving parties permanently. Listed below are hints and suggestions for planning a good children's party.

Planning the Children's Party

1. Keep it simple, with simple refreshments, simple prizes, simple decorations.

2. Keep it full of surprises, which children love.

3. Plan a full program of activities, leaving no lulls where boredom and the resulting impromptu unsocial (to put it mildly) activities take over.

4. Appeal to the children's love of imaginative play.

5. Arrange the party so that food is prepared in advance, leaving the mother (if she is to direct the party activities) free to be with the children from the moment the first guest steps in the door until the last one leaves.

Planning Decorations

The decorations depend on the theme or reason for the party. Is it to be a birthday party or one centered around a holiday such as Saint Valentine's Day or Halloween or Christmas?

Will a meal be served or just light refreshments? If a meal is to be served, will it be served at a table or picnic style on the floor or lawn?

If a meal is to be served, make the table colorful with paper tablecloth, appropriately designed napkins and paper plates. The children will be neither impressed nor careful with your best china, linens or silver. Don't spend hours on an elaborate centerpiece. Spend the time on planning a program of activities.

If the meal or refreshments are to be served picnic style, let the children eat from trays.

Refreshments

Carry the surprise element over into the refreshments or meal. Box lunches or poke lunches are the most fun of all for children. Prepare three or four types of sandwiches that are popular with children: meat, peanut butter and jam and others. Cut each sandwich into quarters and wrap each quarter separately. Fill lunch boxes with quartered sandwiches of several varieties. Children can swap the ones they don't like for the ones they do. There will be less waste and the children will enjoy the element of surprise and the fun of swapping. A hard-boiled egg, a tiny salt shaker to take home, a paper cup of fruit or gelatin dessert, a stalk of celery and some carrot sticks, a piece or two of wrapped candy, a paper cup of baked beans or potato salad all make for pleasant surprise lunches. Any uneaten portion can be taken home in the box (and will be!). Use plastic spoons and forks which can be taken home as souvenirs of the party. If cake and ice cream are to be served, have a not-too-rich cake, colorfully but not too heavily iced. At some birthday parties, cupcakes (each with a lighted candle) are brought in on a tray. The proper blowing-out ceremony and singing of "Happy Birthday" are carried out and then guests receive a cupcake with the candle. Ice cream in cups is more easily served and lots of fun to eat. This kind of lunch, prepared in advance, leaves the hostess mother free to play with and supervise the children and makes serving a simple matter. If hot sandwiches are to be served, use the kind that go into the oven wrapped in foil. Here again the preparation is done early and the serving is simple enough to leave the hostess free.

Planning the Activities

Set up a plan of activities which begin the moment the first guest arrives and continue for the announced period. (Invitations state when the party is to begin and end.) When the party is over the children are expected to go home. Sometimes the unorganized periods of activity after the party is over end unhappily and leave a bad taste for the entire party. If a party is from two to four o'clock, from noon until three o'clock or from four to six o'clock, the children should go home promptly when the party is over as do any polite guests. The hostess mother can politely but firmly speed the lingering child on his homeward way by telling him that the party is over and his parents will be expecting him.

Beginning the Party

When the guests begin to arrive, the child hostess and the mother hostess meet the children at the door and take them to the place where they are to leave their wraps. The guest is then taken to a table on which small cards to be made into name tags are laid out. Crayons, colored pencils, sticker stars or other bright-colored stickers are available for the child to make his own tag and decorate it in any way he chooses.

Wearing the name tag is important. Some children may not know each other. It helps them to remember names. The mother may not know all the children and it helps her to be able to call them all by name. Children behave better when they know that they can be identified and, if a discipline problem arises, the mother is able to call the child by name. The name tags may be of two or three different colors (an equal number of each color) so that after all the guests have arrived and put on their name tags, the various colors make up teams and eliminate the necessity for choosing teams.

Making Hats

At this same table or another, the makings for hats might be provided. Paper plates, colored cardboard or construction paper, newspaper or shelf paper, scissors, cellulose tape, staplers and pins should be available. Each child makes himself a hat to wear at the party. This provides an interesting activity early in the party while the early guests are waiting for the other guests to arrive. The older children may help the younger ones. The hostess should be handy to offer help and suggestions. Not only does this keep the guests busy until the entire group has assembled, but it provides an excellent creative activity which all will enjoy.

Guessing Contests

Set up two or three guessing contests for the children to participate in. These will serve as activities for the early-comers and make for good fun during the party. For each contest provide a pad of paper and pencils for the children to write their names and guesses on. Provide a jar or small box to hold the guesses for each contest. The contest items may be the prizes. Suggested contest items follow. (See Chapter 14 for other suggestions.)

Jar of jelly beans (guess the number)
Piggy bank with tiny hard candies (guess the number)
Cellophane bag filled with kisses (guess the number)
Closed and sealed carton with some toy in it (guess the kind of toy)
Bag or box of peanuts in shells (guess the weight in ounces)

Learning Names Game

The children cover their name tags for this game. The

children seat themselves on chairs or on the floor in a circle. The mother or leader stands or sits with the children as part of the circle, not in the center. Beginning with one child, the leader asks her name. She repeats it a couple of times until she thinks she remembers it. Then she goes on to child #2 and asks her name. She repeats both children's names, pointing to them as she says their names. So it goes all around the circle. When the leader thinks she knows all the names, she covers her eyes and the children change places. The leader tries to name all the children. The children love this game. They conspire to confuse the leader and catch her in a mistake. Invariably, if there are two children with the same first names they will sit next to each other and try to fool the leader. This game is not only fun for the children but helps the leader to learn names.

Guess Who I am Game

Children love to play acting-out games. The leader might start the game out by saying: "I'm going to act out a nursery rhyme. See if you can guess who I am." After the children guess, select a child to act out another puzzler. Play until several of the children have had a turn. Never play any game too long. Work on the children-have-short-interest-span principle and start another activity. This helps to keep interest high at all times.

Where Is It Game

Let the children scatter themselves over a limited area. One child is *It*. He hides his eyes while one of the children takes a beanbag and sits on it. When everyone is ready, with the guilty person trying to look innocent and the innocent guilty, all the children begin clapping their hands softly. *It* then begins to search for the child hiding the beanbag. The closer he comes to the guilty person the louder the clapping becomes. The farther he gets away from the hidden beanbag the softer the clapping becomes. This is a popular game as it is full of the qualities of fooling and suspense both so dear to the hearts of children. When *It* finally locates the beanbag, the child who is caught with the beanbag is *It* for the next turn and the game begins over again. Try humming or stamping feet as variations to clapping.

Button Button Game

Divide the group into two teams. Give team #1 a button to hide while team #2 looks the other way. Hiding is done by giving the button to one child who holds it in his hand. All the players on team #1 then hold their closed hands out in front of their bodies at about waist height, each trying to look guilty. When they are all ready, team #2 stands in a line facing team #1. The first child on team #2 points to a hand of a child on the other team, hoping it is *not* the hand holding the button. The hand is opened and its contents displayed. If it is empty, the child drops that hand at his side. The second player on team #2 picks another hand and so on down the line, or until the hand with the button is picked. When the button is found, the remaining unpicked hands are counted and that number credited to the score of team #2. Team #2 now hides the button and team #1 tries to pick the hand holding the button on its last pick. Play several times and the team with the *lowest* score wins. The object, of course, is to keep the hand with the button until the last. This is another game of suspense.

Musical Partners

This is a very active game which is fun to put into the program to help wear off excess steam so that the children will be ready to enjoy a few quiet games. It's musical chairs without the chairs but with a partner instead, and with or without music. Have the children choose partners. If music is available have someone play the piano. The children, as soon as the music begins, walk *away* from their partners. When the music stops, each rushes toward his partner and takes his partner's hands in his; then both squat. Both are up and away the moment the music starts again. If music is not available, use a signal to leave partners and another to come back to them. A whistle will serve very well for this purpose. Do not use this as an elimination game, as the purpose is to keep all the children playing. Just call out who was the last couple down. The children will play this until they are exhausted, but you as the wise leader will call it quits long before that time. The most fun of the game is when short intervals between getting up and coming back are made. Start the music and then stop it almost before the children have had a chance to get on their feet and move away. Slip these "shorties" in every so often. It's fun to watch and fun for the children. They bounce up and down like rubber balls on the short stops, screaming their heads off.

Treasure Hunt

There's nothing more exciting to the children than a treasure hunt. If the weather is suitable, hide candy kisses and other wrapped candies all around the yard. Hang them in the bushes, hide them at all levels and just everywhere over a particular area. When all is in readiness, tell the children that something wonderful has happened—candy has been found growing on the trees and bushes and on the ground. A word of warning about being careful not to break off branches or trample the flower beds might be in order. Give the boundaries of the treasure trove and turn the children loose.

If this is played within the home, limit the hunt to certain rooms. Play as a team activity. All findings are pooled and then evenly divided among the team members so that everybody gets something.

Breaking the Pinata

This is a traditional Mexican custom at Christmas, but it is fun for anybody at any time of the year. Fill a Pliofilm or heavy Cellophane bag with wrapped kisses or caramels. Do not use hard candies, as these break and make a mess. Tie the bag shut at the top with strong cord. Then tie the bag in the center of a twenty-foot length of wash line. Have two of the older children or two adults stand on chairs at each end of the wash line and hold the line in the air. The bag of candy, or *pinata*, will then be suspended about a foot over the children's heads. The rope holders can lower or raise the height of the bag to suit the individual child.

Blindfold one child and give him a baseball bat to hold.

Have the other children stand well back. Spin the blindfolded child around a couple of times and stop him under the *pinata*. He is allowed one healthy swing with the bat. If he misses, another child is blindfolded and takes his turn. If the bag is hit and breaks, all the children scramble for the contents. Keep a bag of candy in reserve and when most of the *pinata's* contents are retrieved toss the contents of the other bag into the scramble, scattering the candy well so that all the children have a chance to get something.

Bubble Blowing as a Party Activity

All party activities need not be games. With children of almost any age, bubble blowing is wonderful fun. Give each child a bottle of prepared bubble-blowing mixture and his own wand or bubble pipe. Turn the whole gang loose out in the yard or in the playroom.

This is especially good with a group of tiny tots. Adults fill the air with bubbles and children are like puppies in their efforts to break them. This will keep a group of children happy for at least twenty minutes.

Balloons

Where there is a large group of preschool children, give each child an inflated balloon and turn them loose in a large, cleared room. They will play happily for several minutes, kicking, batting and pushing the balloons.

Make-It-Yourself Activity

With small children, crafts activities are excellent activities. Take a group to a table where beads of all colors and shapes and string are provided. Let each child make himself a string of beads to take home.

Indian Headdresses

Cut strips of corrugated cardboard. Let the children decorate these with crayon designs. Provide feathers so they can stick them in the corrugated part of the cardboard to make a headdress. Rubberbands fastened to the cardboard with staplers will complete the headbands so they can be worn by the children.

Beanbag Toss

Take a clean corrugated cardboard carton. Draw a large clown's face on the flat side. Cut a hole for the mouth and a smaller one for the nose. The holes should be large enough for a bean bag to pass through. Color the face with bright-colored paint, chalk or crayons. Tie the box to a chair and let the children throw the beanbags at the face. Give a candy kiss for a successful toss into the mouth. Give a sucker or balloon for every throw that goes through the smaller holes in the eyes of the face. Jar rubbers may be substituted for the beanbags.

Clown Shooting Game

Purchase a cork-shooting gun or one that shoots ping-pong balls. Let the children try to shoot objects into the clown's mouth or nose.

Ball Basket Bounce

Place a wastebasket in the corner of the room or against a wall. Have children stand back a few feet and try to bounce rubber balls of varying sizes into the basket.
Variation: Place the basket on a chair. Try bouncing the ball on the floor in such a way as to have it bounce into the basket.

Coloring Activity

Give each child a new box of crayons and a coloring book which will be his to keep and take home. This will provide quiet activity for a period after active games and will settle the children down until it is time for refreshments.

Finger Plays

See Chapter 10 for finger plays which are excellent and enjoyable activities for young children. Seat the children on the floor or on chairs in a semicircle. Teach some new ones and let them tell you some that they know.

Observation Games

See Chapter 10 for observation games. These are excellent quiet activities which are stimulating and challenging to the children.

Storytelling

Let the children arrange themselves comfortably in a group on the floor. Tell familiar stories if you are a good story-teller. If you feel more confident reading, read simple versions of stories to the children. Your children's librarian will be glad to recommend books suitable for storytelling.

Dramatic Stunts

Dramatic stunts are stories with actions in which the entire group participates. See Chapter 9 for dramatic stunts to use with groups of children.

Word Games

Word games are good activities for children's parties. See Chapter 18.

Finger Painting

Finger painting is a wonderful creative activity that adults as well as children of all ages find fascinating. Just be sure that everybody's clothes are well protected and all will be well. Men's old shirts buttoned down the back of the child and with the sleeves rolled up will cover him from neck to toes. If you are planning this activity, ask the parents to have the child bring an old shirt to play in so that everyone is taken care of.

You can use commercial finger paints or make your own. Shiny shelf paper wet down with a sponge makes a good painting paper.

Place a quantity of finger-paint mixture on the paper. Spread evenly over the surface with one or both hands. Then begin the design. Fingernails, thumbs, full hands, palms, a comb or even arm and elbow can be brought into use in making the design. Two or more colors can be used on the same picture. Let the guests work around large tables or even on the floor, which is well protected with newspapers. To keep colors from getting all mixed up, put quantities of color in muffin tins and put a plastic spoon or knife in each color so that the guests may take the colors they desire without having to wash the spoon. The recipe for homemade finger paints is given below. Remember this is a very messy activity, and be prepared. If you can do it out on the lawn, so much the better. In that case, give each painter a large piece of heavy cardboard as a smooth working surface on which to paint.

Homemade Finger Paints

Make finger paint base by mixing 1½ cups of laundry starch with sufficient cold water to make a paste. Add one quart of boiling water, stirring constantly until the mixture is clear and glossy looking. Cool and add 1½ cups of soap flakes and ½ cup of talcum (optional). The mixture should be thick. Place in jars and cover. Keep in a cold place until time to use. Dip into cupcake tins and color with tempera color.

Dry-Color Finger Painting

Use regular finger-paint paper, wetting it as you would before using paste-type finger paints. Sprinkle wet paper with dry tempera color and work with hands. More than one color can be used. The results are very similar and the dry color is much simpler to use.

Clay Modeling

Protect the children's clothes with aprons and give each a supply of non-hardening modeling clay. Protect the table with oilcloth. Stimulate the children's imagination by telling them a story and having them make the characters and objects in the story.

Singing Games

Singing games are an ever-popular activity with children.

Play Farmer in the Dell, Looby Loo and other less familiar ones. See Chapter 16 for singing games that are easy to teach, quickly learned and a never-ending source of fun and enjoyment.

The Picnic Party

During spring, summer or fall, a picnic party might be planned for a birthday. Take the guests to a near-by park where hiking, hill climbing or playing along a creek or lake shore is possible. Allow time for a supervised but free playtime. Run a series of picnic-type contests and guessing contests. Serve a picnic meal of hot dogs to be roasted over the fire or hamburgers to be cooked in foil, celery and carrot sticks and other relishes, and marshmallows to be toasted and pressed between crackers with a piece of chocolate bar.

The Winter Skating or Coasting Party

If a birthday comes when winter sports are possible, organize an ice-skating or coasting party. Cook part of the meal over a fire and serve hot chocolate out of a thermos.

FAMILY PARTIES

The Free-for-All Family Party

One of the best all-family church parties ever planned was held by Plymouth Church in Shaker Heights, Ohio. It was not *free* in the sense that no charge was made for it. Families paid five dollars at the gate. From then on everything was free. Many of the indoor church facilities were put to use. The outdoor area, lawn and parking lot all were scenes of activity. Carnival skill games of all kinds were set up inside and outside, in the area best suited to the activity. Small prizes were given at each game. A puppet show and a magic show were held inside. Pony rides were available in the parking-lot area. There was square dancing on the green. Tether ball, volleyball, basketball-hoop shooting and golf chipping games were set up in the lawn areas. Refreshments of all kinds were free once the admission ticket was purchased. A huge gunny sack full of peanuts sat in one corner. Small bags were placed near a sign saying: "Help yourself!" The committee rented a commercial popcorn-making machine. Boxes of popcorn were given away as fast as they could be filled. A soft-drink counter dispensed free drinks. A refreshment counter loaded with homemade cupcakes, cookies and candies was set up inside. Ice cream in paper cups and popsicles were also free. Two mechanical ponies were set for free rides. It was literally a fairyland for the children and good fun for the adults. The program went on for a full afternoon. Besides being an excellent medium for bringing family groups together for a program of fun, it proved to be a money maker.

Such a program could be run on a smaller scale in a limited area at a lower cost per family and still be a satisfying experience for everyone. A carnival, a puppet show, a magic show, movies and a refreshment stand could be operated within the confines of a church or school building. A single family ticket paid for at the door would take care of all expenses. Childless couples or those with grown children away at school would be permitted to borrow children for the day. There would be no rule against aunts and uncles playing hosts to nieces and nephews.

Family Play Parties

Churches and P.T.A.'s and other organizations interested in family programs would do well to have occasional family parties. The evening can begin with a pot-luck supper, which in itself is a socializer. The committee organizes the food donations so that there will not be a predominance of salads or rice casserole dishes. Dinner is served buffet style from a long table which is set up with the hot dishes placed near one end and the salads at the other end. Rolls and butter and desserts are put on the tables at each place. Coffee and other beverages are served after the guests are seated. Guests pay a small per-person charge which covers the cost of the food furnished by the organization, since the beverages, dessert, rolls and butter are purchased by the committee in charge of arrangements.

To give the party an international flavor, all hot dishes should be the international type: Mexican chili, German potato salad, Greek pilaf, Spanish rice, Bohemian sweet-sour cabbage, Chinese shop suey, etc. The cooks should telephone to say which dishes they are making, so that the committee will know what kind of food is being brought. Large cards folded into tents are set before each dish announcing the name of the dish and the cook. The cooks outdo themselves to bring something tasty and novel, and since each is identified, recipe swapping abounds and compliments to the individual cooks are passed about. To assure a variety of dishes and a balanced menu, families are asked to bring one of three types of dishes: a hot vegetable, a hot meat dish or a salad large enough to serve ten persons.

To make cleaning up as simple as possible, families are asked to bring their own paper plates and eating utensils, or paper plates and cups can be furnished. All leftovers are taken home in the dishes in which they came so there is no problem of what to do with any remaining food. Most of the work of this type of supper is in the organization. The committee takes reservations, sets up the tables and organizes the serving table as the food comes in. Cleaning up is relatively simple and places no great burden on anyone. Since it is a family supper, everyone is expected to help a little in clearing the tables, putting away chairs, etc.

A play-party program follows the supper. In planning the program when the age range is a great one, as it always is at a family party, the group is divided after the first twenty minutes. The entire group, small children and parents and older children, all play together at first, joining in simple sing-ing games and mixers. The small children then are taken to the nursery room where they may play with toys, hear stories or color with crayons. A selected movie program may be shown to this group. The parents and older children, seven years and over, then have a play-party program together. Rhythmic mixers, games and square dances provide an inter-esting program for this group. Later the entire group may be brought together again for a final community sing and good-night ceremony. A friendship circle and singing of "Taps" or a simple benediction make a fitting ending for such a family party.

Family Progressive Parties

SKILL-GAMES PROGRESSIVE PARTIES

Progressive parties make good family parties because a large number of persons of varied ages can be entertained in such a way as to provide fun for all. Skill games of various kinds are set up all around one room or in a number of different rooms and corridors if no one room is large enough to accommodate the entire group. The smaller children are separated from the group and are entertained in another area with a program of singing games, stories, movies, crafts and arts activities. The older children (seven years and over), and the parents are organized into teams of ten to fifteen persons, with children not necessarily on teams with their parents. Each team is given a number, as is each game. The teams then go to the games with the corresponding numbers. When the group numbers more than fifty persons, it is wise to have a leader stationed at each game who explains to the teams how the game is to be played and scored. Each team carries its own score sheet with it as it moves from game to game. The score sheets may be mimeographed so that they will be uniform. Each team keeps its own scores and numbers its score sheet in the order in which it plays the games. Team #1 goes to game #1. If there are ten games, team #1's sheet is numbered consecutively from one to ten. Team #4 begins at game #4 so its score sheet begins with game #4 and runs consecutively from four to ten and then from one through three. Thus each team plays all ten games. The leader (when all teams are ready) gives a starting signal and all teams begin play at once. All teams play until the stopping signal, whereupon they total their score for that game and write it on the score sheet opposite the number of the game just played. They move on to the next game, where they receive directions from the leader. When all teams are ready, the signal to begin is given and play resumes. The time at each game is from two to four minutes. The faster a team plays, the more turns its players get. The object is to build up as large a score at each game as possible.

It is difficult to say here how long a period should be allowed for play. The best way is to time the game that takes the longest to play, since not all games can be played in the same length of time. A game played with a cork-shooting gun takes longer than a beanbag-toss game, as it takes longer to load the gun and retrieve the corks after each turn. The leader often watches the game of longest play and sets his time by that particular one. He allows the team there to play at least one round. At other games, meanwhile, the players on a team may get several turns before time is called. When time is called and the team moves on to the next game, they do not begin with the original first man on the team but with the player whose turn was just coming up at the last game. This method evens up the players' turns by the time the round is completed.

At the end of the program, the scores are added up and a team prize (bag of candy or small individual prizes for each player) is awarded. A prize may be awarded to the second team or to the team with the lowest score. See Chapter 5 for skill games suitable for progressive parties.

In setting up the party, the leader places all the games before numbering them so that when he finally gives them a number, the numbers run in consecutive order around the course and the teams do not have to hunt for each game. Numbers should be large and easily seen from anywhere in the room. Throwing lines may be shortened for the children at each game just as there are women's tees and men's tees on the golf course. If a child prefers to throw from the adult's line, he of course gets no argument on that point.

This type of party is not limited to family groups, by any means. It can be used for all types of groups.

VARIETY PROGRESSIVE PARTIES

In the variety type of progressive party, large groups can be accommodated. Large church or school parties can use this method to good advantage. Activities areas are set up all over the church or school area. The gymnasium or meeting hall becomes one center of activity, the auditorium becomes another. The social room, the cafeteria and game rooms are all put to use. Much of the success of this type of program depends upon the timing as well as the selection of activities.

SETTING UP THE PARTY

In organizing the party, it must be determined if there is any one room large enough to hold the estimated crowd. For example, if the auditorium is sufficiently large to take care of the entire group, the first order of business might be a variety show made up of selected talent from the children and parents. Such a program should be of high caliber, well rehearsed and timed not to exceed an hour. At the conclusion of this program the group splits into various activities. Social dancing might be held in one room and square dancing in another. The game room might be opened up for ping-pong, shuffleboard, card games, chess and checkers. A movie program might be run off in the auditorium. At the end of a stipulated period, a signal might be given and the groups change from one activity to another. Thus, in an evening, the guests may have participated in two different activities and been spectators at an entertainment. Refreshments may be served after the show or sold during the remainder of the evening.

This type of party requires much planning and a high degree of organization during the program itself. It entails much work but when it is successful it pays off in every way.

THE ONE-ACTIVITY PROGRESSIVE PARTY

At this type of progressive party, only one activity (cards, dice, Chinese Checkers or Anagrams) is the order of the day. The progression is in the movement of the players from table to table, where they meet different partners and opponents.

To set up such a party, the type of activity is decided upon first. Guests, as they arrive, are given tally or score cards showing a table number. When play begins, players take their places at the tables indicated and meet their partners and opponents. After a stipulated period of play each player records his score for that period of play on his score card. Winners move to the next table, where each plays with a new partner.

Losers stay at the same table, but also split up and play with a new partner coming from another table. Thus, in the course of play, guests have a new partner for each period and play against two different persons as well. Since each player has his own score card, prizes are awarded on the basis of the highest and lowest individual scores.

Variation:

This type of progressive party is often made more interesting by having a different type of game played at each table. Chinese Checkers, Five in a Row, Anagrams, various card games, Parchesi, Monopoly, Finance, Money, Cootie, Bunco or other dice games may be used. Parchesi, Monopoly, Anagrams and Chinese Checkers can be purcased at game counters in department or ten-cent stories. Rules for the dice games mentioned above are given in Chapter 8 and rules for Five in a Row in Chapter 7.

The Family Fair

Playground systems, day camps and overnight camps all plan a big blowout for parents and children at the end of the season. A family fair is a good project for the entire camp or group to work on. Everyone—parents, brothers and sisters, aunts, uncles, friends and neighbors—is invited. The children and counselors plan the program together, with each group deciding which booth it would like to set up and operate. At the fair itself, the children are scheduled to work at the booth for a specified period and then are free to enter into the fun.

Booths may consist of carnival games, handicrafts exhibits, refreshment stands and side shows. Prizes at the carnival booths may be novelties, candy or balloons that are purchased, or favors made by the children in their handicraft periods.

Side shows may be set up where dramatic groups present their plays, dancing groups give demonstrations, the tumblers put on their shows and the various sports champions demonstrate their skills at archery, horseback riding, swimming, etc. Each show is repeated at regular intervals so that parents may see all the shows if they so desire.

If the sponsoring organization needs to cover the cost of

putting on the fair, an admission ticket for the entire fair may be sold. This entitles the holder to play at all the games as often as he wishes and to see all the side shows. A family ticket may also be sold. Refreshments are not included in the cost of admission but are sold at various stands.

See Chapters 4 and 5 for suitable carnival games and suggestions for refreshment booths.

The Family Picnic

A family picnic serves as an excellent way of winding up the camp or playground season. The program begins with a father-and-daughter or father-and-son baseball game which is followed by a family swim period if swimming facilities are available. A demonstration program of camp or playground activities such as dramatics, music, riding, dancing and crafts is another important part of the family picnic. A series of picnic games and contests for all members of the family is the climax of the afternoon. The final events are the picnic supper (families bring their own) and a community sing around a campfire.

Such a program provides games and activities for persons of all ages and offers the camp or playground ample opportunity to demonstrate the activities in which the children have been engaged throughout the season. If well planned and conducted, it finishes the season in good style.

See Chapter 14 for ideas and games for picnic programs.

PARTIES FOR YOUTH AND ADULT GROUPS

The Mystery Party (For Adults or Youths)

When you don't know the place, the time or anything about what is going to happen and all you know is that there is going to be a mystery party it's bound to be mysterious.

ANNOUNCING THE PARTY

The first announcement may be made by mail or by announcement in the school or church paper. Only the first clue is given in this announcement and then each guest must work out the details himself. If the party details are to be given through a series of mystery phone calls, the leader must line up a group of willing recruits who will take calls and pass on messages. The first clue will give a phone number to call. This can be in the announcement sent by mail. The first announcement might look like this: (You will have to change the letters in the message, of course, to suit your own situation, but the same questions can be used.)

SAMPLE ANNOUNCEMENTS FOR MYSTERY PARTIES

False-and-True Test Announcement

$\underline{\quad}$ (1) $\underline{\quad}$ (2) $\underline{\quad}$ (3) $\underline{\quad}$ (4) $\underline{\quad}$ (5) $\underline{\quad}$ (6) $\underline{\quad}$ (7) $\underline{\quad}$ (8) $\underline{\quad}$ (9) $\underline{\quad}$ (10) $\underline{\quad}$ (11) $\underline{\quad}$ (12)
$\underline{\quad}$ (13) $\underline{\quad}$ (14) $\underline{\quad}$ (15) $\underline{\quad}$ (16) $\underline{\quad}$ (17)

Fill in the above spaces by answering the mystery questions below:

1. If a fly has four legs put a *B* in the first space; if it has six legs write a *P* there.

2. If Columbus was the first man to set foot in America put a *U* in the second space; otherwise write in an *H*.

3. If bicarbonate of soda is poisonous to humans place an *S* in the third space; otherwise write in an *O*.

4. If oranges are rich in vitamin C write *N* in the fourth space; otherwise write in a *G*.

5. If Eli Whitney was born in 1825 write the letter *G* in space 5; otherwise write in the letter *E*.

6. If purple is made by mixing red and yellow write an *O* in space 6; otherwise leave it blank.

7. If Turquoise is a gem stone as well as a color write the letter *P* in the seventh space; otherwise leave it blank.

8. If this is hard for you to do write the letter *R* in the eighth space. If it is easy, write in the letter *E*.

9. If Michigan is the Hawkeye State write an *L* in space 9. If it is the Wolverine State write in the letter *T*.

10. Who said: "War is hell"? If it was Grant put a letter *O* in space 10. If it was Sherman write in the letter *E*.

11. Who found a plum in his pie? If it was Little Boy Blue

write a *Y* in space 11. If it was Jack Horner write in the letter *R*.

12. If 10 × 0 equals 0 write nothing in space 12. If it equals 10 write in the letter *M*.

13. If Socrates is an All-American football player write the letter *B* in space 13. If he was a philosopher of ancient times write in the letter *G*.

14. If paw-paw is what some children call their father write the letter *N* in space 14. If it is an edible fruit write in the letter *R*.

15. If "r" comes before "p" in the alphabet write the letter *D* in space 15. If it comes after, write in the letter *O*.

16. If an en is half an em, write the letter *S* in space 16. If not, write in the letter *A*.

17. If a hare and rabbit are one and the same write the letter *S* in space 17. If a hare is a tortoise, write the letter *Y*.

If you have done this riddle correctly it will tell you what to do. If it doesn't make sense, you had better work it all over again. When you have a clear answer, follow the instructions and you will receive the next clue. Continue to follow all the clues until you know when the party is, where to meet, what to wear and any other necessary instructions. *But remember*, even when you know all these facts, the rest of the party is still a mystery.

OTHER MYSTERY PARTY ANNOUNCEMENTS

Announcements may be of many kinds. A rebus invitation would take some time to figure out but is not too difficult to prepare if a mimeograph or other type of duplicating machine is available. A rebus, as you know, is a message made partly of words and partly of pictures, or of letters and pictures combined. For example the letter "t" and a picture of a hat make the word "that." If some words are hand drawn and combined with pictures and printed words it looks more difficult and complicated than it actually is. A sample invitation might read like the following:

"You are invited to attend a party on Sunday, the eighteenth of February, at 5 P.M. Telephone MU 1-8890 for details."

In rebus form it would look like the following diagram:

JIGSAW-PUZZLE ANNOUNCEMENT

Print or type the invitations on filing cards or on colored cardboard. You might print the invitations over colored picture-cards. Cut each card into ten or more pieces before placing it in an envelope for mailing. Guests will have to put the puzzle together before being able to read the message.

PHONE-BOOK CODED INVITATION

You can write an invitation right out of the phone book. Look up names (you'll be surprised how clear an invitation you can write using names) and make up the message you want your invitation to give. You'll have to give some directions on the invitations so that the guests will know what to do. The invitation might read like this:

Dear Johnny Gross:

Are you curious? Do you like mysteries? There is an important announcement for you in the coded message below. If you follow directions carefully, you can solve the mystery yourself. Take your alphabetical phone book. Open it to the page number given for each word in the message. Look in the column indicated and count *names* only, counting from the top down or the bottom up, whichever it tells you to do for that word. Use only the last name or surname in the line indicated for the code word. When you finish, the message should be clear to you. Call the phone number indicated in the message for further information. The directions for finding the words are listed below, word by word. As you find the proper word, write it on your invitation so that you can see the whole message at the end.

Here is the message:

First word: Page 196, col. 1, line 26. Count down from the top.

Second word: Page 718, col. 2, line 47. Count up from the bottom.

Third word: Page 754, col. 4, line 72. Count up from the bottom.

Fourth word: Page 150, col. 3, line 52. Count down from the top.

Fifth word: Page 446, col. 3, line 27. Count down from the top.

Sixth word: Page 227, col. 4, line 17. Count up from the bottom.

Now you should know what this is all about. If you can't make sense out of it, call WA 6-6657 and you will be instructed further.

Note: The message above was made up from words actually in the Cleveland telephone book, though the columns and line number given here are not accurate. It was possible to give this message: "Come. Mystic Partee. Call host (name follows)," the last words being the name, address and phone number of the host. The phone number given in case of complete confusion on the part of the guest is also the host's number. However the host, on ascertaining that the guest had not bothered to work out the code or couldn't understand it, would tell the caller how to decode the message and ask him to do it over again. If the host feels sorry for the guest, he might tell him the necessary information without making him go to all that trouble.

CROSSWORD-PUZZLE MYSTERY INVITATION

Prepare a simple crossword-puzzle invitation and let the guests figure out what's cooking. A sample invitation is given below.

If this is a mystery to you, work out the crossword puzzle below and do exactly what it tells you to do. Most of the words in the puzzle, when put together in the proper order, give you an important message.

When you have worked out the puzzle, call (give a phone number here) for further information. Write down all the information you receive so you can keep all the details straight.

THE MEETING PLACE OF MYSTERY

The meeting place may not be the place of the party at all. Here the assembled group may be given the first clue in a mystery journey which may be made on foot, by auto or by public transportation, depending on the age or kind of group. At the conclusion of the mysterious journey, the leader may be waiting to conduct the guests to the mysterious location of the party. In one instance, the young people walked over a treasure-hunt type of trail and were met by cars which then took them to the place, which, in this case, was only two houses down the street from the end of the trail. The cars were headed the other way up the street and traveled to an intersection, then turned down the same street and back to the mysterious house. The guests were still guessing when the cars stopped in front of the correct house.

THE MYSTERY PARTY PROGRAM

A clever invitation is only the beginning of the party plan. The proof of the party lies in the program. Announcements, refreshments and prizes are necessary parts but minor details.

It's the games and activities that make the fun part of the program. Using *mystery* as a theme, let the games and activities be of the mysterious type. Every other aspect of the party can be mysterious: the refreshments, the prizes and even the guests.

When guests finally arrive at the party divide them into teams of equal numbers. All activities are team activities. All of the guests are sure to have a good time since no one guest is asked to do something alone. Some people freeze when expected to be clever and become embarrassed at their poor showing in contests and games. Having guests work in teams avoids this problem.

Mysterious Who Are We?

Send teams to card tables, (one team per table) that are equipped with old newspapers, scissors, cellulose tape, staplers, pins, etc. Given fifteen minutes, each team is to make one costume out of the newspapers for one of its members depicting a character in a nursery rhyme, song or book. Since time is limited, simplicity of costume is the keynote.

When time is called the teams line up in different parts of the room and each team tries to guess the identity of the costumed person. Each team has to tell only what category is depicted; i.e., nursery rhyme, song or book. A prize might be given to the cleverest costume, not necessarily the hardest to identify. Prizes should be simple. A bag of kisses for the whole team to divide, or a balloon or pencil for each team member is suitable.

MYSTERY CONTESTS

Set up three tables and divide your group into three teams. Give each team a sheet of paper and a pencil. Each team elects a secretary to record its results. Send each team to one of the tables. At the end of five minutes have the teams rotate. When all teams have visited each of the tables, score the results and give prizes to the teams having the best score for each contest. See contests listed below.

Mystery Sniffers

Prepare ten small bottles or vials by filling each bottle with a different brew, all of which have a distinctive but elusive odor. Number each bottle so that teams can identify the smells, and record their guesses. Since it is groups of people playing together each answer ought to be the consensus of the entire group. There will be arguments but that's half of the fun. Disguising the contents by adding vegetable coloring will add to the confusion. Some suggested liquids to pour into the bottles are:

Vinegar, diluted ammonia, mouthwash, cold coffee, peppermint, vanilla, rubbing alcohol, lighter fluid, dry-cleaning fluid, nail polish remover, almond flavoring, gardenia toilet water, bleaching fluid.

Mystery Tongue Ticklers

Prepare ten custard cups or small bottles with contents to be tasted. Liquids are more easily disguised than solids or soft solids. Vegetable colors help disguise the contents. Number each container. Leave a box of toothpicks on this table. Contestants use a *fresh* toothpick for each taste. When this is played as a team game, the final decisions represent the taste consensus of the entire team. Disguised tongue ticklers might be:

Red vinegar, blue-colored lemon-flavored gelatin in a liquid state, green milk, pink orange juice, cold coffee, cold green tea, root beer, red pineapple juice, juice from maraschino cherries, yellow saltwater solution, pink sugar water, alum solution, licorice dissolved in water.

Mystery Feelers

Take ten large brown bags. Place a familiar or common article in each bag, twist the top of bag and fasten with rubber band or string. Number each bag clearly. Players attempt to identify the contents of the bag by squeezing or feeling. Caution! Do not use toothpaste or shaving cream tubes as one of the items or there will be disastrous results. Contents of the bags might be:

Egg beater, darning ball, wooden salad fork, spatula, pot holder, empty salt shaker, percolator top, measuring spoon, custard cup, empty Coke bottle, cellulose sponge, typewriter eraser, ash tray, partly used roll of paper towels, dog's bone, beanbag, small frying pan, large can of fruit juice.

Variation Mystery Feelers

Blindfold all the members of the team after they have removed one shoe and stocking. Take ten articles and give them each a number. Pass item #1 around the circle, allowing the players to touch the articles with their toes only in attempting to identify the articles. After all have had a chance to identify the article, record what the group decision is for the item and then pass around the next item. Suggested articles are:

Tea bag, safety pin, paper clip, fur-lined gloves turned inside out, piece of sand or emery paper, nail file, plastic spoon, can opener, hand brush, piece of velvet, key, wrist-watch band, napkin ring.

Mysterious Sounds and Rattles

Prepare a variety of containers by placing in each something that will rattle when the container is shaken. Use empty cold cream jars or any opaque glass containers so that the contents cannot be seen. Number each container. Players are to try to guess the contents or type of material in the container by the sound. Containers may be rattled but not squeezed! Containers and contents might be:

Metal washers in a cloth bag, nails in a glass jar, thumb tacks in a paper cardboard box, rice grains in a paper box, wooden safety matches in a paper bag, keys in a coffee can, sugar or salt grains in a paper bag, jingle bells in a cardboard carton.

Mysterious What's My Occupation (A Mixer or Icebreaker)

This is a game to play as guests are gathering. As the guest comes in the door give him one of the articles listed below (or any others you may think of) to wear *in plain sight* but nevertheless in a hard-to-see place. Each guest retires to another room or dark corner to put on his mystery article so that other guests may not see what he is wearing or where he puts it. When all the articles have been given out and most

of the guests have arrived, give each guest a pencil and a list
such as shown below. Each is to find someone wearing an
article appropriate to the occupation listed below. When he
finds such an article, he asks the wearer to sign his sheet on
the proper line or merely asks his name and writes it in himself. The guest *does not point out the article in question* so
that others may see it. The first guest to complete the list correctly wins a prize. Number the lists as they are turned in so
that you will know the order in which they were completed.
Use more than fifteen articles in a group numbering over
fifty and about ten in a group numbering fifteen to fifty persons. While only a few guests wear the mystery articles, all
can play since none knows who is wearing what article. A
suggested list of articles and the occupations they might
represent follows: (In your printed list you would list only
the occupation and not the article to look for.)

1. Baby tender (safety pin).........................
2. Gambler (poker chip or playing card).............
3. Typist or secretary (typewriter eraser).............
4. Seamstress or tailor (needles and thread)...........
5. Hairdresser (bobby pin or hairpin)................
6. Cook or chef (small spoon).....................
7. Shoemaker, shoe salesman (small pair of doll shoes).
8. Bookkeeper or accountant (red pencil)...........
9. Laundress or laundryman (doll clothespin or small bar
   of soap) ....
10. Ticket seller (theater stub)......................
11. Dollmaker (small doll).........................
12. Musician or band leader (small costume-jewelry in-
    strument or any musical symbol)................
13. Matchmaker (match) ....
14. Carpenter (toy hammer).......................
15. Cowboy (toy gun, cowboy tie)...................
16. Bookie (player carries book around with him)......
17. Record breaker (piece of broken record)..........
18. Datemaker (small calendar).....................
19. Knitter (knitting needles).......................
20. Barber (razor, comb)..........................

Note: Look through your junk drawers, jewelry box or dresser drawers. Pick out ten or fifteen articles that you have on hand and make up your own list. It's easier to take the articles and make up a list than it is to make up a list and then try to find suitable articles. The above list ought to give you plenty of ideas. This may be played as a team game with five or more players working together to fill in the list.

Mysterious Musical Occupations

Divide your group into teams and give each a pad and pencil. If you have an accomplished musician in the group who can play parts of many songs, recruit him for this game, but do it well in advance so he has some warning as to what is expected of him. The teams select a captain, who numbers the pad from one to fifteen. Tell the teams that the pianist will play a portion of a number of songs. Each song represents a mysterious occupation. ("Three Blind Mice" suggests a rat catcher, exterminator, butcher or farmer's wife.) The teams are asked to name only one for each song. If they don't recognize the song, they can't arrive at an answer. That's half the battle. At the end of the game, allow time for the team to ask for repeats on some of the songs for which they ask by number. Give a team prize to the team with the most correct numbers.

Given below are a number of familiar song titles that suggest occupations. If you do not have a pianist in the group, play the game by giving the teams ten minutes to name fifteen songs which suggest fifteen different occupations.

Occupations in Songs

1. Dancer	The Band Played On; After the Ball; Sailor's Hornpipe
2. Jeweler	Rings on Her Fingers and Bells on Her Toes; Ring Around the Rosie
3. Boatman	On a Sunday Afternoon; Sailing, Sailing; Volga Boatman
4. Florist	When you Wore a Tulip; Rose of Tralee

5. Farmer	Old MacDonald
6. Bicycle rider	Daisy Bell
7. Rancher or cowboy	Home on the Range, or any cowboy song
8. Snow-plow operator	I'm Dreaming of a White Christmas
9. Taxi driver	Darktown Strutters' Ball
10. Engineer or conductor	I've Been Working on the Railroad
11. Milliner or model	In Your Easter Bonnet
12. Miner	Clementine
13. Shepherd	The First Noel
14. Teacher	School Days
15. Miller	Down by the Old Mill Stream
16. Pilot	Air Force Song
17. Hunter	John Peel

For more mystery-type musical games see Chapter 12.

Mystery Names

As guests assemble, have each prepare a name tag to wear in plain sight. Divide groups into teams and give each team five slips of paper on which are written, in jumbled form, the names of five of the guests present. At the signal to go, players rush around trying to figure out what the jumbled names are. By looking at the name tags of other players they may be able to figure them out faster. As soon as a team has five names correctly unscrambled the game is over.

Secret Objects

Divide the group into teams. Tell teams that each member is to select something small that he is wearing or carrying in pockets or purse and hold it in one hand. The selection and movements of putting the object in the hand must be done as secretly as possible, each member of the team hiding his selection from the others. When all are ready, tell all the members to lay their things out in front of them. One player is elected as captain and scoring is done in the following fashion:

1. Ten points for every different type of item. (A watch is different from a ring. Coins of different denominations count as different items. A man's handkerchief is different from a woman's handkerchief, but two women's hankies, however different, count as the same type of item.)

2. Count ten points for every pair of similar items: i.e., two watches (men's or women's), two hankies, two pennies, two knives count as pairs.

3. Ten points for something red. (Red earring, red match folder, red hanky.)

4. Count twenty-five points for any article that is considered a lucky piece by the team member.

5. Give ten points for every watch that has a second hand on it.

6. Five twenty-five points for every set of triplets, or three-of-a-kind, on a team. (Note: if in item #2 some items were counted in pairs they can be counted again if they can be regrouped into triplets.

7. Lay all the items end to end to make the longest line possible and measure the length of each team's line. Take the total number of inches as the score for this item.

8. Score ten points if any of the items is edible. (Gum, candy, pill or cough drop.)

9. Score ten points for every item having to do with personal toilet, such as comb, file, emery board, manicure scissors, nail clippers, dental floss or compact.

10. Score twenty-five points if any item is an honor key, school pin, ring, fraternity or sorority pin.

11. Score ten points for any item made of silver.

12. If an item has a precious stone set in it, score ten points.

13. If it is a souvenir from a trip, score ten points.

14. Score ten points for any handmade item in the collection.

15. Have each team make the collection of secret items into as small a pile as possible. Give ten points to the team with the *largest* pile of items, or vice versa.

16. At the signal to go, have players retrieve their items as fast as possible. When all items are back with the rightful

owners, have the team stand to indicate it is finished. Give ten points to the first team finished and five points to the other teams. Note: Use ten or twelve of the above-mentioned methods of scoring only at any one party.

Mysterious Refreshments

This stunt is possible when the group is not too large. Tell guests that they have a choice of four out of ten items for refreshments but they must order sight unseen by number. Seven of the ten possibilities are edibles while the others are jokes. Each guest is served what he ordered. Later, of course, you can take pity on the poor unfortunates and give them something to eat if their selection has been poor. If your refreshments are cookies, ice cream, coffee, tea, milk, candy, nuts, the other three items could be water, toothpicks and dried prunes. Give each item a number. When a guest is served he does not know which item is which number so that the next guest will not be warned by his predecessor's selection. One guest may get coffee, tea, a prune and a glass of water; another may get a piece of candy, a toothpick, ice cream and a prune.

The Musical Mystery

Divide group into teams and give each team paper and pencil. Have the captain of the team write the numbers from one to twelve, one below the other, down the sheet. The leader tells the mystery story and fills it with a portion of a song, playing it on the piano or humming it. The teams attempt to fill in the necessary part of the story which they get from the words of the song or the title.

Given below are the main characters and events in the story as they can be found in songs. Alternate song titles are given in most cases:

1. The heroine in the case.   It Was Mary; Sweet Adeline; Charmaine; When You and I Were Young, Maggie; or Sweet Rosie O'Grady

2. The hero in the case. Little David, Play on Your Harp; My Bill

3. Who was found dead? Poor Jud Is Dead; Joe Hill; John Brown's Body; Old Uncle Ned

4. Where was the body found? Down in the Valley; On Top of Old Smoky

5. When was the crime committed? In the Gloaming; Perfect Day; In the Good Old Summertime; After the Ball; While Strolling Through the Park One Day

6. Where was the crime committed? In the Blue Ridge Mountains of Virginia; Down by the Old Mill Stream

7. Who was the detective on the case? Captain Jinks; Dragnet Theme

8. Who was the likeliest suspect? John Peel; When Johnny Comes Marching Home

9. What was the murder weapon? Johnny, Get Your Gun; Grandfather's Clock; The Old Oaken Bucket; Little Brown Jug

10. How did he make his getaway? Darktown Strutters' Ball (I'll be down to get you in a taxi, Honey); In My Merry Oldsmobile; I've Been Working on the Railroad

11. Where was he finally apprehended? Coming Through the Rye; Tavern in the Town

12. What did the detective say? Tell Me Why

13. What did the murderer say? You Made Me Love You; I'm Sorry, Dear

14. Where did he end up? The Prisoner's Song; Water Boy

15. When did this all happen? Long, Long Ago

For other mystery-type games see the Peculiar Leader Game, the Peculiar Letters of the Alphabet Game, Mystic Mind Reader, Historic Twenty Questions and Mystic Number Game in Chapter 18.

Mystery Person

Players stand in a small circle facing in. *It* is blindfolded and given two large serving spoons. *It* turns around three times in the center of the circle and then advances toward the players. Using only the spoons to feel with, he attempts to identify the player he is "spooning." The player may stoop to disguise his size, but otherwise he cannot back away from the spoons. If *It* can identify the player the two exchange places; otherwise *It* must move on to another player.

Help-a-Friend Work Parties

A successful party isn't always one where guests play games or watch entertainers or have elaborate refreshments. All it takes to make a good party is a group of congenial people joining together in a common activity and enjoying each other's company. To the uninitiated reader, some of the following parties may sound more like work than fun, but actually they are modern adaptations of the old-fashioned corn-husking bees, barn-raising or quilting parties where groups of people got together to perform useful services and made a real social affair out of what might have been work if it had not been so much fun.

WALLPAPER-REMOVING PARTY

Do you have a friend who is moving into a house where the old wallpaper has to be removed before the necessary redecorating can be done? With your friend's permission, of course, organize a paper-removing party. Invite special friends who all know each other and will enjoy an old-fashioned "bee." Tell them all to wear their oldest clothes and come prepared to work, bringing their own work bucket, sponge, scraper and ladder. Many hands make short work of an otherwise lengthy and back-breaking job. Jokes, stories of real-life adventures and songs make the usually tiring work fun to do.

At odd intervals, time is called and all descend from their ladders or get up off their knees and sit on a dry spot on the floor for a cigarette, cup of tea or coffee, a soft drink or other tasty refreshments. Lunch is a one-dish affair such as chili, hamburgers, hot dogs or sandwiches eaten while seated on the floor. At the end of the day, the muscles may ache, but ah, the heart is light and the naked walls are proof that a hard job has been completed.

COMMUNITY OR CHURCH WORK PARTIES

Churches and similar organizations would do well to organize work parties when painting or landscaping or some such job needs to be done, particularly where the hands are many but the budget insufficient to have the job done by hired help. Each person wears the proper costume and brings his own tools. The job must have a well-organized plan with a boss-manager on the job to see that everyone gets a job and knows what to do and how to do it. Another committee keeps the coffeepot full for coffee breaks and serves a simple but hot and tasty meal. The work will get done, people will have fun and, best of all, a good feeling between members is built up. Nothing builds good fellowship faster than a good and worthy service project.

MOVING PARTY

Moving day with all its tasks and mixed emotions can be made hectic or pleasant by events leading up to the day. Organize a Help-a-Friend-Pack Party. Bring boxes and packing materials, such as old newspapers, cord and twine, stickers and marking pencils. Help her pack her breakables. Organize a caravan of cars to haul the things never trusted to the movers. Help prepare cupboards, floors and windows of the new home for the big day. On moving day, arrange a lunch that can be served to the moving family so they won't have to worry about where to go to eat or what to prepare. Take it to the house and have it ready when they get there. Invite the moving family to dinner, or better still take a dinner in to them so they won't have to dress up to go out to eat. You will be remembered for your good deed for many a moon.

Hard work? Sure! But the good feeling it gives you can't be bought for any money.

Money-Raising Project Parties

Church groups and service organizations are always looking for ways to augment their treasuries. Handmade or homemade items which can be offered for sale on an occasional basis are among the best methods for making money. If a group can select a particular time for its project such as Christmas or Easter and make decorations or items peculiar to that season, the chances for making money are enhanced. If the day for making the items can be given a party flavor, the work gets done and people have fun all at the same time.

Everybody's Birthday Party

Some clubs and organizations have an Everybody's Birthday Party once a year when every member's birthday anniversary is remembered at one big celebration. Twelve tables are decorated, one for each month, with appropriate and unmistakably representative decorations. Guests sit at their birth-month table. Presents are chosen from a selection of "white elephants" which each guest has brought.

Since this party entails considerable preparation in the matter of refreshments and table decorations, it is necessary to know not only how many guests are coming but what their birth months are so that each table has places for the expected guests.

The kind of food served depends upon whether the party is a luncheon, dinner or merely a dessert party. In any case the dessert must be ice cream and cake with the cakes properly decorated with candles and other birthday paraphernalia.

GAMES AND ACTIVITIES

If such a party is primarily an eating party and the only open space is taken up with refreshment tables, many of the games are played at the tables with each table constituting one, two or even three teams depending on the number of players at the table. Ten is about the maximum number of players on a team; any more, and the whole purpose of helping people get acquainted is defeated.

Birthday Statistics

Give each team a scratch pad and pencil. Have teams appoint captains who act as secretaries. Ask secretaries to number a sheet of paper from one to fifteen, one number under the other down the long side of the sheet. The total score for item #1 is written after #1 and the score for item #2 after #2, etc. At the end of the game the total score is determined. If it has been impossible or inadvisable to take the time to organize teams of equal numbers, have the secretaries divide the total score by the number of players on the team to determine an average score for each team.

1. Five points for each different birth city represented on the team. (If five out of ten players were born in different cities, the score would be twenty-five points for that team. If all were born in the same city, the score would be five points.)

2. Ten points for each different birth state represented.

3. Ten points for each different country of birth.

4. For every player born on or before the fifteenth of the month, ten points. For every player born on or after the sixteenth of the month, five points.

5. Ten points for every player born on a national or legal holiday. Count Flag Day, Washington's or Lincoln's Birthday, Arbor Day, Veteran's Day.

6. Ten points for every player who was married on her birthday.

7. Twenty-five points for a woman who has a child born on her birthday.

8. Twenty-five points if there are two players on team having the same birthday.

9. Counting one point per year of membership, add the total number of years guests have been members of the particular organization giving the party.

10. Fifteen points if there are any mother-daughter com-

binations on a team. Other relationships such as sisters, sisters-in-law also count fifteen points.

Birthday Musical Game

See Birth-Month Song Game in Chapter 12 for use at an Everybody's Birthday Party.

Chapter 3

Active and Quiet Games

THERE IS A TIME and place for group games in any social occasion for children where the entire group plays together in non-competitive fashion. If there is plenty of space, these games help to work off excess steam and energy. When the space is limited or the weather warm, group games of a less active type are employed by the wise leader.

Many of the games given here are tried and sure-fire games which always bring pleasure. These are as important a part of our heritage as folk songs or folk dances. They have brought joy to children in the past and will continue to bring pleasure to those in future generations.

The games given here are classified for your convenience into three groups: Active Games; Quiet Games for Limited Spaces; and Run and Hide Games. All are suitable for boys and girls to play together. Where the games can be used for groups of children and adults playing together as they do at family parties, that information is given after the title of each game.

ACTIVE GAMES

Jump the Shot

Players form a circle around the leader, who stands in the center of the ring. The "shot" is a beanbag tied to the end of an eight-foot length of wash line. The leader swings the beanbag-weighted rope around the circle no higher than six inches off the ground. On the first few swings around the circle, the players stand back until the leader has gotten up momentum and has the bag under control. At a signal from the leader, the players must step in close enough so that they will be hit by the shot unless they jump at the proper moment. Any player hit by the beanbag below the knees is eliminated; a hit above the knee does not count. After the first player is hit, however, if the bag bounces off that player and hits a second, the second player is not eliminated. It is usually better not to eliminate any players for the first few rounds until they get the hang of the game. Then the leader announces that the practice session is over and any player hit will be eliminated. The game goes on until one player is left. The game may be played several times and the champion jumpers of each round then compete in a final round.

Whirling the shot takes skill and practice on the part of the leader. The best way to maintain a certain height and still be able to speed up or slow down the shot for a confusing change of pace pattern for the players is from a stooping or kneeling position. The leader does not turn with the rope but changes the rope from hand to hand. A loop or large knot tied near the end of the rope makes it easier to hold and tends to keep the rope from slipping out of the hands on the changes. Usually four rounds is enough for this game. It's harder on the leader than on the players, particularly if the group is a large one.

Fly Away

An active game for a large group of children. Depending upon the size of the group, number the children off by threes or fours. Players stand in single circle formation, facing in. The leader calls out, "ones." All number ones turn to their right and run once around the circle and back to their original places as fast as they can, attempting to catch the player ahead and trying not to be caught by the player behind. Any players caught must go into the center of the circle and become prisoners. The leader then repeats the process, calling out another number. At the end of the game those in the center must pay a forfeit for having been caught, or better, an exchange of prisoners may be made at the end of each run around. Those in the center are released if there are prisoners to take their places. By the latter method, no child remains in the center for too long a period.

Spud (Children and Adults)

Spud is a popular favorite. Number off the players so that

each player has a different number. If the leader is playing, he also must take a number. The leader throws a large rubber ball high into the air and calls a number at random. The player with that number attempts to catch the ball on the fly while all the other players scatter over a limited play area. As soon as the player has caught the ball he calls, "Spud." All other players must stop running. If the ball has been caught on the fly, the player catching the ball can take a giant step toward another player. From that position he attempts to hit the nearest player with the ball. That player may dodge the ball but cannot move his feet in doing so. If the thrower misses, he has an "S" scored against him. If he hits the other player, the player hit has an "S" scored against *him*. If the player whose number has been called could not catch it on the fly but had to catch it on a bounce, he must throw from the spot where he caught it. The player, after throwing the ball, retrieves it and then throws the ball into the air and calls another number and the game resumes. Those players who have accumulated four points against them, or enough to spell out the word SPUD, are lined up against a wall at the end of the game with their backs to the other players. The non-SPUDS then have the privilege of throwing the ball at the SPUDS, trying to hit them if they can.

Buddy Spuds

This game is played as described above except that each player has a partner. Thus there are two number ones, two twos, etc. When a number is called, one partner (by pre-arrangement) catches the ball. He then passes the ball to his partner, who throws it at the closest players. All penalties accumulated count against both partners regardless of which made the error or which was hit.

Beat and Swat (Children and Adults)

The group stands in a large circle, facing into the center. The only equipment needed is a beater which is made from a roll of newspapers held together with several rubber bands. All players stand with their eyes closed and their hands behind their backs. *It* moves around the outside of the circle, keeping a close watch for the peeping players. If he sees anyone with open eyes he is permitted to tap him on the head with the beater as a penalty for peeking. Very quietly he slips the beater into the hands of one of the players. This player becomes *It* and immediately turns to his right-hand neighbor and begins hitting him below the hips in good spanking fashion. The neighbor begins to run around the circle to avoid being spanked. He is followed by *It*, who is as determined to swat his neighbor as his neighbor is determined to get away. The player being chased must make one complete round of the circle and get back to his place. *It* then continues the game by placing the beater in another's hands and the chase begins again. The important thing to remember in this game is what happens to the old *It*. He must step into the place of the person to whom he gave the beater and he must do this quickly or he will be in the way of the runners, who are most anxious to be on their way and may not have time to stop and apologize for knocking him down should he be in their path of flight.

This is a hilarious game and wonderful for all except very young children and those who consider themselves too old to run. If played inside on slippery floors, slow the run down to a fast walk. It's just as much fun and much safer.

Dodge Ball (Team Method) (Adults and Children)

This is an old favorite which can be played in several fashions. Players stand in a single circle, facing into the center, and are counted off by twos. The ones enter the circle and the twos make a circle around them. A large rubber ball is given to the players in the outside circle. At the signal to begin, the player holding the ball throws it at the players in the center, attempting to hit one below the hips. (Hits above the hips do not count.) Players hit either by the ball with a direct hit or by the ball bouncing off another player are eliminated and become spectators. The leader keeps time to determine how long it takes for the entire team except one to be eliminated. The last player left competes against the last player left on the other team after the second team has had its turn in the center. By this method you determine not only the best team but the best dodger.

Dodge Ball (Individual Method)

This game is played very much like the one described above except that the eliminated players join the circle as soon as they are eliminated and become throwers. The game continues until the last player is eliminated. To make the game more exciting, use two balls instead of one.

Chain Gang Dodge Ball

Three players are selected to make a chain in the center of the circle. They stand one behind another, holding on to the waist of the player in front. The players standing in circle formation throw the ball, attempting to hit the end man of the chain gang. The player who threw the ball which hit the end of the chain goes into the circle and stands at the head of the chain. The end man who was hit rejoins the circle and becomes a thrower. The threes in the chain must be very agile and active, swinging from side to side and dodging as best they can in an attempt to protect the end man. The players on the outside will find it best not to try to make direct hits every time but to pass the ball quickly around or across the circle until a thrower has a good chance to hit the end man. The passing gives every player a chance at the ball and keeps the chain gang on the move.

Skin the Snake (A Stunt Game)

Divide group into teams of seven or eight players. Have members of teams stand in files, one player behind the other in close formation. At a signal to hook on, players bend forward slightly, put their right hands between their legs to be grasped by the player behind and, at the same time, grasp the right hand of the player ahead of them in their left hands. Thus all members are joined together. When all are in proper position in the manner described, the end man very carefully lies down, still holding the hand of the player ahead. For this to happen, the man next to the end must walk backward carefully with feet astride over the body of the end man, carefully pulling the man ahead of him backward. As soon as he can lie down without breaking the chain, the second man from the end does so. This process continues until the whole team is lying on the floor, still with hands joined. When all are down, the end man is now first in line and the first player is at the tail end. The movements are now reversed and the last man to go down gets up carefully and walks forward with feet astride over the body of the second player, pulling him up to his feet. This motion continues until all the players are standing up again, still with hands joined. The trick is to go down in proper fashion and get back to the original position again without letting go of hands. If you have more than one group, this can be run as a relay, with one team racing *slowly and carefully* against another. But win or lose, just to be able to do it at all is a good trick.

Slap Jack

This is a game which can be varied in so many ways that it seems like many games. Players stand in a single circle, facing in, with hands behind their backs. *It* starts around the circle in either direction, slaps a player's hand and continues around the circle in the direction he was moving. The player whose hand was slapped leaves his place and runs around the circle in the opposite direction from *It*, attempting to get back to his original place in the circle before *It* can get there. The last player back to the proper place is *It* for the next time.

Variation of Slap Jack

Play as above, but when the two runners meet they must take hands and stoop before proceeding around the circle to their destinations.

Another variation that is fun is to have the players join both hands with each other when they meet and run around in a little circle three times before proceeding in the proper direction (if they still know which is the proper direction).

Double Slap Jack

Number players off by twos so that each has a partner.

Players stand beside their partners in a single circle holding inside hands. Play the game in the same way as Slap Jack except that there is a double *It* and two players must run around the circle, holding hands as they run. The double *It* touches off another pair of players and each couple, with hands joined, proceeds around the circle in opposite directions. Add the variation of having the players take hands when they meet in their trip around the circle and circling three times around before they can proceed to the proper place. Running with a partner is harder than running alone and adds to the fun.

Tandem Slap Jack

Play in the same manner as described in Double Slap Jack except that the partners stand one behind the other, with the one behind holding on to the hips of the player ahead. All running must be done in this fashion. The *It* is a double one and must also proceed around the circle in tandem fashion.

Tandem Tag

Have each player take a partner. One partner stands behind the other with hands on the hips of his partner. The player behind must have a tight hold. There is one *It* in this game. He runs from couple to couple, attempting to hook on to the player in the back. To hook on, he must have hold of that player's hips with both hands. When *It* has hooked on to a player properly, the front player is released and becomes *It*. To make it hard for *It*, all couples swing and turn from side to side to keep from being caught. In large groups use two *Its*.

Whistle Groups (Adults and Children)

Players stand in an unorganized group in the play area. The leader signals by blasts of the whistle what size groups are to be formed. If the leader blows twice, players must form circles of two. If the leader blasts the whistle five times, players must regroup into little circles of five. The leader ends with the size group desired for the next game. If she wants them in teams of ten she can blow ten times, or she can finish with groups of five and join two groups together to make teams. If a partner game is to follow this game, the leader ends the game with two blasts. Children love this game. At a party in a home, chords on the piano may be used instead of whistle blasts.

Two Deep

Players take partners, one standing behind the other, with the couples in circle formation. The player who is *It* begins chasing another player. This player attempts to avoid being caught by running to the head of any group of two. This gives the runner immunity from being caught but immediately makes the tail partner on the outside a runner. *It* tries to catch this new runner. No runner may cut through the circle but must run around the outside until he desires immunity. Only then can he step into the circle and in front of a couple. Should a runner be caught, he becomes *It* and must chase the old *It*. When one *It* becomes too tired, the leader may blow her whistle signaling runner and *It* to reverse positions and directions. The runner becomes *It* and begins chasing the old *It*, who can then step in front of a couple and release a new runner. If a group is too small to play this game with partners, the same procedure may be played in a single circle of players. The runner, by stepping in front of a player, makes him a runner. Similarly, if the group is very large, the game may be played as three-deep with three players standing in each group.

Squirrel in a Tree (Adults and Children)

Organize group into small groups of three and give each child a number from one to three in each group. Have the ones and twos join hands to make a tree. Number three in each group is the squirrel and stands in the little circle formed by the ones and twos. Have two or three other players who are the extra squirrels. At a whistle signal from the leader, all the squirrels must change trees. The extra squirrels, of course, try to get a tree. After several changes, have the number threes exchange places with the number twos so that they get a chance to be squirrels. And after a time, give the ones a chance to be squirrels.

The couples need not stand in circle formation, but should remain within a limited playing area.

QUIET GAMES FOR LIMITED SPACES

Fool Ball (Adults and Children)

The leader stands in the center of the circle with a large rubber ball. Players stand in a large circle facing in, hands behind their backs. Leader indicates which is the player who is to have the first turn and which direction the play will go around the circle. When this is done, the leader explains that he will make the motions of throwing the ball to player after player in turn, attempting to fool them into thinking he is going to throw the ball. The players must stand motionless without making perceptible movements of the arms unless the leader actually throws the ball to them. If the ball is thrown the player must catch it. If a player is fooled into moving his arms or fails to catch a thrown ball, he is eliminated from the game. He stays in the circle but sits down in his place or, if the ground is wet, stands with his arms folded on his chest to indicate to the leader that he is out of the game. The last player becomes *It* for the next game. If the leader makes a poor throw that is impossible to catch, the player who misses the ball is not eliminated. This is a good game for indoors or outdoors and one that offers much challenge to the players. Last player left standing is the fooler for the next game.

Have You Seen My Lost Sheep?

Players sit in a large circle facing in. *It* stands behind one player and this conversation goes on:

It: "Have you seen my lost sheep?"

Player: "No. What does it look like?"

It then begins to describe the clothes of a player. As soon as the player being described as the lost sheep recognizes himself, he jumps up and begins running around the circle followed by the first player. *It* meanwhile sits down in the place of the player doing the chasing and gets out of the way of the runners. If the lost sheep can get back to his own place before being caught he remains there and the new *It* goes to another player and the same process is repeated. If, however, the lost sheep is caught he must go in the center and stay until another player is caught and can come into the center to replace him. The fun in the game comes when the lost sheep being described is seated very close to the chaser. The chase then becomes very exciting and the lost sheep is more apt to be caught than if he were seated across the circle from the chaser.

Who Is Leading? (Adults and Children)

The players stand in a single circle facing into the center. One is chosen to be *It* and retires to a safe distance until he is called back. While *It* is out of hearing, a leader is chosen by the players. He then begins some repetitive motion which the group picks up. A good leader constantly changes the motions. Meanwhile *It* has come back to the circle and attempts to discover who is starting all the motions. He has only three guesses in which to come up with the right answer. A tricky leader will make a change of motion even if *It* is looking directly at him because *It* can never be sure that he is looking at the leader or someone who is merely imitating the leader. It is not as easy to pick out the leader as one might suppose, particularly if all the players do not watch the leader but watch other players who are following the motions of the leader.

Human Puzzle (Adults and Children)

Players stand in a single circle, facing in and holding hands. *It* remains outside the circle and retires to a safe distance with eyes closed until he is called. The circle of players, meanwhile, *without letting go of hands* proceeds to tangle itself up and tie itself up into a tight knot. This is done by having players (while holding hands) coming from across the circle and pulling part of the circle through an arch formed by two players. A similar tangle is made in another portion of the circle. In a good tangle a player often has difficulty in knowing who has hold of his hand. *It*, when called back, must untangle the snarled-up circle without breaking the hand holds. The author has seen a group get itself so tangled that the *It* has given up in despair. If *It* should give up, the circle must untangle itself before his eyes to prove that it can be done. Remember, all tangles must be made without players breaking hand holds.

Variation: Begin this game from a line formation instead of a circle. Tangle must be made without breaking hold of hands.

Button Snap

This is a wall game. Each player has a button or a coin. One player lays his button or coin near the wall. The other players in turn snap their playing pieces against the wall from a line about six feet away. A playing piece that lands within a span of the hand (distance between outstretched little finger and thumb) of the target scores two points for the thrower. A coin within two spans scores one point. If a coin hits the target and bounces within one span away it counts four points. If it hits and bounces within two spans it counts three points and if farther than two spans it counts only one point. Players should agree on a game score, twenty-five or fifty points, before beginning the game. The first player to reach the total wins the game. (Note: Playing pieces are snapped from the thumb and not tossed at the target.)

Club Snatch

Divide group into two equal teams and line them up facing each other about twenty-five feet apart. At the center point between the two teams draw a thirty-inch circle and place an Indian club in it.

Number the players on each team, with the number ones on each team being at opposite ends of the line in this manner (X represents the Indian club):

1 2 3 4 5 6 7 8

X

8 7 6 5 4 3 2 1

The leader calls a number. The player with that number on each team advances to the Indian club. With caution and cunning, each player attempts to snatch the club from its place and carry it back to his team without being touched or tagged by his opponent. Faking and fooling plays a prominent part in this game in the effort to confuse the opponent. Neither player may step into the thirty-inch circle during the fooling or snatching process. If a player succeeds in snatching the club and getting back to his team without being tagged or caught, a point is scored for his team. If he is tagged or caught, the opposing team scored a point.

May I?

The players stand in one long line facing a finish line some fifty feet away. It stands facing them. He tells the first player he may take a certain number of baby steps or giant steps. The player must ask a polite "May I?" before he takes the prescribed number of steps toward the finish line. If he fails to say the magic words, It immediately sends him back to the starting line. Each player, in turn, is then given permission to take whatever number of steps It tells him to. The first player to cross the finish line is It for the next game. There is a sneak play permitted in this game. While It is busy with one player, any other player may attempt to inch forward. If, however, he is caught in the act, It sends him back to the starting line as a penalty for stealing.

Grunt, Pig, Grunt

Players stand in a small, tight circle. It stands in the circle blindfolded. Someone turns him around several times to confuse him and then lets him go. It then walks forward with arm outstretched until he can touch a player with his index finger. It then commands the player he is touching to "Grunt, pig, grunt." The player must comply by grunting. It tries to guess his identity. He may ask him only three times. If he cannot guess the person, he must move on to another player. It is permitted only to poke a player with his finger. He cannot feel his clothes or face in his attempt to identify him.

RUN-AND-HIDE GAMES

Tap the Icebox

It stands at the goal and covers his eyes. The other players stand around him. One gives him a poke. If *It* guesses who poked him, the guilty player becomes *It*. If, however, *It* cannot identify the player who poked him, he must stay *It*. He must then cover his eyes and count loudly to some agreed-upon number while the others run and hide.

When *It* has finished the count he yells: "Here I come," and begins looking for the hidden players. When he finds one he races that player back to the goal. If *It* touches goal before the other player, that player is *It* for the next round. Meanwhile, when *It* is out hunting for players, any hidden player may attempt to sneak back to the goal when *It* is not looking. As soon as *It* has caught one player, he calls: "All-ee, all-ee in free," which is the signal for all the hidden players to come back to the goal without penalty of being caught. Should *It* fail to catch at least one player, he must be *It* for the next round. This is a wonderful old game to play around houses and garages just about dusk or at camp where plenty of hiding places are available.

Kick the Can

This is another exciting hide-and-seek game. A tin can is placed next to the goal. *It* hides his eyes and counts aloud to an agreed-upon number while the other players hide. At the end of the count he may or may not announce that he is coming and begins hunting. If he locates a hiding player, he races him back to the goal. If *It* tags the goal before the other player, he has captured a prisoner, who must stay near the goal while *It* begins hunting again. While *It* is on the prowl, another hidden player may sneak back to the goal and release the prisoner by kicking the can and yelling "Kick the can" as he does. The freed prisoner and the player who released him then hide anew. *It* must continue to hunt until all players are made prisoners. The first player to have been made prisoner is then *It* for the next round. One round may last all evening if the players are cunning and *It* is a little slow.

Chapter 4

Bazaars and Fairs

CHURCHES, P.T.A.'s and other organizations which have annual money-raising programs will find that the family bazaar is the most fun of all. It is planned for and by men, women and youths so that there is something of interest for persons of all ages and so that all members of the family will have a part in it.

When it is decided to have a bazaar, a planning committee should be organized months ahead of the bazaar date. The types of booths and activities should be planned then so that some groups may begin working on their projects. Some booths sell handiwork that is made by the women's groups. The articles to be sold are made over a period of months by groups of women working together at regularly scheduled meetings or by women working individually in their own homes. However this is done, some advance planning must be done so that the handiwork booth will contain a variety of things.

Color, sounds and pleasant and appetizing smells are important parts of every bazaar. Colorful decorations and signs; the sounds of the hawkers shouting their wares; the music of the roving accordionist; the voices of many people all talking at once; the tantalizing odors of fresh popcorn, hot coffee and hot dogs; balloons floating in the air; visitors, loaded with purchases, rushing hither and yon; pushcart peddlers in colorful costumes; all these make a bazaar a fascinating place to spend time and money. In the early planning, the sights, sounds and odors should be given important consideration. The more color and the more atmosphere that can be created, the longer people will want to stay.

If a bazaar is to be a family affair the children must be considered. Having a fish pond for the children is all very nice, but once the child has spent his money, what then?

Children have ways of finding something to do if nothing is provided. Children underfoot and getting into mischief are a worry to their parents and a nuisance to everybody. Such a situation is unnecessary and unfair to the children. With proper planning many behavior problems never develop. In the section on Special Services, a number of activities and programs are suggested for the children.

Listed below and described in detail are the kinds of booths and activities that help to make a family-type bazaar a success. No matter how much or how little money is made, or how much work is entailed, the biggest asset of a bazaar is the fellowship and togetherness that is developed through large numbers of people playing and working together in one joint effort. The money made is just so much extra dividend.

THINGS-FOR-SALE BOOTHS

Home Crafts

Home-sewn and handmade articles of all kinds needed in the home—aprons, pot holders, hot mats, place mats, hand-embroidered tea towels, tablecloths, bridge sets, etc., are sold at this booth. These products are in the making for months and require long-range planning. Aprons made from inexpensive remnants can be sold cheaper and thus more readily than ones made from expensive yard goods. Pot holders made from scraps rather than from materials especially purchased for that purpose cost little or nothing and can be sold cheaply but with good profit.

Tote Bags and Carryalls

Certain kinds of articles can be purchased only at bazaars and visitors look forward to buying such articles there. Tote bags are dressy shopping bags that make practical purchases and welcome gifts and are always good sellers. If these can be made from donated materials or inexpensive remnants, the selling prices can be made more attractive and the profits realized are just as great.

Dolls

Funny, lovable rag dolls are fun to make and sell well at

fairs and bazaars as they have a charm all their own not always found in the commercial rag dolls. Commercial dolls dressed by the women of the organization are also good sellers, particularly if the clothes are the kind that can be taken off and washed by the little owners. Beanbag toys are also good sellers.

Green-Thumb Booth

Every organization has its green-thumbers who will raise healthy plants at home especially for the bazaar which they pot attractively and donate for sale. Others make up interesting and beautiful floral arrangements from straw flowers, grasses and field flowers that make excellent winter bouquets. The chairman of this booth may want to make arrangements with a local florist to sell plants and dish gardens on a commission basis so that an ample supply of plants is available. Dried field flowers for winter bouquets, colored gourds, Christmas greens and wreaths (if the bazaar is held near Christmas) and other seasonal decorations might be sold at this booth.

The Arts-and-Crafts Booth

Every organization has its artists and craftsmen who will donate articles they have made for sale. They will bring other articles such as paintings, ceramics, enameled metal, photographs, etchings, etc., to place on sale on a commission basis. Such a booth not only adds to the color of a fair or bazaar and gives another sources of revenue but also helps members to become acquainted with and aware of the talents of the various members.

The Businessmen's Booth

The businessmen of any organization can bring products of various kinds to sell, some of which they may donate or bring on a commission basis, and give all of the profit over and above the wholesale price to the organization. Again, such a booth not only adds to the variety of articles sold at the fair but acquaints members of the organization with the businesses of the various members.

Talent

A group of musical members may form a quartet or orchestra just for this occasion and perform at certain times during the day. Guests may toss coins to the musicians. All money collected goes into the general fund.

Wandering Minstrels

An accordionist and singers may act as strolling musicians, singing requested selections. They will not refuse coins tossed into the proffered hat.

Homemade Goodies

Mrs. Jones' homemade bread, Grandma Smith's cherry pie, cakes, cookies and specialties from the ovens and kitchens of the good cooks and bakers always provide a quickly purchased stock for a goodies table. Jams, jellies, relishes, canned fruits, pickles and sauces are seldom left unsold.

Some organizations have special stickers made with the organization's name with which they label all the donated jellies and canned goods. Since some of the articles purchased are given by the buyers as gifts to their friends, the fair or bazaar is remembered for months afterward.

Specialty Sales

Sometimes arrangements are made with companies that sell jewelry, cosmetics, novelties, greeting cards and gift wraps, spices and condiments to have their products for sale on a consignment basis. All unsold articles may be returned for credit and the organization keeps the profit on the articles sold.

Popcorn, Peanuts, Candy and Candied Apples

Popcorn, particularly if donated by the group taking over the booth, is a good money maker. Its delicious odor wafts all over the room and is hard to resist. Peanuts and homemade or commercial candy may also be sold at this booth. If candy can be sold from a penny up, little children will have a chance to buy. Candied apples will sell well and at a good profit.

Balloons

Air-inflated balloons tied on a stick are good money makers at a bazaar, particularly if the child's name is written on the balloon with a felt marking pen. A balloon is hard to resist but when it has one's own name on it, it's even more wonderful. Balloons add to the color of the bazaar and make it more fun for the children.

Grab Bag or Surprise Grab

Articles of all kinds are wrapped and placed on the table or are wheeled around in a decorated cart. Children may buy a surprise for a few pennies.

The Toy Shop

Children of the organization are urged to bring toys (still in good condition) that they no longer play with or books and records they are tired of. These are put on sale at reasonable prices. All money taken in is profit and the children have a wonderful time browsing around for "new" toys to buy.

White-Elephant Table

One of the most popular booths at a fair or carnival is the white-elephant table. Here members assemble all the still usable odds and ends no longer wanted or never wanted in the first place. The articles are then priced by the committee which works on the principle that what is one man's junk is another's treasure. Even the most unlikely-to-sell piece is eventually carried off in triumph by someone.

Experience has proven that the more jumbled the appearance of the table the surer the prospect is of making a "find." All mixed up with no apparent order are pie plates, odd cups, salts and peppers and children's rubbers. Pictures framed or unframed are hung where they can be seen. Sooner or later most pieces are sold. What is left can be put in a carton and shipped off to the Salvation Army, Goodwill Industries or Volunteers of America.

The Haggle Table

The most-fun-of-all way to handle the white elephants is

to haggle them away instead of selling them. The odds and ends are all put together under a sign that reads: NOTHING IS PRICED. MAKE US AN OFFER. Buyers make an offer on a piece and the seller tries to get a higher price. The haggling goes on and eventually a price is agreed upon. The fun in this type of selling is that the offer made is often more than the committee would have dared to ask for the article. The seller sometimes feels obliged to say that the offer made is too high and may suggest a lower price. This technique so confounds the buyer that he comes back to the table again and again just for the fun of haggling.

Some customers, however, are too shy to make an offer. They are afraid that their offer will make them look ridiculous, and will actually walk away from the table rather than haggle. The technique to use in this instance is to say, "Well, if you won't make an offer, let me ask you this: 'Is it worth a quarter to you?' " This usually encourages the prospect a little and the haggling process is again in motion.

The Book Table

The book table is one of the more popular booths. Everyone has books that are still in good condition but, having been read, are no longer wanted. Paper-cover mysteries, book-club selections, old reference books all take their place on the book table. What actually happens is that the visitors just exchange books. One member brings in a box of books and eventually goes out with an armload. He gives his away and buys someone else's. Everybody is happy and the organization is money ahead. Leftovers may be given to libraries and other organizations wanting books of all kinds.

Shopping Bags

What is handier to have and harder to find at a fair or bazaar than a paper shopping bag? Organizations are wise to buy a supply of these and decorate them with sketches, pictures and the name of the organization. The bags can be sold at every booth and by a roving salesman with a loud voice and winning ways. The bags are useful souvenirs and sell at a profit as well.

The Parcel-Post Booth

Some organizations give absent members opportunities to participate in annual fairs through the parcel-post method. Members who are away for the season and former members who have moved away are all contacted and asked to send gifts and white elephants valued at twenty-five cents or more through the mail. These packages are sold for a stipulated price, sight unseen. Instead of a pig in a poke it's a surprise in a parcel-post package, since the packages are sold in the original wrappings complete with stamps. There is nothing in the rules that prohibit buyers from swapping with other buyers or donating their purchases to the white-elephant table.

The Herb Booth

The herb gardeners and herb cooks love to have a chance to promote their favorite sport. These enthusiasts prepare their dried herbs in attractive packets that prove very salable. Herb-cookery booklets and charts can also be sold at such a booth. Jars of potpourri and sachet packets and pomander balls make this booth even more interesting.

Pomander balls are made by sticking whole cloves into small oranges. The fruit is literally covered with the spice. Decorated with colorful ribbon bows, these spicy balls make attractive gifts. The oranges dry out and give off a pleasant fragrance when hung in linen closets. One group might make this a money-raising project for its part of the fair.

Food Concessions

What fun are fairs without food? Some organizations serve complete meals during fair day and whole families can come for the noonday or evening meals. Snacks should be available for the visitors who come for an hour or so and do not intend to stay for a meal. The old familiar hot dog or hamburger is always a welcome snack. Ice cream, homemade cake and cookies sell well for the afternoon-tea snack.

Hot Waffle Concession

Nothing tastes better than a hot sugared waffle in the hand. Members bring waffle irons and make the waffles to order.

Hot Doughnuts

With the small deep-fat fryers that are now available, a stand is easily set up where fresh doughnuts are made to order. These may be hard on the digestive system, but at a bazaar all such thoughts are put out of mind.

SPECIAL SERVICES

Movies

Free or inexpensive movie programs may be provided for the children at various times during the day. If activities are provided for the children, the parents feel free to bring the children when they come. They stay longer and thus often spend more.

Puppet Shows

A group in the organization may prepare a puppet show especially for the fair. This can be given several times during the day for a small admission fee.

Baby Parking

A room or two ought to be set aside where the babies and young children can be taken care of by volunteers who work only an hour or two at a time. If parents bring the car bassinets or folding buggies the children can sleep comfortably while the parents enjoy the fair. Toys and equipment from the nursery or kindergarten of the church or school can be used to keep the two- and three-year-olds happy for an hour or so. A charge can be made for this service or it can be provided free in an effort to attract the parents of young children to the bazaar.

The Children's Carnival

Bazaars are usually not much fun for the children unless special attention is given their needs. Organize a carnival where volunteers who come for scheduled periods are in attendance for the entire period of the bazaar. Eight or ten games are set up. Children may win little prizes at a game or accept tickets instead which, when they are through playing, they may turn in for prizes which have been donated or purchased. Prizes are given ticket-value prices. For example, a wastebasket is priced at twenty-five tickets, a pencil at three tickets. Thus a child may spend all his winning tickets on a big prize or take ten small ones if he so desires. Prizes may be samples brought in by businessmen or souvenirs given by companies for which members work. Boxes of crayons, candy bars or other inexpensive articles may be purchased. An admission charge is made at the door of fifty or seventy-five cents, which entitles the child to stay and play all day if he wishes. If he wants to leave for awhile and then come back, this is also permitted. The games are set up all around a room which can be easily supervised by someone at the ticket table at the door. Volunteers work at each game on a scheduled basis for no longer than two hours at a time. One particular score at a game entitles a child to a tiny prize: a candy kiss, a balloon or a sucker. A better score entitles him to a ticket. Everybody wins something, and the child who works at it can go home with a basketful.

A carnival not only provides interesting activity for the children for many hours, but proves to be a money maker as well. See Chapter 5 for games suitable for a children's carnival.

Photo Booth

Members who own cameras that make instant pictures can set up booths and do individual and family portraits. Amusing backdrops add to the fun and the resulting pictures make good souvenirs of the fair.

Silhouettes

Organizations who have silhouette makers among their members will find such a booth to be a successful venture.

Amateur Astronomers

When there is an amateur astronomer in the group who has his own telescope, a concession is set up and proves a profitable and interesting part of the fair. If the weather conditions are not suitable the telescope is turned toward familiar landmarks. Telescopes never fail to fascinate.

NOVELTY AND SPECIALTY BOOTHS

Fortune-Telling Booths

Tea-leaf-reading, fortune-telling and palm-reading booths make money and provide entertainment for visitors at fairs and carnivals. No fair is really complete without one or more of these features. The more atmosphere that can be created by use of colorful costumes, decorated booths, crystal balls, etc., the greater the fun.

The Make-It-on-the-Spot Shop

The church bazaar or P.T.A. fair need not be a boring affair for the children and the men who sometimes feel "dragged" there and spend hours waiting while the mothers and wives do their stint in the kitchen or in one of the booths. For those who will spend a long period of time at the fair, the Make-It-on-the-Spot Shop will prove novel and interesting. Here a visitor may spend several hours making some leather project such as a belt, coin purse or key case, or assembling a pair of moccasins. Not only is a useful article made but often a new skill is developed and a new interest born. Now, with the small portable enameling-on-metal kilns available, projects in this field may be completed even by a beginner in an hour. If the bazaar is near to Christmas, simple Christmas decorations may be one of the make-it-yourself projects. Materials may often be obtained from local craft houses at a professional discount and on a consignment basis. All unused projects can be returned. Volunteer craftsmen run the booth and sell supplies on a cost-plus basis. Extra projects to make at home and perhaps even tools and supplies can be sold. The shop does more than fill in hours pleasantly for visitors; it opens new doors to creative endeavor and may even make a little money.

Chapter 5

Skill Games for Bazaars, Fairs and Progressive Parties

SKILL GAMES are wonderfully versatile. They can be used at bazaars and fairs, at progressive parties and as preparty activities. In the following pages, each will be discussed in detail to demonstrate how these activities can be used to the best advantage.

SKILL GAMES AT BAZAARS

The Children's Carnival at a Bazaar

Skill games can be put to good use in setting up a children's carnival which will not only provide many happy hours of play for the children but will prove profitable. Sometimes it is difficult to find ways of putting the husbands and fathers to work at a bazaar. The carnival is a good spot for that purpose. The men can be placed in charge of various games. If this is done on a short-period schedule basis, no one person need work too long. If the carnival is run for seven or eight hours, as might be necessary for an all-day bazaar, the men might be scheduled to work in two-hour shifts.

Parents will have fun taking their children into the carnival and playing with them. By placing starting and throwing lines back for adults, the games will be equally challenging to adults and children.

How a carnival is incorporated into a bazaar program is discussed in Chapter 4.

SKILL GAMES AT PROGRESSIVE PARTIES

Skill games are the basis for one of the types of progressive parties. See pages 33 to 37 for full description of a Skill-Games Progressive Party.

SKILL GAMES AS PREPARTY ACTIVITIES

Skill games make good activities for the preparty period when the guests who arrive on time are waiting for the latecomers. A few games of the most challenging variety will intrigue your guests and keep them busy until you are ready to begin the main events of the party.

SKILL GAMES AS BAZAAR OR FAIR FEATURES

Some of the booths at a bazaar might employ skill games set up as concessions. The skill-game booths can be scattered around the bazaar headquarters and operate on an individual basis like any other booth. The selection of the individual games should be done carefully so that balls or corks or other paraphernalia would not be flying all over the room and getting underfoot. Such games add to the fun of a bazaar and make for interesting variety.

SKILL GAMES AT FAIRS

Fairs are usually money-raising projects which some organization holds to secure funds for some community purpose. A fair, then, is one big carnival with skill-game booths scattered all over an indoor or outdoor facility. Intermingled are refreshment booths and concessions with rides for the children. For this kind of project, the skill games are set up each in an individual booth. To avoid all booths having to keep money on hand for making change, one or two ticket booths may be set up at advantageous points and all tickets handled through them. Play at any booth is by ticket only except where the player's own pennies are used for throwing pieces. In those games, pennies thrown into play are retrieved by the booth manager and "sold" back to the players who need change.

Descriptions of skill games follow. Winning scores are given in terms of prizes and tickets where the system of play permits players to accumulate tickets to turn in for larger prizes. When this system is not used, and less valuable prizes are given at each individual game, the higher score should be used as the determining factor and no other prizes given.

Distance of throwing or pitching lines is to be considered as variable. The leader in setting up the game tries to determine where the line should be by playing the game from several distances. The line should be set so that no one wins all the time and no one loses all the time. Separate lines may be set up for children and adults if desired.

GAMES OF SKILL

Beanbag Bowling

Set up three wooden bowling pins or milk bottles near a wall. Set the bottles just far enough apart so that a beanbag can pass between without touching the bottles or pins. Make a mark on the floor once the position of a pin is determined so that when a pin is knocked down, the game tender knows where it is to be reset. Players stand back about six to eight feet and attempt to slide three beanbags down the floor between the bowling pins without knocking them down. Two out of three wins a small prize; three successful tosses wins a ticket.

Beanbag Toss

Fasten five tin cans (gallon size with edges cleanly cut and smoothed down) to a square frame. Set the board against a chair or prop it up so that it will be tilted away from the player. Players stand back about eight feet and attempt to throw three beanbags into the cans. If a beanbag lands on the edge of the can and is not knocked off in the process of play, it counts as in. Two out of three successful tosses wins a little prize. Three out of three wins a ticket.

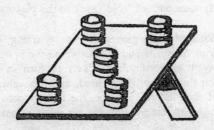

Clown Shoot

See page 27 for description of this game.

Hoop-a-leg

Turn a chair over so that it rests on its back with the legs pointing toward the players. Players stand back about eight feet and attempt to ring the legs with four embroidery hoops. Give a little prize for two out of four ringers and a ticket for three out of four ringers.

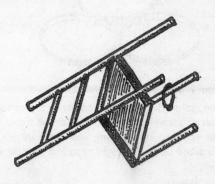

Ball-and-Glass Game

Take a small cardboard carton, preferably one in which glass jars were packed. Put heavy drinking glasses or small jars in the box until the box is full. With a little experimenting you can get just the right-sized carton which will hold twelve glasses or jars. Place the carton with the glasses on a four- to six-foot-long table. Prop it up so that it is tilted away from the players. Players standing at one end of the table attempt to toss or bounce five ping-pong balls into the glasses. Give a small prize for two out of five successful tosses and a ticket for three out of five.

Ring Target Toss

Fasten three embroidery hoops together in a flat triangle. Cellulose tape will make a good fastening agent. Lay the hoops on the floor near a wall. Players stand back about ten feet and attempt to toss five jar rings into the hoops on the floor. Give a small prize for two out of five. Give a ticket for three or more out of five. Always give the benefit of the doubt and eliminate arguments. If the jar rubber lands on the edge of a hoop, score it as in the hoop.

Variation: Poker chips or heavy washers might be substituted for the jar rings.

Hoop and Pan Toss

Fasten three embroidery hoops together in a row with cellu-lose tape or electrician's tape. Then fasten the three hoops to a board about eighteen inches long and three inches wide so that the hoops stand up in a straight row. Put the row of hoops

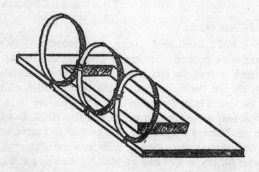

near the end of a six- or eight-foot table with the end of the table against the wall. Behind the hoop and also against the wall place a large rectangular cake pan or cookie sheet. In other words, the hoops are standing just in front of the cake pan. Players stand at one end of the table and attempt to toss bottle caps or metal washers *through* the hoops into the pan.

A loud "clunk" heralds the successful throw and adds to the pleasant noises of any carnival. Give players five washers. Two out of five wins a little prize; three out of five, a ticket.

Balloon and Bag

Inflate a six-inch round balloon and tie the neck of the balloon to hold in air. Tie a twelve-inch string to the balloon. Weight the other end of the string with a washer. Prepare at least a dozen such contraptions so that you have extra on hand in case of breakage.

Players stand back about ten feet and attempt to throw three balloon contraptions into a wastebasket or cardboard carton placed against the wall in a corner. Two out of three wins a small prize; three out of three wins a ticket.

Bird in the Basket

In this game the bird in the basket is worth three in the hand. Players stand back about ten feet and attempt to toss three shuttlecocks or badminton birds into a wastebasket or small carton. Two out of three wins a small prize and three out of three wins a ticket.

Sailing Saucers

Paper plates are unpredictable things when thrown at a target. Give players five six-inch plates. From a line about ten to fifteen feet away, they attempt to sail the paper plates into a carton or wastebasket. Three out of five wins a small prize; four or more wins a ticket.
Variation: Suspend a hoop in a doorway or from the ceiling. Players attempt to sail the plates through the hoop.

Hit the Funny Face

Make a hole in the center of an old sheet, large enough for a person to put his head through, or pin two blankets together leaving an open space large enough for a head in the center of the seam. Hang the sheet or blanket on a wash line held in place by two volleyball standards or poles driven into the ground (if the activity is to be used outside). Players stand back about ten feet and throw ping-pong balls or cellulose sponges at the funny face. The "clown" wears a catcher's mask. Loud yells from the clown add to the fun. Three throws are permitted each player. Give a small prize for one hit out of three and a ticket for two hits.

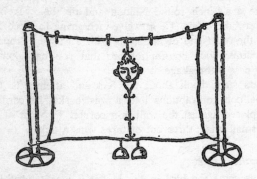

Pin and Silver Dollar

Where plenty of space is available and hard balls can be thrown without endangering bystanders or marking walls, this is a good carnival skill game that is fun for children and adults alike. A platform about a foot high and about three and one-half to four feet square is set back about fifteen feet from the throwing line. A regulation bowling pin is set in the center of the platform. A silver dollar is placed on the top of the pin, which may have to be flattened somewhat to hold the coin. Players attempt to hit the pin with the baseballs and knock it down in such a way as to have the silver dollar roll off the platform. This is not easy to do, so a good prize ought to be given for each successful hit. The prize may be the silver dollar itself. Regulation baseballs are used. If no platform is available a three-and-one-half- to four-foot area might be marked off on the floor or the ground.

Cork Shoot

Cork-shooting guns are usually available at toy counters. Set up a shooting gallery where players shoot corks at targets which come with such a game. A box with holes cut into it might be used as a target. Players shoot five corks per turn. Three out of five successful shots wins a prize. Four out of five wins a ticket.

Rubber-Dart Shoot

Guns which shoot darts with rubber suction-cup tips are available at toy counters. Players shoot darts at targets hung on a wall or backdrop. These are much safer to use than sharp pointed darts but precautions must still be taken that no bystander gets hit by a flying missile. Dart games of any kind must be roped off to insure safety at all times. One accident can ruin an otherwise successful occasion. Each player shoots three darts. Two out of three wins a ticket.

Dart and Balloon

Where it is possible to use the pointed darts safely, rig up a dart-and-balloon game. Use an archery target and hang four or five inflated balloons at a time. Do not blow up the balloons to the maximum. Players throw three darts at the target, attempting to break the balloons. Two out of three wins a ticket. Caution: Rope off such an area to protect spectators and players from wildly thrown darts. If used inside protect the floor with a heavy covering.

Archery-Target Balloon Shoot

Use regulation archery target and hang balloons on the target as described above. Use a child's toy bow-and-arrow set. A regulation bow would be too dangerous in a limited area. Score as indicated in previously described game.

Angel-Tin Penny Throw

Place an angel-food-cake tin or large hollow-center mold as a target on the floor or at the end of a table. Players throw pennies or washers into the center of the mold. Two out of three wins a ticket. Players might throw their own pennies into the mold if the game is being used as a money maker. All pennies falling into the ring would be retained by the organization. All pennies going into the center would also be retained but a candy bar or some small prize might be awarded. At a children's carnival, pennies, washers or bottle caps can be furnished to the children for the game.

Bottle Lift

Equipment for this game is a Coke bottle or any sturdy bottle up to a quart size and a three-foot stick with a three-foot string tied to one end. A rubber jar ring or a metal ring about three inches in diameter is tied to the other end of the string.

Players holding the stick stand back from the bottle about three feet. They attempt to place the ring on the neck of the bottle, which is *lying down* (this is not hard to do), and they attempt to pull the bottle up to a standing position (this is hard to do). Allow each player three attempts.

This is also a good preparty-activity stunt or parlor stunt. On a hard uncovered floor, it is very difficult to do. It is an easier trick on a rug.

Hoop-and-Bottle Toss

Take three soft-drink bottles and place them in a close triangle on the floor. Players from about eight to ten feet away attempt to toss an embroidery hoop in such a way as to ring all three bottles with one hoop. Give each player three hoops for a turn. One out of three wins a prize; two out of three wins a ticket.

Goldfish Catch

The successful player in this game wins the target. Cover a small table with small goldfish globes, each partially filled with water and each containing a fish. Players stand back ten to fifteen feet and attempt to throw ping-pong balls into the globes. The successful thrower wins the globe and fish. In this game it would be well to permit each player to win only once at this game although his *attempts* to win need not be limited.

Penny-and-Water Toss

A player kneels on the seat of a chair and rests his arms on the back of the chair. He attempts to drop pennies into a glass below. The catch is that the glass is resting in a large globe filled with water. It's hard enough to drop a coin into a glass but when there is water between the glass and the penny, it's even more difficult. In this game the organization conducting the game might keep all the pennies that fall outside of the glass into the surrounding water. The player uses his own pennies. When he makes a successful drop into the glass he might be awarded a five- or ten-cent prize. At a children's carnival the pennies would be furnished to the players.

Squirt and Douse

This is a wet but full-of-fun game. It is better played in an outdoor area. Set up three lighted candles on a table. The area will have to be protected from wind and drafts. Players stand back about ten to fifteen feet. Each is given one water pistol fully loaded and the player attempts to shoot out the three candles with well-aimed streams of water. Two out of three should win a prize or a ticket.

Chip-Shot Golf

Using regular golf clubs (niblicks or other chipping irons), give players five balls and let them try to chip them into bushel baskets fifteen to twenty-five feet away. If played indoors, players might chip from a fiber door mat. If played outside, any grassy or sandy area is suitable. Use *celluloid or cotton practice balls only* and play in a roped-off area. One out of five is a good score and probably represents more luck than skill.

Chip-Shot Target

Using regular golf clubs (niblicks or chipping irons) and practice-type golf balls only, have players attempt to chip the balls through a hole in a canvas or sheet suspended from the wall. If it is an outside area, suspend the canvas between two volleyball or badminton standards. One out of five bull's-eyes is a good average, depending upon the size of the hole.

Driving for Accuracy

Cut three small garage doors in the side of a cardboard

carton just large enough to permit a small toy car to be rolled through it. Set the box at the end of a six-foot table. Players stand at the other end of the table and attempt to send three small cars into the garage, via the doors, of course. These are the push type cars and not the wind-up-motor variety. Two out of three is a fairly good average for a winner. The cars are as unpredictable in their steering as most new drivers are.

Bounce in a Basket

Set two hassocks, foot stools or small chairs and one wastebasket in a row about three feet apart. Players stand about three feet in front of the first stool and throw a ball in such a way as to make it bounce between the two chairs or stools, over the second chair and into the basket. Small rubber balls are suitable. Three throws per turn should give the players a fair chance. Two out of three is a good average and wins a ticket. Boxes may be used instead of chairs.

Lemon Roll

This sounds like something to eat but it's just another carnival skill game. Lemons make unpredictable rolling objects. Place a box with two doors cut in one side at the end of a six-foot table. The table should be placed against the wall with the box tight against the wall. Players stand at the other end of the table and attempt to roll three lemons through the holes into the box. Two out of three should be considered a winning score for a small prize or a ticket.

Variation Lemon Roll

Draw three parallel lines on the floor with chalk, the first one about a foot from the baseboard, the second about two feet in front of the first line and the third a foot in front of the second line. About ten feet away draw a starting line. Players toe this line and attempt to roll three lemons into the middle area between the first and second line. If the lemon touches either line it also counts as a successful roll. Two out of three is good bowling.

Dart Blowing

Give each player a large malted-milk straw and three regular drinking straws. The player puts the little straw into the big one and attempts to blow the little straw into a target area drawn on the floor about ten feet away. Two out of three is good shooting and worthy of a ticket or a prize. Each player gets a new blowing straw, but the other straws can be used over and over again so long as they are not bent or broken.

Shuttlecock and Hoop

Hang a hoop in a doorway or suspend it from a rope stretched across the corner of a room. Have players stand back about ten feet and attempt to throw three shuttlecocks through the hoop. Two out of three wins a small prize; three out of three wins a ticket.

Variation: Give players paddles and have them try to hit the "birds" through the hoops.

Swing Bowling

Set up ten small bowling pins on the floor in a doorway. Hang a ball on a rope suspended in the doorway. The ball should be about twelve inches off the floor. Players stand behind the bowling pins and swing the ball on the rope in such a way as to have it swing around in front of the pins, hitting the head pin on the back swing. Allow three swing throws to knock all the pins down.

Disc and Target Toss

Draw a target on the floor or paint it on oil cloth and lay it on the floor. See diagram below. Players stand back ten to fifteen feet and throw five discs at target. Give a prize for a certain score and a ticket for higher scores, the winning score depending on how you number the particular areas in the target.

Ball and Hazard Roll

Take three shoe boxes and cut out one end, leaving each a three-sided box. Place these boxes in a triangle pattern on

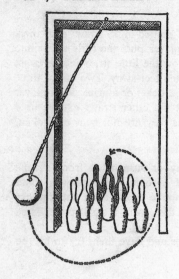

the floor; one box in front, two behind. Place a piece of wood about two feet in front of the boxes to act as an obstacle. A broomstick would serve. Players stand back about ten feet and attempt to roll three old tennis balls over the stick into the boxes. Give a prize for one out of three and a ticket for two successful throws out of three. Ball does not need to stay in the box to count.

Variation: Large tin cans laid on their sides and anchored to a board will serve as targets. The same rules apply as in game described above.

Chapter 6

Card Games and Tricks

CARD GAMES

THE CARD games with which we are concerned here are those which have simple rules, are easily learned and which may be played by family groups. Their simplicity of rules in no way detracts from the fun which the element of chance and the spirit of competition provide. Many parents will discover that an evening of fun with their children will bring satisfaction that can be gained in no other way.

The games which follow are particularly good when two or more families get together for a family party. Most of the games do not limit the number who can play. In fact, the more players the merrier the occasion will be.

Wheel of Fortune

Prepare a diagram such as is shown here on a large sheet of cardboard or poster paper, or procure a yard-square piece of white oil-cloth and mark with a china-marking pencil.

A straight deck is used. Four to seven players can play. Give each player thirty poker chips or matches. Before each hand is dealt, every player must ante one chip into each of the six areas on the playing wheel.

The dealer deals out the cards one at a time to the players around the table, making one extra hand as he goes around. When all cards are out (some players will have an extra card) the players examine their hands. The cards indicated on the wheel are pay cards. The dealer examines his hand. If he has a good hand he will offer the extra hand for sale to the highest bidder. The dealer does not have to sell the extra hand, however; if he has a poor one he may discard the first hand he picked up and use the extra hand himself. The discarded hand then remains out of play for the remainder of that round.

Play begins with the player to the left of the dealer. He must play the lowest card in his hand. To play it he lays it face up in front of himself and calls out what it is. The player who has the next higher card in that suit plays it from his hand and calls it out. Play continues in this manner until a dead spot is reached. This will happen occasionally because of the extra hand which is out of play. If in the process of play a pay card is laid down, the player wins those chips on the card in the wheel. When a dead spot is reached, the player who has played the last card starts a new series. He must play the lowest card in his hand of the opposite color of the last suit just played. For example, the first player has begun the game with a four of hearts (his lowest card). Play on the four goes up through the nine, where a dead spot is reached. The player who played the last card (the nine of hearts) must begin with the lowest black card in his hand. If he has no black cards, play moves to the player on his left. He plays his lowest black card. If he has no black cards he must pass and the next player gets the privilege of play.

In this game ace is high and the deuce is low; thus the ace ends a sequence. Should play on any one series go to the ace, the person playing the ace starts another series, playing his lowest card in a suit of the opposite color.

The round continues until one player has played all his cards. He collects the money in the *pot*. If some pay cards were not played during the round, the money accumulates on the wheel.

Dive and Swim

Any number may play but each must have his own deck of cards, which he deals into five stacks of seven cards each. These he places face up on the table in front of himself. The remainder of his deck is placed face down and is his "dividing pile." When all players are ready, at a signal, each turns up a card from his dividing pile and yells, "Dive and swim." The players begin playing on their own or opponents' cards from their five stacks. Play may go up or down on any one card and the directions may change as each person plays as fast as he can. A four may be played on a three regardless of suit and then another four played on that three. Play continues in wild confusion until a stalemate is reached and no more cards can be played. The players all yell "Dive and swim" again and play resumes. The first player to play out his thirty-five cards wins.

This game is best played on the floor and with old cards.

Twenty-nine

Four people playing as partners will find this a good game.

The dealer deals the cards around until all cards are out. Play is to the left and begins with the player to the left of the dealer. It is not necessary to follow suit at any time. The object of the game is to play the card that will make the total of twenty-nine points. Ace, king, queen and jack count one point each; all other cards count their own number values. For example, the first player plays a ten. The second plays a four, the third player plays another four. It is impossible for the fourth player to make twenty-nine so he plays a six. The next player luckily has a five, making the total number of points of that trick twenty-nine. He takes the trick. The game continues until eight tricks are taken. Partners add up the number of tricks they have taken and score one point per trick on their score pad. Set a game limit of thirty or thirty-five points.

If by any chance a player cannot play a card which will either bring the total to twenty-nine points or keep it below, that round comes to an end and the remaining unplayed tricks are given to the opposing team.

If playing this game with three players, remove one ten from the pack. If five are playing, take out a ten and a nine. Where an uneven number play, there can be no partners and it is every player for himself.

Hearts

This is an excellent game for four to six players. It may be played as an individual game or with partners.

The dealer deals one card at a time to the left around the table. Any extra cards are kept in the *kitty*. Each player examines his cards and then selects three cards from his hand and passes them to the player on his right. At the same time he receives three cards from the player on his left. Since the object of the game is to avoid winning any hearts or capturing the *black widow* (the queen of spades), players always give away their high hearts and spades.

The player to the left of the dealer begins the game. There are no trumps. Everyone follows suit when possible, but no player needs to play a higher card than those previously played, if he does not wish to take the trick. When a player cannot follow suit, he may play any card he chooses. In this manner he may rid his hand of any dangerous high cards, the *black widow* or any hearts. The player taking the first trick also gets the *kitty*. The players then examine the cards in the tricks they have taken. Any heart taken counts one point. The *black widow* counts thirteen points. When one player has scored fifty points the game is over. The lowest score is the winning one.

While the object is to try to avoid winning any tricks with a heart or the *black widow* in it, if a player has the kind of hand with which he can *go for broke* he can attempt to take all the hearts and the *black widow*. If he is successful in this venture he has no points scored against him for that hand but all the other players have twenty-six points scored against them.

Rhymes Are Rampant

Any number of people may play this game. Deal out all the cards in a straight deck two at a time. Players take up their hands and examine them. The player on the dealer's left begins the game. He takes a card from his hand and lays it down face up for all to see, and in so doing says the first line of a four-line verse. For example, he plays a ten of diamonds. He might say: "A diamond ten I offer you." If the player to his left has a ten, she plays it but must add a line to the rhyme as she plays. She might say: "Lucky for me, I have one too." If that player has no ten, she must pass and play moves to the next player. The third player, who also has a ten, adds another line: "Here's another bone to chew." The player who plays the fourth may answer: "I have one too, whoop ti doo." In no case may the rhyming word be the same as one used previously. The player who plays the fourth card then begins the next round by playing another card and starting a new rhyme. He may begin with: "I can't think of a decent line." This may lead to: "I've got a card, I'm doing fine."

The game continues until some player has played out all his cards, which makes him the winner of that round and gives him one point. Play until one player has scored eight or ten points.

Remembered Pairs

Two or more players may play this game. The one with the best memory wins. All cards are dealt face down in five rows of ten cards each, with the two remaining cards placed anywhere. The first player turns up any two cards. If he happens to turn up a pair, he removes these cards from the rows and keeps them as a trick. He then has the privilege of another turn. This continues as long as he turns up pairs. When, however, he fails to turn up a pair, he turns the two cards face down again, leaving them in their original places. The next player takes his turn, trying to remember which cards have already been turned so that he can find the second of a pair should he turn up a card similar to the one turned up by the previous players.

The game continues until all of the cards have been taken in tricks. The player with the most cards wins that round.

Menagerie

This game is as much fun as the zoo and almost as noisy. Each player selects the name of an animal, and the longer the name the better for him. All players try to familiarize themselves with every other player's name. When all are ready, the cards are dealt out around the table one at a time until the deck is used up. For four to six players, one straight deck is used. For more players, use two decks. Each player takes the cards dealt to him and without looking at them places them in a little pile face down. The first player turns up the first card on his pile for all to see and places it on the table just in front of his pile of cards. The second player does the same. Whenever a card is turned up that is the same as another card on the table, the two players owning those cards attempt to call each other by their animal names. The first player to call out his opponent's name wins that little battle and is thereby privileged to give all his turned-up cards to his opponent of the moment. Since the object of the game is to get rid of all your cards first, everyone must pay strict attention to the cards as they are turned up or he will find himself with all the cards before long. In turning the cards, the player must turn the card away from himself with a quick motion so that all can see the card at the same time. There will be much yelling, much stuttering and a great deal of pointing of fingers at players (as if that helped in remembering their names).

I Doubt It

This is the game to use that old poker face in or you'll lose for sure. Each player (and there may be four or more) is dealt cards one at a time until all the cards give out. Two players may have an extra card but this will make no difference. The object is to get rid of your hand as soon as possible. The player to the left of the dealer begins. Since in this game aces are one and the kings are high, the first player must attempt to get rid of any aces he has. He does this by taking

his aces out of his hand and placing them face down on
the table. "These are aces," he says. However, if he has no
aces, he takes any other card he has and pretends it is an ace.
He may take from one to four cards from his hand to bluff
with. If the next player believes they really are aces, he may
pass. The next player who has reason to doubt the cards
may say, "I doubt it." The first player turns the cards over. If
all are aces, the doubting player must take those cards into his
hand. If they are not aces, then the first player must take
them back into his hand. The game resumes with the second
player laying down from one to four cards and calling them
deuces. The passing or doubting goes on until these cards are
taken into someone's hands. The third player must play or
fake threes, the fourth must play or fake fours. Play proceeds
in this fashion until the kings have been played and the play
goes back to aces again. The game continues until one player
has managed to get rid of all his cards.

War

Young children will enjoy this game. They need only know
the values of the cards. Ace is low, king is high. Two or more
players may play. The cards are dealt around until all are
distributed. The players do not look at their cards but put
them in a little pack face down on the table. All players turn
up their first card and leave them face up on the table. The
highest card wins all the others. The winner takes these cards
and adds them to the bottom of his pack. When two cards
of the same value are turned up, the owners of those two cards
are at war. They leave the duplicate cards on the table and
on top of them place a card face down. Then they take another card from their packs and turn it face up. The higher
card wins all the cards in play in this little battle. Or if they
turn up duplicates again, another card face down is added to
the pile and the fourth card is turned up with the higher card
winning all the cards on the table. Play continues until one
player has won all the cards. If this seems to be taking too
long, play for a certain period of time. The player with the
most cards wins this game.

Wandering Cards

In this old German game, the cards seem to be wandering back and forth from player to player. Any number can play. For more than four use the whole straight deck. For four or less, use only thirty-two cards, taking out all cards under the sevens.

The cards are dealt around until all cards are distributed. The player to the left of the dealer begins by playing any card. The other players must follow suit if they can. If this is the case, the highest card takes the trick and those cards are put out of play. If, however, a player cannot follow suit, he must pick up any cards that have been played in that round and put them into his hand. He then must lead off with a card of another suit. For example, player number one leads a spade. The second and third players also play spades. The fourth player has no spades, so he must pick up the three cards which have been played and put them in his hand. He must then lead out with a card of any suit. The game continues until one player has succeeded in playing all of his hand. He wins that round and a new one is begun.

Scoring may be done in one of two ways. Only the winning player gets a point in each round, or the winning player may get no score and the other players have a point scored against them for every card still remaining in their hands. The first player to score twenty-one points loses the game and the lowest scorer wins.

Stinko

This is a simple contract game which calls for as much luck as sense, thus making it a good game for experienced and inexperienced players to enjoy together. Each game consists of fourteen hands. Any number of players up to seven may play. The dealer deals out seven cards, one at a time, to each player. The remaining cards are set aside with the top card turned up for trump. Each player examines his hand and tries to figure out *exactly* how many tricks he can take. The player to the left of the dealer gives his estimate to the scorekeeper first. Each player in turn makes his bid. When all estimates have been recorded, the player to the left of the dealer leads off. Players must follow suit. If they cannot follow suit they may discard or trump. Any player who takes in exactly the number of tricks he bid gets fifteen points for making contract and one point for every trick. Thus if he bid three tricks and made his contract he would receive eighteen points for that hand. If, however, he takes fewer or more tricks than he contracted for, he gets a neat little goose egg for that hand. If a player bids no tricks and takes none he can still win fifteen points that round.

In the second hand only six cards are dealt out per player. Each succeeding hand contains one card fewer until the play is down to one card. The next hand is also a one-card hand. Each succeeding hand contains one more card. The game continues until the fourteenth hand, which has seven cards.

Sometimes this last hand is played as a no-trump hand for variation. For easy scoring, a score card as pictured below is recommended.

NAME	B	S	B	S	B	S	B	S	B	S	B	S	B	S	B	S	B	S	B	S	B	S	B	S	B	S	B	S
Paul	2	0																										
Mike	3	18																										
Johnny	2	17																										
Peter	0	15																										
Jean	1	16																										
Julie	1	16																										

Winner Stays Longer

From four to six players may play this game, the object of which is to stay in the game the longest period of time.

Use a straight deck. For four players, deal nine cards per hand; for five, deal eight cards; for six, deal seven cards each. The remainder of the cards is set aside in a pack with one card turned up for trump.

The player to the dealer's left leads off. Players in turn must follow suit if possible; otherwise, they may trump. The highest card of a suit takes the trick unless the trick has been trumped. When a player wins a trick, he picks the cards up

and lays them aside out of play. His reward for winning the
trick is the card on the top of the pack, which he adds to his
hand. Play continues in this manner until only one player is
left with cards. The other players, meanwhile, drop out of the
game when they have played their last card. The last player
with cards in his hand wins that round.

Pig

For five or more players use the entire straight deck. For
less than five take out cards in "sets" of fours, such as four
aces, four tens, so that you have only thirty-two cards. Deal
out cards around the table until the entire deck is distributed.
At a signal to play, each player passes a card to his right-hand
neighbor and at the same time receives a card from the neighbor at his left. Each player is trying to get a "set" of four
aces, tens, deuces or whatever. As soon as he has four of a
kind or a set, he gently lays his hand down and puts a finger
to his nose. The other players may not notice him do this and
will continue to play. Suddenly someone notices and immediately puts his hand down and puts his finger to his nose.
The last player to notice has a "P" scored against him. The
game continues until a player is a full PIG. He is eliminated
from the game and a set of four cards is removed from the
deck. The game continues until most of the players are
eliminated. If you prefer not to eliminate players, just keep
score for the player and play for a limited period of time. At
the end of the time, the player with the fewest number of
points wins the game.

Spools

Spools is a wilder variation of the game of Pig. Place a
number of empty sewing-thread spools in the center of the
table, one spool fewer than there are players. Play as in the
game of Pig except that now when a player gets a set of four
cards, he grabs for a spool. Immediately all other players
grab. One will be left without a spool. He has a point scored
against him. Play for a limited time. The player with the
lowest score is the winner.

This is a very strenuous game. In the mad scramble for the

spools some accidentally get knocked on the floor. The game of Hide and Seek the Spool is soon added to the fun of the card game.

CARD TRICKS AND STUNTS

The tricks here are simple to do but baffling to the person being tricked. Practice a trick so that you can do it without hesitation. Some tricks should never be repeated. Others can be done over and over again without giving the trick away. With practice you will know which not to repeat. Probably the most fun of any trick is that it starts the ball rolling at a gathering. One trick leads to another and before the evening is over you will have learned a couple of new ones and everyone will have had fun. Any activity which draws others in and gives them a chance to share their knowledge with someone else is a good activity. In some instances, some of the tricks shared will have been taught to that person by his grandfather or grandmother and the sharing will not only help to insure the preservation of that trick but will start off a chain of reminiscenses.

Bright Eyes

This is one of the simple but baffling tricks which require a little practice and deception. Shuffle the deck and place it on the table face down. Have someone select a card and show it to the others but not to you. Then have that card returned to the deck at the bottom.

The deck is cut once with the bottom being placed on the top, which places the selected card somewhere in the middle of the deck. You have merely to take off cards one at a time until you come to the selected card, which you immediately identify. The trick is simple. In placing the shuffled deck on the table, you take a quick look at the bottom card. The selected card will be the one immediately following that card. This is definitely one trick you should not repeat immediately.

Card Spelling

Arrange the cards from any one suit in this manner: 3, 8,

7, A, Q, 6, 4, 2, J, K, 10, 9, 5. Place them in a stack face down with the three on top and the others in the order given. Take the top card and call it *A* and place it on the bottom of the deck. The next card call *C* and place it on the bottom of the deck stack. The third card is *E*. Since you have spelled ace the next card on the top is the ace. Turn it up and there it is. Take it from the stack and leave it face up on the table. Continue spelling, taking the top card each time and putting it on the bottom. The second word you spell is "two." Sure enough, after you have spelled "two" the next card is the deuce. Take it from the deck. Continue in this manner, spelling three, four, five, six, seven, eight, nine, ten, jack and queen, removing the proper card each time. The last card turned up will be the king.

Magic Card Selector

The trick that is always fun to do is this simple trick. Shuffle a deck of cards until you have a picture card or an ace on the bottom. Lay the deck face down on the table and begin questioning your victim in this manner:

Leader: "Name two suits in the deck."

Victim: "Clubs and diamonds."

Leader: "Take one of those two." (The card at the bottom of the deck is the ace of clubs.)

Victim: "Diamonds."

Leader: "That leaves clubs?"

Victim: "Yes."

Leader: "Select two of the four highest cards in the deck."

Victim: "Ace and king."

Leader: "Select one of these."

Victim: "Ace."

Leader: "Look at the bottom card."

The victim is amazed to find the ace of clubs. You have, of course, made him pick the correct card by a careful process of elimination. Since you know the correct card, this is not difficult. Had the victim named hearts and spades as his first selection, you had only to say: "That leaves clubs and diamonds." You have thereby brought the selection partly along the way. If the victim selects the wrong suit a second time, you can bring him to the right one by saying: "That leaves clubs. Name two high clubs." Sometimes, however, the victim will unerringly pick the correct suit and the correct card without any help from you. The trick is more baffling than ever, since you don't have to work the elimination process at all. It is wise to have an ace at the bottom since most players will pick an ace as their choice.

To make the trick more mystifying, select your card and ask your victim to hold it in his hand without looking at it until you have finished questioning him. At the end he will find that he is holding the card he last named. Or place the card in an envelope and seal it. This makes the trick appear magical. Don't repeat this one more than once at any one time.

Slide and Reverse Puzzle

Pick the thirteen cards of any one suit from the deck and take out the two and the three. Take the remaining eleven cards and place them in three rows on the table with four in the top row, four in the second row and three in the third row, leaving the remaining space at the lower right-hand corner. The cards would be arranged in this order:

A K Q J
10 9 8 7
6 5 4

In other words you have twelve spaces in your little arrangement. Eleven spaces are filled with cards and one remains empty. Move one card at a time, filling up an empty space with each move, but keep all your moves within your twelve-space arrangement. With practice you can move the cards so that you will end with the cards completely reversed in numerical order with the final arrangements looking like this, but with the empty space in the second row:

4 5 6 7
8 9 10
J Q K A

In other words you have gone from this:

A K Q J	to this	4 5 6 7
10 9 8 7		8 9 10
6 5 4		J Q K A

pushing one card at a time within your twelve space arrangement.

Play with it for awhile and see if you can figure out the trick. If you can't, you'll find the solution below.

Solutions: 4 5 6 10 9 8 7

4 5 6 10 9 A K Q J

4 5 6 10 9 A K Q J

4 5 6 10 9 A K Q J

4 5 6 7 9 A K Q J

4 5 6 7 10 A K Q J

8 9 10

When you have mastered the trick, just to be extra fancy, turn the cards face down and work the trick. When you have finished, turn them face up and see if you have done it correctly.

Sixteen Cards

Select sixteen cards from the deck and lay them out in four rows of four each. Have the victim select a card and tell you which row it is in. Be sure he understands what you mean by a row, whether it is a vertical or horizontal row. Once you know the row, you are on the way. You know that the correct card is one of the four cards. Take that row up first and pick up the other cards with equal care to confuse the watcher. In laying out the cards the second time, keep the four key cards separated so that each appears in a different row. Note where you have placed these in the layout. Now when your victim tells you which row his card is in, you know the card since it is the only one of the important four in that row. You do not tell your victim you know the card yet. You really want to baffle him. Pick up the cards with what appears to be careless abandon but actually is extreme care, placing the correct card on the top or the bottom of the pile. Begin now to lay the cards face down in four little crosses each made with four cards. Keep track of the magic card. With all cards in place, have the victim point out two of the four piles. If the card is in one of those two crosses, discard the other two. Have him then select one of the two remaining crosses. If the card is in the cross he selects, discard the other pile. Now have him narrow it down to two cards. Discard the two you do not want and keep the two, one of which is the right card. Have him select one card. If he selects the correct one, say, "This is your card." On turning it over, he'll find that it is. This trick is one of elimination at the end. You can do this better and with less giveaway if you practice a bit. In laying out the cards for the second time, while they are still face up you can use any fancy method you like so long as you get one of the four correct cards in each row. They can be laid diagonally across the set of four from corner to corner or down the left edge or the right edge if the selection is made on the basis of horizontal rows.

Don't do this more than twice in succession with any victim. He'll begin to give you an argument in the matter of discarding the cards at the end of the trick. He'll say: "I selected these two and you kept them one time. The next time you discarded the pile I selected." You may have to give out with some fine double talk to get around that kind of reasoning.

Twenty-one

One of the author's grandfather's favorite card tricks was the one using twenty-one cards. Any twenty-one cards are selected. The trickster lays them out face up in three vertical rows of seven each. The victim selects a card and indicates which row it is in. The cards are carefully picked up, with the row with the selected card in it being placed between the other two rows. The cards are laid out again in three rows. The victim again points out the row with his card in it. The cards are picked up again in rows with the selected row again being sandwiched between the other two. The third time the cards are laid out, the selection is again made. The correct card will be the fourth from the top. The trickster does not then identify the card. In stacking them, he puts that row between the others as he did before. Then he begins counting the cards from the top. The eleventh card will be the correct one.

Be careful to deal from left to right across the top. Proceed in this manner until all twenty-one cards are placed. This same procedure must be followed with each deal.

For a confusing variation, deal out the cards as described above and let the victim select his card. Pick up these seven cards first and place the remaining cards underneath. Lay out the cards in the prescribed manner. The selected card is one of the first seven cards which will come out in this manner: three will be in the first row, and two in each of the second and third rows. Now when the player points out the row in which his card now lies it will be one of three, if it is in the first row, or one of two if it is in the second or third rows. Pick up the row with the selected card, keeping track of the two or three special cards. On the next deal, be sure that each of the special cards goes into a different row. Now when your victim shows you the row with his card in it, you know the card. Allow the victim to shuffle the cards. Go through the cards until the right one turns up and name it. With practice, you can do this trick differently every time. Depending upon where you place the row with the selected card in it after each pickup you can make that card appear at the top of the row, in the middle or at the bottom of a row in the third and final deal.

Trick Pairs

Arrange cards in a straight deck so that the cards in each suit are in this order: 2, 3, 4, 5, 6, 7, 8, 9, 10, J, K, Q, A, with the two at the bottom. Stack one suit on top of the other in the deck. Have players cut the deck any number of times, always taking more than one card on a cut and always placing the cards taken off the top under the one on the bottom of the stack.

After the cuts are completed, dealing from the top, place the first twenty-six cards in three rows, dealing from left to right, one under the other, with the cards not overlapping or touching each other. The first two rows will have nine cards in them and the last only eight. Now take the remaining twenty-six cards and, dealing from the top and in the same manner as before, cover each of the first twenty-six cards. When all the cards are placed, allow players to turn over any pair. The surprise will be that the cards are actually pairs, with the two appearing together and all the others appearing in pairs.

Variation: If in stacking the deck in the beginning you alternate the suits as to color, red and black, the pairs will come out all red or all black. If you place the two red suits on the top and the two black suits on the bottom or vice versa, the pairs will come out with one red and one black card.

There is no particular trick involved here. This will work out every time if you stack the cards properly and follow the directions.

Amazing Pairs

Select any twenty cards. Deal them out in groups of two, face down. Up to ten players may participate in this trick. Each player takes up a pair, examines it and turns it face down, memorizing the combination he saw. When all players have done this, the trickster takes them up two at a time, in any order so long as he keeps the pairs together. He then lays out the cards face up in five horizontal rows of four cards each. Each player tells the trickster in which row his combination appears. From this identification, the trickster can tell the player which are his two cards. By the same token, he can identify the cards of the other players.

The trick is done in this manner. The trickster keeps this formula in mind in laying out the cards face up:

TILE
GOES
HIGH
ALAS
TODD

With this picture of the words in mind, he assigns a letter value to each pair of cards. If you examine the words you will note that there are twenty pairs of letters represented in

the four words. There are two "S's," two "T's" two "H's" etc.
Consider the first two cards as "S's." Place them where these
letters appear. Place the next two where the "T's" appear,
and so on until all cards are placed. Now when a player tells
you that his cards appear in the first and third rows, the pair
would be the cards in the position of the "I's." Similarly, if
the combination appeared in the fourth row, the cards would
be the two in the same position as the "A's," etc.

This is a good trick because so many persons can participate. The trickster should practice this several times so that
he can place the cards quickly and without too much delibera-
tion.

Card Tossing

This is a game of skill rather than a trick. Give a player a
deck of cards. Place an open box or a hat upside down at a
point about five feet from the player. He may sit or stand.
Throwing one card at a time as rapidly as possible, he attempts to throw the cards into the hat. The player making the
most successful tosses wins.

Card Tents

A stunt that will fascinate children and keep the baby sitter
busy, too, is card tentmaking.

Take two cards and make a tent of them. Set up another
with the bases of the tents touching at some point. Long lines
of tents can be made. When a long string is up, the child
pushes over or blows at the end tent. The whole line will go
down like a row of wooden soldiers. If the child is old enough
let him make his own tents. This will keep him busy for a
long period.

Variation: Take old cards and fold them down the center
vertically and open up to a right angle. The card will then
stand alone. Set one folded card next to another in long and
curving line. A push at the last card will send the whole row
down, much to the delight of the child.

Chapter 7

Checkerboard Games

A CHECKERBOARD is the most versatile of all playing boards. A number of games may be played on it which will have appeal for children and adults of all ages and varying playing skills. The checkerboard is, therefore, a valuable piece of equipment for the home, playground, church, camp or recreation center.

The games described here have a number of things in common. They all use a checkerboard. The rules of the game are simple, making the games easy to learn quickly, but they are not simple games. They "grow" on the discerning player, who soon realizes that the more skill that is developed the more complicated and challenging the game becomes. Herein lie their charm and their value.

Checkerboard Chinese Checkers

Equipment: Checkerboard and twenty playing pieces, ten of each of two colors.

Rules: The board is set up as shown in the diagram with four checkers in the king row, three in the next row, two in the next and one in the next. Each player's pieces are arranged in a triangle with the apex of each in the center of the board.

The object of the game is for one player to move his pieces to the other side of the board so that his pieces are in the same position as his opponent's before his opponent can do the same. In other words the triangles just change places.

All play is on the black squares only. A man may move one square forward or backward. He may jump over a man of his own color or one of the opposite so long as the square into which he jumps is open. Double or triple jumps are legal. The men jumped over are not removed from the board but remain there, since the object is not to eliminate the opponent's men but merely to exchange positions on the board.

The first player to get his men in the proper position wins

the game. Players will find that it is better to play an offensive rather than a defensive game. Leaving a man in the last row just to thwart the opponent will prove foolish. The dog-in-the-

manger play may keep the opponent from winning but it also keeps the other player from winning. Such tactics result in a draw game and outraged feelings on the part of the opponent.

Checkerboard Galloping Chinese Checkers

Equipment: Checkerboard and twenty playing pieces, ten of each of two colors.

Rules: Playing pieces are placed as in Checkerboard Chinese Checkers. (See diagram above.)

The object of the game is for the player to shift his triangles to the opposite side of the board before his opponent can do the same. This game differs from Checkerboard Chinese Checkers only in the method by which the men can be moved. Movement rules: No checker may be moved from square to square; it must jump. In other words, the only legal move is the jump. The jump may be over one checker or over three so long as the move follows the diagonal and the square into which the piece is to be jumped is vacant. Double or triple jumps are possible and since a piece may now jump forward or backward, a piece can travel a considerable distance in one move. Actually a piece could jump from one king row to another by a double jump if the proper conditions exist.

The trick to this game other than the long and unusual jumps is that no single move from square to square is legal. The players will find that although the long jump makes the game proceed fast at first, the trick of getting the last piece into place with a jump requires some fancy engineering. Sometimes a whole game is replayed to get the last piece into position.

As in Checkerboard Chinese Checkers, the offensive game rather than the defensive game is important. Just get there the fastest and leave intrigue for another game.

Five in a Row or Japanese "Go"

Equipment: A playing board marked off into 150 squares, 10 squares wide by 15 squares deep. The squares must be carefully ruled off so that the vertical, horizontal and diagonal rows of squares run in true rows. The squares should be large enough to accommodate a checker or bottle-top playing piece. Approximately sixty playing pieces, thirty of two colors, are needed. When bottle caps are used, one player uses the top side and the other, the cork side of the cap.

Rules: The players, taking alternate turns, place one man at a time anywhere on the board, each trying to get five men in a row either on a diagonal, horizontal or vertical line before his opponent can. The first to get five in a row wins the game. Any more than five in a row, however, does not constitute a win. For example, in placing his men, a player has three pieces in a row and then an open space and then another two men in the same row. Placing a man on the empty space in between would make six in a row. Six in a row cannot win the game.

When any player has three pieces in a row, he must announce this fact to his opponent and point out the place. If his opponent does not heed the warning and "stop" that row with one of his own playing pieces, his opponent can go on to win the game without hindrance. This simple little rule makes this game one of skill, as it forces a player to win by skill rather than a chance oversight on the part of his opponent.

Players will soon learn that, while the rules of this game

are not difficult, this is not a simple game. Players will develop skill as they play, making each game more challenging than the last.

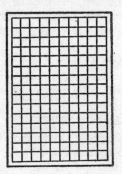

Variation: Three or four players may play this game under the same rules, each playing for himself and each using a different-colored playing piece.

A checkerboard may be used as a playing board for two players, but as they gain in skill they will find the sixty-four-square board too confining for a good game.

Fox and Geese

This is the simplest of all games played on a checkerboard. Young children can learn the game readily. Adults will find that it is a tricky little game of skill. It is a good lead-up game to Checkers as it teaches children the movement of the places of the king and the other pieces on the board.

Equipment: A checkerboard, four geese (black checkers) and one fox (red checker).

Rules: Place the men as shown in the diagram, with the four geese in one king row on the black squares. The fox is placed on any square in the king row on the opposite side of the board. Play is on the black squares only. Neither the fox nor the geese can jump. No men are removed from the board. The fox moves forward or backward one square at a time. The geese move forward only one square at a time. The object of the game for the fox player is to break through the line of geese. Once he has done that, he has won the game no matter where the breakthrough occurs on the board.

The object for the geese is to pen the fox up in a corner so that he cannot move. If the geese are successful in doing this, they win the game.

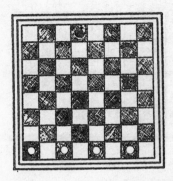

The geese usually have the first move. Players switch after each game. The novice usually protests that the geese don't have a chance to win. With careful play they can win. The fox plays an offensive game pushing into the line of geese, retreating only when necessary. The geese must play a defensive game, always wary lest the fox find a hole to slip through.

Checkerboard Friends

Equipment: A checkerboard and about sixty playing pieces which are a different color on the top side than they are on the bottom. Bottle caps can be used since they are different on the top and bottom.

Rules: Four playing pieces are placed, as shown in the diagram, in the center of the board before the game begins. From then on, one piece is placed at a time by each player with the players taking alternate turns. Play is on both red and black squares.

The object of the game is to make as many "friends" as possible during the course of the game. The player with the greater number of "friends" wins the game. A player can make a friend in these ways:

1. By catching an enemy between two of his own pieces either on a horizontal or vertical line. (No captures are made on a diagonal.) When this happens, the player turns over the enemy piece and makes it his friend.

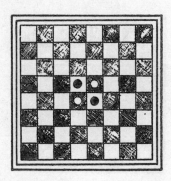

2. If a player has one of his pieces at the end of a row of two or more of his opponent's pieces, by placing a piece at the other end of that row, he may capture the entire row and turn the pieces over and make them into friends.

3. If in placing a piece a player has a choice of directions in which he may make a friend, he takes the choice giving him more friends since it is not possible to capture in two directions on one play.

4. A player must be able to make a friend on a play or he must forfeit his turn. Occasionally the pieces are so placed that the player whose turn it is cannot win a friend. The other player then takes an extra turn. If after that move the other player still cannot make a friend, the opponent continues to take turns until it is possible for the other player to make a legal move.

The game continues until neither player can make a legal move or until the board is covered with pieces. The player with the larger number of friends wins the game.

Players will note that pieces are turned over and over during the course of play as friends become enemies and are won back again. Note: If no checkerboard is available, a board may be made by ruling off one hundred or more squares on a piece of cardboard or wood. A checkerboard is suggested here since it is a common piece of game equipment and is often available or can be readily and inexpensively purchased.

Giveaway

This game is played exactly according to the rules of Checkers except that the purpose of the game is just the opposite. A player, instead of trying to eliminate his opponent's men, moves his men in such a way as to force his opponent to eliminate them. The first player to have his men captured wins the game. After a game or two, the experienced checker player will find that Giveaway requires as much skill to win as Checkers does.

Cornerwise Checkers

Equipment: A checkerboard and eighteen checkers, nine of each color.
Rules: The pieces are placed on the board as shown in the diagram.

The play is on the black squares only and the object is to eliminate the opponent's men by jumping them as in Checkers. In this game, however, the upper right-hand and the lower left-hand corners are the only squares in which a king can be made.

The men move on the black squares one square at a time unless they are jumping. Movements for the single man are forward or sideways but not backward. A king may move forward, backward and sideways. The first player to eliminate his opponent's men wins the game.

Chapter 8

Dice Games

SINCE DICE GAMES require more luck than skill in most instances, children and adults can play them together with equal enjoyment. The games given here are particularly good for family home play or for party groups. They are simple to learn, require little or no equipment and may be used by large or small groups.

Contract Dice Game

Players can play as partners or as individuals. If the game is played on an individual basis, each player receives a score sheet such as shown below. If played on a partner basis, each two players have one score sheet between them and pool their scores on the one sheet.

The game is played with five dice. Players take turns throwing, the play moving clockwise around the table. Any number may play, but at a progressive party the number at a table would probably be limited to four players. The players have thirteen contracts to make in a game and only thirteen throws in which to make them. After each throw a player decides where he wants to score the throw. He tries to score it where it will give him the highest score.

The twelve contracts are as follows:

1. Ones	8. Four of a kind
2. Twos	9. Little run (consecutive series of four)
3. Threes	10. Big run (consecutive series of five)
4. Fours	11. Full house (triple and a double)
5. Fives	12. Two pairs
6. Sixes	13. Contract (five of a kind)
7. Three of a kind	

The player must enter a score on his sheet after each throw. In the early part of the game he has many choices but as the game progresses the chances are narrowed down. For example, on his first throw a player throws three fives and a one and a three. He can score the three fives as a triple or he can score it under the "fives." In either case the score is fifteen points (three fives equals fifteen). His next throw may be a nondescript collection such as a six, one, four, two, five. He can score the one under the "ones" and hope for better luck next time. In other words he is not required to fill in his score sheet in any particular order but is given a choice as to where to score each throw. As the game goes on, and he throws combinations which cannot be scored in the remaining places, he is forced to take a zero in one category or another. He takes a zero in the spots he thinks he is most unlikely to make a contract. However, if he puts a zero in one category, and on the very next throw he rolls such a score, it is just too bad. No score can be changed after it is once entered.

No matter how carefully one plays this is still a game of chance, so what looked like a smart move may prove to be a foolish one before the game is over. That's what makes it so much fun.

Dice Cootie

Cootie is an old dice game but always fun. Each player has a score sheet. If played as a partner game, two players pool their scores on the same sheet. A "cootie" is made up of thirteen parts, with each part being represented by a number on a die. The body is a one, the head is a two, each leg is a six, the tail is a four, the eyes are threes and the feelers are fives. Each player takes turn in rolling one die. He must first roll a one to make the body since he can't put legs, a tail or a head on a body that isn't there. Once he has the body he can begin adding the other appendages, but he cannot put in the eyes or the feelers unless the head has been made.

Each player rolls the die once for each turn. The first individual player or first team to complete a cootie wins the game. In a progressive setup, when a cootie is completed at one table, play stops everywhere. Each individual and team counts up the number of parts his cootie has by scoring each part as one point. That score is entered on the individual tallies and the high-score partners split up and move on to a new table. The low-score partners split up but stay at the same table.

Variation: Some games of Cootie allow a player to continue to roll the die so long as he rolls a number he can use. This will make a faster game.

Roll the Bones

Give each player a tally card which he numbers from one to twelve consecutively down the left side of the card. Any number of players may play. If there are more than six playing, however, it would be wise to split up the group into tables of four. A player, in turn, rolls two dice. He is permitted one roll per turn unless he rolls a double; then he gets another turn. With each roll, he adds up the spots and crosses the corresponding number off his tally. For example, if he rolls a four and a three, he crosses off the seven on his tally. Any double may be scored for number one. The first player to cross off all twelve numbers wins the game.

Bunco

This is an old and familiar dice game that is always good fun. Three dice are used. Any number of players may play. It is better, however, if the group numbers more than six to set up groups of four so that players get more frequent turns. At the beginning, one die is rolled to determine the "bunco" point. Once that is determined, the game begins. For example, the bunco number turns out to be a four. The first player rolls the three dice. If he rolls a four, he scores one point and gets another roll. A triple roll (three of a kind) counts five points and allows another roll. If three fours are rolled, however, the player yells "Bunco!" and wins the game. The player who first scores twenty-one points or rolls a bunco wins. At the completion of a game, a single die is rolled for a new bunco point and the game begins all over again.

If this game is used in a progressive-party arrangement, two players play as partners. During play, their scores are pooled.

At the end of each game, the pooled score is entered on each player's score card as his total at that game. Winners move on to another table and split up, taking new partners. Losers remain at the same table, but also split up and take new partners.

Chapter 9

Dramatic Stunts and Games

DRAMATIC STUNTS are wonderful activities not only because they furnish fun to any group but because they fit into those places that are often difficult to fill in a party or social recreation program.

Does the leader want an activity that is fun for a large number of adults and children to do together? The dramatic stunt fits in that situation. Does he want a group activity to use in an auditorium or crowded dining room where the group must remain seated or where its actions are limited? The dramatic stunt fits there. Does he want an activity that will help children to get rid of excess energy and steam while remaining in one spot? The dramatic stunt does the trick. Does he want an activity which brings satisfaction to the participants and offers much challenge? A dramatic stunt or game fills the bill. The wise leader uses this type of activity often. Familiarity of the group with a particular stunt does not breed contempt; rather, the reaction is much like that of a child toward an old, familiar and well-loved story. "Let's do that again!" or "Are we going on a Lion Hunt again today?" or "Can we play charades?" your group will ask during a play period. They'll want to do them over and over again.

DRAMATIC GAMES

Dramatic Charades

The best-loved of all dramatic games is Dramatic Charades. Divide the group into teams. Give teams five minutes to select a word and prepare a dramatization of it for the rest of the group, who try to identify the word from the performance. The rules of the game are simple:

1. Every member of the group must participate in the dramatization.

2. The word must contain two or more syllables.

3. At the beginning, the captain of each team must tell how many syllables are in the word and then announce each one as it is demonstrated.

4. Syllables may be dramatized individually or two may be done as one. The captain must announce when two are being combined.

5. The team must dramatize the entire word in some way after doing each individual syllable.

For example, the word selected is "snapshot." The first syllable might be enacted by the group's just snapping their fingers. The second might be a dramatization of holding a gun and firing a shot. The entire word might be enacted by the group's appearing to take pictures with various kinds of cameras.

Speedy Team Charades

Divide players into teams. Have teams seat themselves in tight little groups around the room about equal distance from the center of the room, where the leader is stationed. In placing the chairs, each team should be seated in circle formation with an opening toward the center of the room so that the acting players can move quickly from their groups to the center of the floor and back again.

When all is in readiness, the leader calls for one member of each team. These gather around the leader in football-huddle style. The leader announces a classification to the teams so that they know what kind of title to expect. When the groups know the category to be used, the leader then gives the actual title (book, movie, song, play or musical) to the huddled players. The players all run back to their respective teams and begin acting out the title. The first team to guess the correct answer yells out the answer. Repeat the procedure using different players from the teams.

Suggested titles which are fun for acting out are:

Titles of Books, Movies, Musicals or Plays	Song Titles
The Egg and I	Silent Night
The King and I	Down by the Old Mill Stream

The Good Earth
Earth and High Heaven
The Waste Land
The High and the Mighty
Cannery Row
Spoonhandle
The Blackboard Jungle
The Caine Mutiny
Battlecry
From Here to Eternity
The Fourposter
Not as a Stranger
The Cry and the Covenant

Daisy Bell
The Surrey with the Fringe on Top
School Days
I'm Forever Blowing Bubbles
Smoke Gets in Your Eyes
Tea for Two
When the Moon Comes over the Mountain
She'll Be Comin' Around the Mountain
'Round Her Neck She Wore a Yellow Ribbon
Oh, What a Beautiful Morning
Come to Me, Bend to Me

Speedy Drawing Charades

Play as Speedy Team Charades but provide each team with a pad and pencil. The performing players must draw a picture illustrating the title instead of acting it out. The titles listed above are suitable for either acting out or drawing.

Combination Charades

Divide the group into teams and give them five minutes to work out a word, song title, proverb or book title using a combination of objects and actions. For example to demonstrate the word *high-hat*, a team need only hold a hat high in the air. A chair held high in the air is a *high chair*. A group saying "e-e-e" and holding books would demonstrate *bookies*. The family cat and a number of combs being held would be *catacombs*. Try this as a variation of acting charades and see how ingenious people can be.

Silent Charades

Divide group into teams and allow time for them to prepare a silent dramatization or pantomime of a word or book, song, play, movie or musical title. Each group then performs for the others, who try to identify the word or title. Since this all must be done silently, the group indicates by gesture

whether it is a word or a title. If it is a word, they point to
the palms of their left hands with their right forefingers. They
hold up a number of fingers to indicate how many syllables
are in the word. Then they begin the pantomiming of the
various syllables. If it is a title to be dramatized, they indicate
book title by making a book of their hands and showing by
fingers how many words in the title. A movie is indicated by
making a camera lens with the hands and peering at the
audience. A play title is indicated by a dramatic pose struck
by all the team members. Motion with the mouth and a dance
step or two with the feet indicate a musical. A song title is
demonstrated by elaborate motions of the mouth. In each
case a show of fingers tells how many words are in the title.
The rules ask merely that all members of a team participate
in the dramatizations.

Speedy Mystery Pantomimes

Divide group into two teams. Have each prepare a list of
three words, song titles, book titles, musical or play titles.
Proverbs, famous sayings or advertising slogans may also be
used. Each of the selections is then written on a separate piece
of paper and each is folded two or three times. The teams
then exchange selections. The leader decides which team is to
begin and acts as a timer, as this is a game against time. One
member of the beginning team then selects a piece of paper
and silently reads what is written there. He then indicates
to his teammates the nature of the word or title to be dramatized. He does that in this manner:

Book	Hands held up shaping book
Word	Finger in palm of hand
Song title	Mouth making singing motions
Musical	Mouth making singing motions and body held in mock dramatic pose
Play	Body held in mock dramatic pose
Proverb or saying	Index finger in palm of hand and mouth making speaking motions
Advertising slogan	Fingers making motion of handling much money and mouth making speaking motions

The number of syllables in a word is indicated by the number of fingers held in the air. The number of words in a saying or title is similarly indicated. After each signal, the pantomimist waits for his team to venture a guess. If correct he nods yes and proceeds to the next phase of the game. If the team guesses wrong, he so indicates. If they are warm but not quite correct he waves his fingers at them to tell them to keep guessing until they hit the right word.

Once the team has determined the category and the number of syllables or words involved, the player goes on from there. The other team watches closely, trying to determine which of their selections is being dramatized. Once they recognize its identity they have all the fun of watching the other team trying to guess the answer in record time.

As soon as the correct word or title is identified, the other team takes its turn. The teams alternate guessing until the three selections have been identified. The total guessing time for each team is determined and the team with the shortest time record wins.

Players will discover many ways to get past difficult spots as they play. Short words or short syllables are indicated by holding the forefinger and thumb together to indicate brevity. Hands held far apart indicate long words.

When a team gets near to the solution everyone is yelling at once. The pantomimist will be waving the warm ones on and wiping out the wrong guesses. This is definitely not a quiet game.

DRAMATIC STUNTS

The Lion Hunt

A lion hunt is probably the most loved of all dramatic stunts. It is often used with groups of adults and children together. It is a welcome part of the family party, the children's party, the camp program and wherever children, or children and adults, gather to play together.

The leader sits facing the audience. The whole stunt is done with the participants seated in chairs, or on the floor if children are seated on the floor. He asks the group if they would like to go on a lion hunt. The initiated need no explanation. To the uninitiated this explanation is given:

"When we go on a lion hunt, we all go together. Hunting lions is a very dangerous business, so it is important that we stay together and follow all the directions of the head hunter (that's me). You will say everything I say and do everything I do. Is that understood? Shall we begin?"

Leader: "Do you want to go on a lion hunt?" (At this point, the children very often yell, "Yes!" This is not correct so the leader reminds the children that they are to repeat only what the leader says and then begins again.)

Leader: "Do you want to go on a lion hunt?"

Group: "Do you want to go on a lion hunt?"

Leader: "Well, then, let's go."

Group: "Well, then, let's go."

This procedure is followed all through the hunt, with all words of the leader being repeated by the group. The leader often gives spoken directions which the children repeat. All this makes for fun and hilarity, especially when the children get carried away with the fantasy and often give a fervent answer instead of repeating the leader's query. Once the group has the idea, the hunt continues over hill and dale complete with motions and appropriate sounds as indicated in the following description of the hunt. From here on only the leader's directions are given, but the reader understands that all lines spoken by the leader are always repeated by the group, as are all the actions. The asterisks mark the place for a pause allowing time for the response of the group. The motions are parenthesized.

Leader: "Let's start walking."* (Walking sounds with feet on floor.) "We'll have to cross a bridge."* (Hit palms on thighs to simulate sound of feet on bridge.)

Leader: "Now we're across the bridge.* Horses are waiting for us here.* We'll ride part of the way."* (Hold reins with hands. Bounce up and down on chair.

Make clucking sounds with tongue against roof of mouth to simulate sounds of horses' hooves on hard ground. Give an occasional "giddap" and "hiya, hiya" yell.)

Leader: "This is as far as we can go with the horses.* We'll have to walk from here."* (Walking sounds with feet.)

Leader: "Oh!* It's beginning to rain."* (Rub palms together in circular motions, making sounds of rain.)

Leader: "It's getting muddy.* We'll have to walk in the mud.* It's hard going."* (Hit fists on chest in slow walking rhythm.) It's getting soupier and soupier."* (Make claws of hands, turn palms down and make motions in walking rhythm as if pulling each foot out of boggy, sloppy mud. This is accompanied with a juicy, slurpy sound made with the mouth.)

Leader: "In fact, we're walking through a bog."* (Continue slurping sounds and same motions.) "The mosquitoes are biting."* (Slap at face and neck and arms, scratching here and there. Between scratches and slaps continue slurping walk through the bog.)

Leader: "We're finally on dry ground now.* We can walk a little faster."* (Walking sounds with feet again.)

Leader: "Oh, oh! Wait a minute.* I think I see something."* (Hand held to eyes.) "Yes, I see a stream.* Shall we take a run?* And jump over it?* Ready?* Here we go."* (Running rhythm, slapping palms on thighs. Raise palms in mid-air, hold for a moment and then hit thighs again as if hunters had taken a run and jumped over the stream.) "We made it."*

Leader: "We'll have to walk through the reeds."* (Movement of hands in front of face as if parting reeds to permit passage through them.)

Leader: "Now we're on clear ground again."* (Walking sounds with hands slapping thighs.)

Leader: "Stop!* Wait a minute.* I see a big river.* Let's take a long run.* And a big jump.* If we don't make it we'll have to swim.* Ready?* Run!'"* (Running rhythm, slapping palms on thighs. Suspend hands in mid-air for a moment.) "We'll never make it.* We'll have to swim."* (Hold nose with hand as if jumping into water. Make spluttering noises and begin swimming, crawl style, making "blub, blub" sounds when face is turned down in water.)

Leader: "We can walk the rest of the way."* (Slurping sounds with mouth, hands clawlike, palms down, slow, painful walking rhythm.) "Well, we made it to shore."* (Wring out clothes and hair and shake self.)

Leader: "It ought to be easier going from here on.* Let's go."* (Walking rhythm with feet.)

Leader: (Hands to eyes.) "Hold it.* I see a cave.* Shall we go in?* Careful now, here we go."* (Hands cupped around mouth while speaking in cave.) "It's dark in here.* I wonder if there's anyone in here.* Yoo hoo"* (Louder) "Yoo hoo!* I hear an echo.* Yoooooo hoooooo.* Hey!* I just happened to think of something.* There may be bears in here.* Let's get out of here."* (Running sounds with feet.) "Phew.* I'm glad we got out of there safely."*

Leader: "We'll have to climb this hill."* (Slow walking rhythm of feet on floor.) "It's getting steeper and steeper.* We'll have—to—go slower—and—slower.* Phew.* We're almost to the top.* Just a little farther."* (Foot rhythm gets slower and slower.)

Leader: "Now we're at the top.* Let's rest a minute.* Take a deep breath."* (Loud and long sniff.) "Take another one."* (Louder and longer sniff.) "Isn't the air wonderful?"* (Hit hands on chest.) "Makes you feel so good.* Look at the beautiful view."* (Hands to eyes, turning complete circle as if looking all around.)

Leader: "Everybody rested?* Shall we run down the hill?* Ready?* Get set.* Go!"* (Running rhythm with feet on floor.)

Leader: "Shhhhhhhsh!"* (Finger to mouth.) "We're near lion country.* We'll walk through this tall grass.* Grass makes a swishing sound."* (Slap palms together back and forth in swishing, not clapping sound. Make swishing sound with mouth to accompany movements.)

Leader: (In whisper.) "Stop!* This is where I last saw a lion.* Let's climb this tree."* (Curve arms as if grasping trunk of tree. Move hands up higher and higher, stand on chair to get even higher.) "Careful, don't fall, now.* Hold on tight."*

Leader: (Holding on with one hand, puts other to eyes.) "Let's look in this direction.* See anything?* I don't see anything.* Let's look in this direction.* See anything?* I don't see anything.* Look over here.* Can you see anything?* I don't see anything.* Now look this way.* Shuuuuuuush!* I think I see something.* It has two big eyes!* And a long tail.* It's waving back and forth.* Back and forth.* It looks like a lion.* It *is* a lion.* Hand me the gun.* I don't have the gun.* Do you have the gun?* *You* don't have the gun? Let's get out of here!"* (Motion of sliding down the tree. Whole party retraces steps in a mad dash, running up the hill, down the hill and into the cave.)

Leader: "Let's wait here.* The lion may not find us.* Shhhhhsh!* Now carefully, let's tiptoe out."* (Tiptoe walking with feet.) "Now hurry."* (More retracing of route in double time, swimming the river, running over hard ground, running and jumping the small stream, walking through the reeds, over the dry ground, through the rain sounds, walking in mud, walking through the bog, riding horses, running over bridge, etc.)

Leader: "We made it.* But if I *ever* go lion hunting with you again, I'll be sure to take the gun.* You can get killed going hunting without a gun!"*

This entire stunt is done in place, with audience seated on the floor or in chairs. Leader tries to retrace steps as accurately as possible. If he misses on the return route some child will be sure to tell him what the deviation was or what was left out.

The leader's only recourse is to say: "Well, we took a short cut back."

Once in a program is enough for the lion hunt. Don't repeat it. Save it for another time.

The Shopping Trip

This is a good stunt for a children's group or one which has adults and children in it. The leader tells the story about the shopping trip. Each purchase he makes has an accompanying motion. The group mimics the motions made by the leader. Each motion, once started, is continued after the next is begun so that before the end of the story, hands, feet, head and jaws are in motion. Players are all seated and remain seated throughout the story.

The story goes like this:

We're all going on a shopping trip in the big department store. (Name a local one.) We're going to buy a pair of scissors first (Cutting motion with forefinger and middle finger of right hand simulating blades of scissors.) We need a new set of steps for the back porch. (Walking-up-steps motion with feet.) There was a sale of rocking chairs so we bought one. (Rocking motion back and forth in chair while walking with feet and cutting with fingers.) We got thirsty walking around and put a big piece of bubble gum in our mouths. (Make lump in cheek with tongue and begin chewing as if on a big wad of gum. All other motions are continued.) At this moment our heads began to itch. (Scratch heads and continue all motions.) The salesman comes up to us and asks if we wanted to buy anything else and we all said, "No." (Shake head from side to side and continue all motions.)

My Pioneer Grandmother

This is a dramatic stunt suitable for children's groups or mixed groups of adults and children. The leader tells the story. Motions to fit the action of the story are made by the leader and imitated by the group. Action is added to action so that soon hands, feet, head and body are in motion.

The story goes along like this:

My grandmother was a pioneer who traveled west in a Conestoga wagon. One day she was sitting rocking in her rocking chair which was in the wagon (leader makes rocking motion with body and group imitates). It was getting close to time for making camp for the day and Grandmother picked up her old coffee mill and began to grind some coffee for supper. (Motion of grinding coffee with left hand; rocking motion continues.) My Uncle Alf, who was just a little shaver then, came in and said: "Maw, I've wore a hole in the seat of my pants. Can you put on a patch?" Grandma found a patch but discovered that she was out of thread. "I'll have to spin some," she said. (Movement of right foot and right hand as if spinning thread is added to coffee-grinding motion and rocking.)

Just then the baby began to cry and Grandmother reached out her left foot and began to rock the cradle nearby. (Cradle-rocking motion added to all the others.)

Grandma loved to chew on things as she rode along so she popped a dried prune into her mouth and chewed and chewed. (Chewing motion added to others.)

Grandpa looked back from the driver's seat and asked: "Need any help, Maw?" Grandma just shook her head. She didn't need any help; she was getting along just fine. (Shaking-of-head motions added to others.)

The Busy Farmer's Wife

This is a dramatic stunt where the leader tells the story and demonstrates the actions. The group mimics the actions, which become accumulative.

The farmer's wife has many duties. She keeps busy all day long. The other day I visited a friend of mine and found her in the kitchen. She was standing at the stove stirring a big pot of apple butter. (Stirring motions with right hand.) The churn was standing nearby and she was pumping the handle up and down as she stirred the apple butter. (Pumping motion up and down with left hand.) One of the girls came in with a piece of taffy she had made at a taffy party, and put a piece in her mother's mouth. So there my friend stood, stirring and pumping the churn and chewing. All of a sudden she noticed that the screen door had been left open and chickens were coming in the kitchen. She couldn't leave her churning and apple butter, so all she could do was stand there shaking her head at the chickens and yelling, "Shoo, shoo, shoo." (Head moving up and down as if gesturing toward the door while making shooing sounds.)

The Rocket Trip to Mars

(With thanks to Pilot Kay Benko)

This is a dramatic stunt suited to children's groups or family groups with both adults and children. As in the Lion Hunt, the leader tells the story with the children repeating every word the leader speaks and mimicking all the actions. For example, the leader says: "Let's take a rocket trip to Mars." The children repeat the statement: "Let's take a rocket trip to Mars." The story written below gives just the leader's instructions and story. The asterisks indicate where the leader pauses and the group is given time to repeat the statement just as it is made by the leader. The motions are parenthesized. The group is standing at the beginning.

Leader: "All aboard the rocket for a trip to Mars."

Leader: "Climb up the ladder."* (Motions with feet and hands of climbing a ladder.)

Leader: "Everybody take your seats."* (All sit down.) "Fasten safety belts."* (Motions of fastening safety belts.)

Leader: "Fire one!"* (All make motions of pulling lever. Jerk in seats.) "Zo-o-om!* Fire two!"* (Motion of lever.) "Zo-o-om!* Fire three!"* (Pull lever.) "Zo-o-om!* Fire four."* (Pull lever.) "Zo-o-om!* We're off!"*

Leader: "We're going through a cloud."* (Peering as if to see through the mist.) "Now we're out in the clear.* Look! That little ball down there. That's the earth."*

Leader: "Look out that window. There's the moon. Let's zoom over this mountain into that crater."* (Motion of heading down and then up again.) "Look out.* We almost hit that mountaintop.* Phew."* (Motion of wiping forehead.) "That was close."*

Leader: (Quick jerk of head to other side.) "Look there.* There goes a shooting star."*

Leader: "What was that? We've just hit a small meteor."* (Motion of rocking ship.) "It knocked out the number-four rocket.* We're leaning to the left."* (All lean to the left.) "No danger! We can still make it to Mars.* We can fix it there."*

Leader: "See that red ball there?"* (Pointing.) "That's Mars.* Put on the brakes."* (All lean back in seats.) "We're heading down now."* (All lean forward in seats.) "Don't scrape the bottom."*

Leader: "Look out."* (Cross arms across face.) "We're coming in now. We're going to be okay.* Bump! Bump!"* (All bounce up and down in seats and lean back with a jerk.) "We're safely down."*

Leader: "Put on your space helmets."* (Motion of putting on helmets.) "Turn on oxygen."* (All put hands cupped over mouth and talk that way to give hollow-voice effect of talking from inside helmet. Group now standing.)

Leader: "Let's fix the number-four tube.* Got a wrench?* Let's tighten up this nut."* (Motions of working with wrench with one hand, other hand still cupped over mouth.) "Now this one.* There that does it."*

Leader: "Okay, let's have a look around before we leave.* Let's walk over here."* (Heavy walking sound with feet.) "Look at this beautiful vine."* (Pointing to ground.)

Leader: "Wow! That isn't a vine. It's a huge snake.* Give me the ray gun!* I haven't got the ray gun!* You don't have the ray gun?* Let's get out of here."* (Hurried but heavy running motion with feet. Group still in standing position.)

Leader: "Hurry! Up the ladder."* (Motion of climbing ladder in double time.) "Get in your seats."* (All sit down.) "Fasten your safety belts."* (Motion of fastening belts.)

Leader: (In rapid fashion.) "Fire one. Zoom!"* (Group jerks in seats.) "Fire two. Zoom."* (Group jerks in seats.) "Fire three! Zoom!* Fire four. Zo-o-om!* We're off!"*

Leader: "Gosh! The earth is certainly going to look good to me.* I'll tell you one thing. I'll never go to Mars again without my ray gun."*

Old Si Just Went By

This is one of those stunts where the leader makes a statement and the group asks a question. The leader in answering the question does so with gestures. The group takes up the gesture of the leader and the whole process is repeated with new gestures being added in accumulative fashion. Few groups ever make it to the end of the story. Try it and see if you can.

Leader: "Old Si just went by."

Group: "How?"

Leader: "With his neck held awry." (Hold head to left as if suffering from a stiff neck.)

Group: "Oh." (They mimic action of leader.) "That's how he went by with his neck held awry."

Leader: "Old Si just went by."

Group: "How?"

Leader: "With his neck held awry and his right hand held high." (Right hand raised above shoulder, neck still awry.)

Group: "Oh. With his neck held awry and his right hand held high." (Mimic actions of leader.)

Leader: "Old Si just went by."

Group: "How?"

Leader: "With his neck held awry, his right hand held high, winking one eye." (Right eye winking in rapid fashion with right hand high in air and neck still awry.)

Group: "Oh. With his neck held awry, his right hand held high, winking one eye." (Mimic actions of leader.)

Leader: "Old Si just went by."

Group: "How?"

Leader: "With his neck held awry, his right hand held high, winking one eye and one foot in the sky." (Neck awry, right hand held high, eye winking and left foot held up in the air.)

Group: "Oh. With his neck held awry, his right hand held high, winking one eye and one foot in the sky." (Mimic actions of leader.)

Leader: "Old Si just went by."

Group: "How?"

Leader: "With his neck held awry, his right hand held high, winking one eye and one foot in the sky with his mouth full of pie." (Neck awry, right hand in air, right eye blinking, left foot up in the air, mouth blown up and talking as if mouth were full.)

Group: "Oh. With his neck held awry, his right hand held high, winking one eye and one foot in the sky with his mouth full of pie." (Group mimics actions of leader, talking as if mouths were full.)

Leader: "Old Si just went by."

Group: "How?"

Leader: "With his neck held awry, his right hand held high, winking one eye, one foot in the sky with his mouth full of pie, going rockaby. (Neck awry, right hand held high, winking right eye, left foot in air, talking with mouth full and rocking back and forth.)

Group: "*Oh*. With his neck held awry, his right hand held high, winking one eye, one foot in the sky with his mouth full of pie, going rockaby." (Mimic actions of leader.)

The Mortgage Is Due

Three characters form the cast in this playlet. All parts are played by all the group, with each part being represented in a different manner. The villain is a grim-looking character who scowls under his eyebrows and speaks in a nasty voice with arms crossed on his chest. The heroine speaks in high voice dripping with woe, with hands clasped dramatically under her chin. The hero speaks manfully, striking a noble pose, one hand on chest and the other raised aloft.

The leader performs the entire playlet once for demonstration. Then the group join him, all speaking in unison. For extra effects, in a mixed group have the men speak the heroine's part and the women the villain's part with both joining together on the hero's part.

The Playlet

Villain: (Assuming correct pose) "The mortgage is due. I've come to foreclose."

Heroine: (Piteously) "Oh dear! I can't pay it now."

Villain: "The mortgage is due. I've come to foreclose."

Heroine: "Oh dear. I can't pay it now."

Villain: (With great emphasis) "The mortgage is due. I've come to collect."

Hero: (Manfully and with great nobleness) "I've arrived just in time. Here, I'll pay what's due."

Heroine: (Throbbing with joy and gratitude) "My hero! My hero! My hero!"

Villain: "Curses! Curses! Curses! Out-maneuvered again!"

I Knew an Old Lady

The lady in this story had a terrible time, as the story bears out. The leader speaks a line and the group answers. For the first time through, of course, the leader explain how the story is to be told and where the group is to make responses. He does not tell the punch line, however. He saves that as a surprise for the uninitiated.

For variation, this might be used as a choral-speaking trick with different children speaking the leader's line as solo lines. Variations in the ways of telling the story will add to the fun once the group knows the story. As the children become familiar with the story they will soon be speaking all the lines.

All lines are spoken with proper expressions of excitement, amazement and sorrow. Put great emphasis on the word "buzzin' " when it appears in the script.

Leader: "I knew a girl who swallowed a fly."

Group: "Swallowed a fly! Why would anyone swallow a fly?"

Leader: "I don't know why she swallowed a fly. But that isn't all. She swallowed a spider that went way down inside her."

Group: "Swallowed a spider, way down inside 'er?"

Leader: "She swallowed the spider to get the fly that was BUZZIN' inside 'er. But that isn't all. She swallowed a bird which was really absurd."

Group: "Swallowed a bird! It was absurd to swallow a bird."

Leader: "She swallowed the bird to get the spider to get the fly that was BUZZIN' insider 'er! But that isn't all, she swallowed a cat. Think of that."

Group: "Swallowed a cat!"

Leader: "She swallowed the cat to get the bird to get the spider to get the fly that was BUZZIN' insider 'er. But that isn't all. She swallowed a dog; whole hog, she swallowed a dog!"

Group: "Whole hog, she swallowed a dog."

Leader: "She swallowed a dog to get the cat to get the bird to get the spider that followed the fly that was BUZZIN' inside 'er. But that isn't all. She swallowed a cow! I can't tell you how but she swallowed a cow."

Group: "Swallowed a cow! Wow, Wow!"

Leader: "She swallowed the cow to get the dog to get the cat to get the bird to get the spider to get the fly that was BUZZIN' inside 'er. But that isn't all. Quite by mistake, she swallowed a snake."

Group: "Gracious' sake. She swallowed a snake?"

Leader: "Yes. Quite by mistake she swallowed a snake to get the cow to get the dog to get the cat to get the bird to get the spider to get the fly that was BUZZIN' inside 'er! But that isn't all. She swallowed a horse! Without remorse she swallowed a horse."

Group: "Swallowed a horse, without remorse. Is there anything worse than to swallow a horse?"

Leader: (In a matter-of-fact voice.) "That killed her, of course!"

The Old Ice Wagon

The words are sung to the tune of "Ten Little Indians." All players imitate the leader, who sits with hands as if holding reins. All bounce up and down on chairs while singing, which gives a rather quavering quality to the words. This is to be expected, of course, as ice wagons don't have springs.

Group and leader: "Jogging along in the old ice wagon, jogging along in the old ice wagon, jogging along in the old ice wagon. Hear my tale of WHOA!" (Motion of pulling up horse to stop.)

Leader: (Calls in huckster fashion) "Any ice today, lady?"

Group: (With great emphasis) "*No!* Your ice melts."

Leader: (With great disappointment) "Giddyyap, Napoleon!" (Motion of cracking whip and slapping of hands to make whip snap. Take up reins again.)

Group and leader: "Joggin' along in the old ice wagon, jogging along in the old ice wagon, jogging along in the old ice wagon. Hear my tale of WHOA!"

Leader: (With pathetic hopefulness) "Any ice today, lady?"

The game continues with the leader becoming more plaintive and the group more emphatic. After three times or so, the leader cracks the whip, shouts to his horse and then stops suddenly. Usually the group is taken by surprise with their mouths open ready to sing again. The leader may say: "You wouldn't buy any ice, so I'll give you no more rides on my wagon today."

My Uncle Ike

"My Uncle Ike is a fabulous character who could do wondrous things. Well, it wasn't that what he did was so difficult. It was just that he could do so many different things at the same time, as this story proves." The leader gives this explanation and describes how the story is to go. The leader will make a statement. The group will answer in the manner indicated below. Motions are added to the words, with all motions being accumulative so that at the end of the story everyone will know just how fabulous a character Ike was.

Leader: "A fabulous character is my Uncle Ike."

Group: "What could he do, your Uncle Ike?"

Leader: "First of all, he could ride a bike; one-handed he could ride a bike." (Motions with feet of riding a bike one handed.)

Group: "So your Uncle Ike could ride a bike." (Take up bicycling motion.) "What else could he do?"

Leader: "What else did he like to do? Well, I remember that he liked to chew." (Motions of chewing added to bike riding.)

Group: "Oh. He liked to chew. Was there anything else he liked to do?"

Leader: "He was mighty good at fly casting, too." (Casting motion with right hand.)

Group: "Your Uncle Ike could ride a bike, he liked to chew and he was good at fly casting, too. Was there anything else? Could he do more?"

Leader: "When he was asleep, he sure did snore." (Snoring sound added to motions.)

The Peculiar Language Tale

This is a tongue-twisting tale which a leader tells to the group. The leader stops occasionally and asks the children to repeat some of the odd names. At the end of the story, the leader might ask the children to say the tongue-twister language over with her.

The Story

Once upon a time a traveler still a long distance from his destination stopped at a farmhouse and asked for food and lodging for the night. The farmer grudgingly gave him supper but did not want him to stay for the night. He began to make excuses. "We really do not have a place for you to sleep," he told the traveler.

"Oh, that's all right," said the traveler. "I can sleep here by the fire in the rocking chair."

"I wouldn't want you to do that," replied the farmer. "Besides, we have such a peculiar way of talking, you would find it difficult to understand us. I'm sure you wouldn't be very comfortable here."

"Tell me about it," the traveler asked. "Such things always interest me. Just how is your way of talking different from mine?"

"Well," the farmer answered, "I am called Master Courageous and my wife is Mrs. Dame Gracious."

"That's simple enough," said the traveler. "You are Master Courageous and your wife is Mrs. Dame Gracious. What's so difficult about that? I'm sure I can remember to call you by your correct names."

"That's just the beginning," said the farmer in desperation. "My daughter is called Betty Pretty-Patience and our cat is called Puss Nimble-Foots."

"How interesting! Let me see, now. You are called Master Courageous, your wife is Mrs. Dame Gracious, your daughter is Betty Pretty-Patience and the cat here is called Puss Nimble-Foots." The traveler was beginning to enjoy this more and more.

The farmer was frantic now. His plan to confuse the traveler and discourage him from staying the night was not working at all. He tried again. "Oh, that's just the beginning," he said. "The fire is called glory, the thatched roof is the hamiltycot, my bed is called easy degrees and my pants are my persuages."

"Very clever of you to call your pants persuages. And glory is a good name to give the fire. But how did you arrive at hamiltycot for the thatched roof? And who thought of calling the bed easy degrees?"

The farmer saw there was nothing to do but allow the stranger to stay the night. He called to his wife and daughter and they went to the loft where they had their beds. The stranger sat back in the rocking chair and settled down for the night before the fire.

Soon all was quiet. Only the sounds of the crackling fire and the farmer's snores broke the silence. The stranger dozed off, only to be awakened by the cat rubbing against his legs. After being awakened several times the traveler lost patience and gave the cat a shove with his foot. The cat fell back into the fireplace and her tail caught on fire. With a yowl she ran up the stairs into the loft and onto the thatched roof. Soon the whole roof was ablaze.

The traveler, aghast at the suddenness of the disaster, stood speechless for a moment and then he began to shout at the top of his lungs: "Master Courageous, rise up from your easy degrees and put on your persuages. Call Mrs. Dame Gracious and Betty Pretty-Patience for Puss Nimble-Foots ran up into the hamiltycot and it is all glory!" (This last is spoken as rapidly as possible.)

Chapter 10

Finger Plays and Hand Tricks

EVEN BEFORE a child can talk he will enjoy finger plays and action rhymes which the older children in the family or the adult members will play with him. Children enjoy imitating. They love repetition. They will be saying, "Do it again," long after the adult is exhausted. Some of the finger plays given here are old favorites and others are new. Each is classified according to the age of the child. Some, while appearing to be very simple, require rather intricate finger movements so that even adults sometimes have difficulty in making their fingers behave. No matter how often these are repeated they never lose favor.

FINGER PLAYS AND RHYMES FOR VERY YOUNG CHILDREN

Pat a Cake

Adult takes the baby's hands in each of his and claps the baby's hands together for him until he learns to make the motion himself. The verse and the action follows:

Pat a cake, pat a cake, baker's man,	(Clap baby's hands together.)
Bake me a cake as fast as you can.	(Continue to clap hands together.)
Pat it	(Pat hands on table or lap.)
And roll it,	(Make baby's hands circle around each other, the more vigorously the better.)
And mark it with B,	(Motion of making large B with baby's right hand.)
And put it in the oven	(Motion of putting something in oven.)

144

| For baby | (Touch baby's hand to his chest.) |
| And me | (Touch self with baby's hands.) |

How Big Is Baby?

Take baby's hands in each of your own and say to baby: "How big is baby?" Raise baby's hands high over his head and say: "So-o-o-o big!" Do this often. Soon baby will answer the question without any help from you by raising his own hands into the air.

Pease Porridge Hot

Hold baby in your lap with his back to you and hold his hands in each of your own. Have another member of the family face the baby and play the game with him. The verse and actions follow:

Verse

Pease porridge hot,
Pease porridge cold,
Pease porridge in the pot
Nine days old.

Words and Actions

Pease	(Hit baby's hands on his thighs.)
Porridge	(Clap baby's hands together.)
Hot,	(Clap baby's right hand against partner's right hand.)
Pease	(Hit baby's hands on his thighs.)
Porridge	(Clap baby's hands together.)
Cold,	(Clap baby's left hand against partner's left hand.)
Pease	(Hit baby's hands on his thighs.)
Porridge	(Clap baby's hands together.)
In the	(Clap baby's right hand against partner's right hand.)
Pot,	(Clap baby's left hand against his partner's left hand.)

Nine	(Hit baby's hands against his thighs.)
Days	(Clap baby's hands together.)
Old.	(Clap both of baby's hands against both of hands of his partner.)

Repeat game several times, going faster each time.

Here Sits the Cock

Here sits the cock,	(Touch baby's forehead.)
Here sits the fat hen,	(Give baby's nose a little tweak.)
Here's where the little chick-ies run in.	(Touch baby's mouth.)
Chin chopper, chin chopper, chin chopper, chin.	(Take hold of baby's chin and move it up and down in rapid motions.)

When a child has teeth, the teeth click together, much to baby's amusement.

Bowl of Porridge

Stir the pot of porridge,	(Take baby's right hand and make stirring motion.)
Eat it while it's hot.	(Lift baby's hand to mouth as if eating.)
Faster, faster, faster!	(Eating motion speeded up.)
Now lick out the pot.	(Take baby's hand and wipe it across his mouth as if licking out the pot.)

Little Mousie

This is little mousie	(Hold baby's left hand, palm up, in your hand.)
Running round and round.	(Make circular motions in baby's palm with your right index finger.)
He runs from here to over there,	(Run with your fingers up baby's left arm across the back of his neck and down his right arm to his right palm.)

And never makes a sound.   (Tickle baby's right palm with your index finger.)

Nicky-Nack*

Hold baby in lap and say following rhyme:

Knee-nicky-nack,	(Pat baby's right knee.)
Shin-shicky-shack,	(Pat baby's shin.)
Heel holler back,	(Pat baby's right heel.)
Toe tippy go.	(Touch baby's big toe.)
Lay me down by the fire,	(Take baby's foot in your hand.)
Help me up, old Joe!	(Say this in a loud voice while lifting baby's leg high into the air by the big toe.)

Shoe Old Horsie*

Shoe old horsie,	(Pat baby's right sole.)
Shoe old mare,	(Pat baby's left sole.)
Hit a nail here,	(Pat right sole.)
Hit a nail there,	(Pat left sole.)
Let a little colty	(Pat right sole again.)
Go home bare.	(Pat left sole again.)

* From Grandma Mary McKay Clark, who "moved from York State (Poky-Moon-Shine) to Hickory Corners, Michigan, where she lived in Toad Holler," according to her granddaughter, Viola Stevens.

FINGER PLAYS FOR PRESCHOOL AND KINDERGARTEN AGE

The title above should read: Finger Plays for Preschool and Kindergarten Age and Anyone Else Who Wants to Play. The author has never taught adults finger plays to use with children and not had the adults convulsed with laughter before the session was over. They may be activities for small children, but adults find them fun, too.

The Typewriter

The typewriter is a funny machine;	(Make motions of poking a key here and there with index finger.)
Each letter is a key.	
I touch one here and push one there	(Continue motion of typing.)
And it prints the words for me.	(Point to self.)

Mother's Needle

This is mother's needle,	(Hold right index finger up in air.)
This is her darning ball,	(Make fist with left hand.)
She weaves the threads	(Darning and weaving motion with right index finger over left fist.)
And mends the socks	
For Johnny, Peter and Paul.	

Mother Knits

My mother knits my mittens	(Knitting motions with hands.)
From brightly colored yarn,	(Turn hands palms up and palms down as if admiring mittens.)
She knits my socks and sweaters, too,	(Touch socks and run hands down arms and front of body, showing sweater.)
That keep me, oh, so warm!	(Hug body and turn from side to side in chair while hugging self.)

My Favorite Instrument

The fiddle sings twiddle, dee, dee.	(Make motions of playing a violin.)
The flute goes peelee, weelee, wee.	(Motions of playing a flute.)

| But best of all, I like the drum | (Motions of playing a snare drum.) |
| That goes tum-ity tum, tum, tum. | (Motions of playing a snare drum.) |

The Strings in the Orchestra

The Bass Viol

The bass viol is big and tall,	(Children stand and raise left hands into the air, indicating height.)
Its voice is deep and low.	Say "deep and low" in deep tones.)
We have to stand as we play on its strings	(Hold left hand at about ear height as if fingering strings.)
With a large and heavy bow.	(Make bowing motions across strings with right hand.)

The Violoncello

The violoncello is next in size;	(Children, seated, indicate height by holding left hands at about ear level.)
It's also played with a bow.	(Bowing motions with right hand while left hand holds neck of instrument.)
We hold it tight between our knees;	(Sit with knees apart and continue bowing motions with right hand.)
Its tones are sweet and low.	(Lean left ear toward instrument as if listening.)

The Viola

| The viola is just like a big violin. | (Hold hands about 24 inches apart, palms facing each other, to indicate size.) |
| It's played like a violin, too; | (Hold left hand out in front |

of body as if holding the neck of an instrument.)

We sit and hold it under our chin, (Turn head down as if resting chin on chin rest.)

Which is not very easy to do. (Make bowing motions as if playing.)

The Violin

Last of all comes the violin, (Hold hands about 18 inches apart, palms facing each other, to indicate size of violin.)

The baby of all the strings.

We hold this, too, right under our chin. (Hold left hand out in front as if holding instrument and lay chin on chin rest.)

When we play, it almost sings. (Bowing actions with right hand.)

The Mule

The mule has two long ears, (Hold hands at sides of head, making two long ears which move forward and back.)

He's as stubborn as he can be;

All he will say when he opens his mouth (Hold hands together, palms touching. Use wrist as hinge and open and close big mouth.)

Is "hee haw, hee haw, he-e-e!"

Riding a Horse

1. I think it is fun to ride a horse (Children stand beside chairs and make motions of mounting a horse as they sit down on chairs.)

With a saddle on his back.

I sit very straight and take up the reins	(Sit tall and hold reins in both hands.)
And say, "Cluck, cluck, giddyap, giddyap."	(Make clucking sound with mouth for "cluck, cluck" and speak words "giddyap, giddyap.")
2. I swish from side to side when he walks Down the trail between the trees.	(Sit tall, hold reins but rock from side to side.)
I post whenever he starts to trot	(Sit astride chair and make posting motion, rising off seat and sitting again in rapid succession while still holding reins.)
And grip him hard with my knees.	(Grip chair with knees while posting.)
3. When he canters I rock back and forth	(Still holding reins, rock forward and back in easy rocking rhythm.)
Just like a rocking chair. The trees fly by on either side,	(Continue rocking motion still holding reins and sitting straight and tall.)
And the wind blows through my hair.	

The Very Old Man

I wear a big and funny hat	(Make motions of a tall, large brimmed hat.)
And glasses on my nose,	(Make circle of finger and thumb on each hand and peer through them, holding circled fingers close to the face.)
My beard is l-o-n-g and snowy white	(With right hand, run hand length of long beard.)
And reaches to my toes!	(Move hand down length of body to toes.)

The Old Witch

The witch is old, her back is bent,	(Children bend backs and hobble and walk as if with cane.)
She hobbles with a stick.	(Hobble painfully and slowly.)
But if she wants to cast a spell	(Make hands into claws and hold near face.)
She can be so very quick.	(Children rush forward quickly, claws moving rapidly in the direction of another child as if casting a spell.)

The Little Birds

Ten little birdies all in a row,	(Hold up ten fingers.)
They move their heads to and fro,	(Turn head from left to right in rhythm.)
Watching for the hunter with his arrow and bow.	(Make motion of drawing arrow in bow.)
When he comes into sight,	
Away they'll go!	(Flying motion in hurried fashion.)

Grandma

Here are grandma's eyeglasses,	(Make circles of forefingers and thumbs and hold to nose to make glasses.)
This is her lacy cap;	(Curve fingers as if holding large ball and place hands on top of head to make round lacy cap.)
This is the way she folds her hands	(Clasp hands in front of body.)
And puts them in her lap.	(Lay clasped hands in lap while sitting up straight in prim fashion.)

Grandpa

This is grandpa's smoking-pipe;	(Make fist of left hand but stick out thumb to make stem of pipe. Put stem near mouth.)
With tobacco it's packed tight.	(Use right thumb as tamper and make motions of tamping tobacco in pipe.)
He puts the stem into his mouth	(Put left thumb in lips.)
And puffs with all his might.	(Puff on pipe.)

Grandpa and His Cane

My grandpa has a walking cane;	
It's made of wood that's black.	
This is the way he walks along	(Walk about as if with cane, with one hand held behind back.)
With one hand behind his back.	

My Umbrella

My umbrella is a little tent	(Make motion of opening umbrella.)
That I hold up over my head.	(Hold umbrella over head.)
It keeps me dry when I walk in the rain.	(Walk about as if holding umbrella over head.)
The one I have is red.	

Two Bunnies

Two little bunnies, going hop, hop, hop,	(Make hopping motions with both hands.)
Heard a bang from the hunter's gun.	(Clap hands on "bang.")
Said one: "We're in danger, Let's flee from this stranger!	(Spoken with great feeling.)

Let's not hop, that's too slow;
Let us run!"

(Hopping motions with hands suddenly changing into fast scurrying motion as if running away.)

Five Rag Dolls

Five little rag dolls sitting up tall.

(Hold one hand in air with fingers outstretched.)

The first one says: "I think I'm going to fall!"

(Thumb closes in toward palm.)

The second one says: "Don't fall on me!"

(Forefinger closes down toward palm.)

The third one says: "This is fun, whee, whee!"

(Third finger goes down.)

The fourth one says: "Whoops, down I go!"

(Fourth finger closes down toward palm.)

The fifth one says: "I'll give a big blow!"

(Blow hard on fingers.)

And they all pop up in a nice straight row.

(Fingers pop up again straight and tall.)

Five Little Soldiers

Five little soldiers sitting in a row,

(Five children sitting on the floor with legs apart, one close behind the other.)

We count out loud: "One, two, three,"

(Children count together, "one, two, three.")

Then we give a big blow.

(All blow together in one big blow.)

The poor little soldiers,
Down they go.

(The five children fall back slowly until they are lying on the floor, one overlapping the other.)

The Hammer

The hammer is a useful tool
To nail things up tight.

(Make right hand into fist.)

We put a nail in the wood

(Place right index finger into left palm.)

And pound with all our might.

(Pound right fist in left palm.)

The Saw

My daddy's saw sings a funny song;	(Make sawing motions with right hand.)
It buzzes like a bee.	(Continue sawing motion.)
It cuts the wood into different shapes	(Make different shapes with hands.)
To make nice toys for me.	(Point to self.)

This Is My House

This is the house with the sloping roof	(Make roof with fingers.)
Where I live.	(Point to self.)
This is the tree so straight and tall	(Hold hands high over head.)
That shades the house with the sloping roof	(Make roof of hands.)
Where I live.	(Point to self.)
This is the dog with ears so long	(Hold hands at sides of head, pointing up like ears.)
That plays under the tree so straight and tall	(Hands over head.)
That shades the house with the sloping roof	(Make roof with fingers.)
Where I live.	(Point to self.)
This is the cat so furry and soft	(Cradle cat in left arm and pat with right hand.)
That worries the dog with ears so long	(Hands at sides of head for ears.)
That plays under the tree so straight and tall	(Hands straight up over head.)
That shades the house with the slopping roof	(Make roof with fingers.)
Where I live.	(Point to self.)
And last comes me, as you can see,	(Point to self with pleasant look.)
Who loves the cat so furry and soft	(Patting motion of cat held in arms.)

That worries the dog with ears so long	(Hands at sides of head.)
That plays under the tree so straight and tall	(Hands high over head.)
That shades the house with the sloping roof	(Make roof with fingers.)
Where I live.	(Point to self.)

Repeat several times, going faster each time.

This Is the House That I Built

This is the house	(Make roof with arms, touching fingertips together.)
That I built.	(Point to self.)
This is the saw that cut the boards	(Make sawing motion with right hand.)
That went into the house	(Make roof with arms.)
That I built.	(Point to self.)
This is the hammer	(Make fist with right hand.)
That nailed the boards	(Pound right fist into left palm.)
That I cut with the saw	(Sawing motion with right hand.)
That went into the house	(Make roof with arms.)
That I built.	(Point to self.)
These are my hands	(Hold out hands and look at them.)
That held the hammer	(Make fist.)
That nailed the boards	(Pound right fist in left palm.)
That I cut with the saw	(Sawing motion with right hand.)
That went into the house	(Make roof with hands.)
That I built.	(Point to self.)

Ten Little Bunnies

Ten little bunnies all in a row;	(Hold up ten fingers.)

They wiggle their ears To and fro.	(Hold hands to sides of head to make ears and wiggle back and forth.)
They're watching for the hunter with his great big gun.	(Make motion of holding gun.)
When he comes into sight, Away they'll run.	(Make hopping and scampering motions with hands.)

Blowing Up Your Muscle

Put right thumb into mouth and blow hard, puffing up cheeks. At the same time flex your biceps, causing them to stand up as if they were being blown up. Then push on muscle with left hand, making hissing sound as if letting air out, and let muscle relax and flatten.

Magic Arm Bending

This is one of those tricks that look very strange and unnatural and yet involves nothing but normal movements of the arm. Hold left arm straight out in front of body at shoulder level. With right hand held palm open, hit sharply at inside of left elbow as if attempting to break a bone there. Bend left arm up at right angle and hold that position. Now strike sharply at inside of left wrist and cause left hand to bend in toward the face. With right hand, grasp the left hand and turn it at the wrist so that the fingers turn away from the face. Now reverse the movements, turning left hand back toward face, straightening left arm at wrist and then at elbow. The trick is to make each movement look unnatural. For some reason the movements look contorted.

Loose Arm

Hold right arm out at shoulder height with arm bent at a right angle at elbow and hand hanging loosely down like a clock pendulum. With left hand give right hand a push as if to make the pendulum swing. Swing right arm back and forth from elbow. When it appears to be swinging freely, give a bigger push with the left hand, causing the right arm to turn a complete circle. With practice in front of a mirror you can make it appear that your right arm is completely loose and unjointed. This is another one of those tricks that looks odd and is completely silly but nevertheless fascinates children.

One Finger Keep Moving

This is an action song which brings in one part of the body after another. The trick is to move the specific part when it is announced in the words and to keep it moving where the words say "keep moving." As another and another part is added to the song, that portion of the body must be brought into the action at the time it is announced in the words. At the end of the song the whole body is in motion.

This is a good trick to use with an audience that has been sitting too long. It has plenty of action but still can be used in an auditorium or meeting room where the group has to remain in seats. It can be used to get a group which has been sitting a long time loosened up and ready for the action program which is to follow the sitting program.

1. One finger keep moving,	(Hold up right index finger with exaggerated motion on "one finger" and begin wiggling it on "keep moving.")
One finger keep moving,	(Wiggle finger again and stop.)
One finger keep moving,	(Start finger wiggling.)
And we'll all be happy and gay.	(Continue finger wiggling.)
2. One finger,	(Hold up right index finger with exaggerated motion.)
Two fingers	(Hold up left index finger with exaggerated motion.)
Keep moving.	(Wiggle both right and left index fingers.)
One finger,	(Stop motion of both fingers and show right index finger.)
Two fingers	(Show left index finger.)

Keep moving.	(Wiggle both fingers while singing.)
One finger, two fingers keep moving,	(Show right, then left forefinger and keep wiggling both.)
And we'll all be happy and gay.	(Wiggle both index fingers.)
3. One finger, two fingers, one thumb	(Show right index finger, then left index finger and then right thumb.)
Keep moving.	(Move all three fingers at same time.)

4. One finger, two fingers, one thumb, two thumbs keep moving, etc.

ONE FINGER KEEP MOVING

Arr. by Harriet Smith Harris

5. One finger, two fingers, one thumb, two thumbs, one arm keep moving, etc.

6. One finger, two fingers, one thumb, two thumbs, one arm, two arms, keep moving, etc.

7. One finger, two fingers, one thumb, two thumbs, one arm, two arms, one foot, keep moving, etc.

8. One finger, two fingers, one thumb, two thumbs, one arm, two arms, one foot, two feet, keep moving, etc.

9. One finger, two fingers, one thumb, two thumbs, one arm, two arms, one foot, two feet, one head (nod head up and down) keep moving, etc.

10. One finger, two fingers, one thumb, two thumbs, one arm, two arms, one foot, two feet, one head, stand up, sit down, keep moving, etc.

Remember the movement stops at the end of the phrase "keep moving" each time, and each part of the body movement must be added a portion at a time as the words dictate. During the singing of "and we'll all be happy and gay," all the motions accumulated during the last verse must be kept going.

In the music given below, the pattern for several verses is given to show how the music is changed to fit the words.

(Musical Patterns for Verses of "One Finger Keep Moving")

One finger, two fingers keep / moving

One finger, two fingers, one thumb keep / moving

One finger, two fingers, one thumb, two thumbs keep / moving

OBSERVATION GAMES

Observation games are usually trick games. The leader tells a little story, repeats a little rhyme or performs a seemingly simple movement. The guests then try to tell the story, repeat the rhyme or make the motion exactly as the leader did. Sometimes the trick is in the way the leader is sitting (with legs crossed in a certain way or with head cocked to the side.) Sometimes it is in what he does before he says the rhyme (clearing his throat, scratching his head or rubbing his nose). Sometimes the gimmick comes at the end of the trick. It might be a particular movement such as the clasping of hands, folding of arms or crossing of legs.

As soon as a player thinks he knows the trick, he is given the opportunity to demonstrate. If he does it correctly, the leader gives him a nod. If he is wrong the leader so informs him but does not tell him what he did wrong.

Simple Little Trick

The leader says the following words:

"It's a simple trick, but you have to do it twice. It's not hard to do but you have to do it right." The motion that goes with it is as follows:

Make tight fists with both hands and hold fists thumb side up. Hit left fist on right fist on the words "it's a simple." Now turn fists parallel to floor and hit thumb sides together on the word "trick." Turn fists thumb side up again and hit right fist on left fist on the words "have to do it." On the word "twice" hit left fist on top of right fist. On the words, "It's not hard to do, but you have to do it right," the entire set of motions is repeated, and the player ends with his left fist on top of the right one. It's tricky, but there is no catch to this one. You just have to do it right! If it seems easy, try doing it several times in a row in speedy rhythm.

Make a Box

As the leader says these words he is making certain appropriate motions: "With you hands make a box and you make it just so. Back and forth, and back you go."

All through the trick the hands are held out in front of the body in various positions, with hands open, thumb side up and thumbs tight against the hand. The words and the accompanying motions are given below in co-ordinated fashion:

Words	*Motions*

With your hands

Hands in front of body, palms parallel, fingers pointed away from the body. Palms about twelve inches apart as if showing length of box.

Make a box

Right hand moves close to body, fingers pointing to left side of body. Left hand moves parallel to right hand about eight inches in front of it, fingers pointing toward right side of body as if showing width of box.

And you make it

Hands back in first position showing length of box.

Just so

Hands as in second position except that now the right hand is out in front and the left hand is close to the body.

Back and

Move hands in parallel position across body so that the right fingers move toward the left elbow and the fingers of the left hand move toward the right elbow. Move the hands back until the fingers are about two inches apart.

Forth and

Move hands across body again, and back to position except that now the left hand is in front and the right hand is close to the body.

Back you

Repeat hand movement across body, this time with right hand out in front and the left hand close to the body.

Go

Hands are in first position, just as you began.

Variation: To make this more tricky, the leader can tap his foot in rhythm as he says the words, and performs the motions. The toe tapping is done quietly and unobtrusively so that only the most observant player will notice that this is part of the trick.

I Have a Round Head

The leader says slowly: "I have a round head, two big eyes, a big nose and a smiling mouth." With the index finger of his left hand used like a drawing pencil, he makes a motion around his head, holds up two fingers for the two eyes, makes his hand into a fist, holds it close to his nose and then sketches in a smiling mouth. The children try to mimic his motions. The trick is in doing it with the left hand. The left-handed person will do it readily without thinking, but the right-handed one will use his right hand, which is most natural for him.

Chapter 11

Handkerchief and Paper-Folding Tricks

HANDKERCHIEF TRICKS

The Hanky Mouse

No trick is more fascinating to children (and to adults, too, who will admit it) than the hanky mouse. The leader carries on a question-and-answer patter with the children while the folding process is going on. It might run like this:

Leader: "Do you know what this is?" (Holding up the handkerchief.)

Children: "That's a hanky."

Leader: "Are you sure it's a hanky? How can you tell?"

Children: "It looks like a hanky. It's a square piece of cloth," etc.

Leader: "Are you sure it isn't a tablecloth?"

Children: "It's too small to be a tablecloth."

Leader: "It might be a tablecloth for a fairy's table," etc.

By this time the folding process is nearly at an end and the attention of the children is complete. The leader has only to tie in the ears of the mouse. She may even pretend to slip a Mexican jumping bean into the folds. The leader then lays the mouse on the palm of her hand and begins gently to stroke it. When it jumps the children usually are so startled they jump with it.

The trick of folding the mouse is not difficult, but takes a little time and patience to learn. The patient reader who works out the trick for himself will find himself amply rewarded by the pleasure of the children who enjoy the antics of the mouse.

Use a medium-sized cotton or linen handkerchief with a plain edge. Lay it in your lap or on a flat surface with one corner toward you and one away from you. (Note: If, in following the directions while learning, you print the letters shown in the diagram on your hanky with a pencil, you will

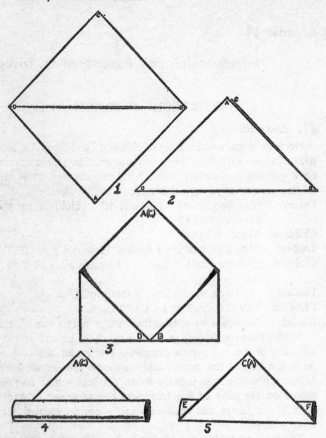

find following the directions easy. You will soon discover that the trick is easier to do than to describe.) Call the corner closest to you *A*, the one to the right *B*, the top corner *C* and the one to the left *D*. (Figure 1.) Now fold the hanky in half, bringing point *A* to point *C*, so that a triangle is formed. (Figure 2.) Fold corner *D* into the center of the bottom edge and do the same with corner *B* so that corners *B* and *D* touch. (Figure 3.) Keeping the hanky in the same position, make

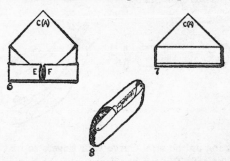

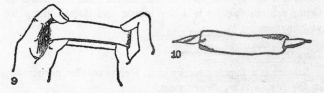

a one-inch fold up from the bottom and smooth. Make a second fold and smooth. Now make a third fold. (Figure 4.) Now turn the handkerchief over, keeping the point *CA* at the top. (Figure 5.) Bring the two little rolls *E* and *F* into the center so that they touch. (Figure 6.) Holding the little rolls firmly, turn them up one fold from the bottom toward

point *CA*. Now turn point *CA* down and tuck it into the space between the fold and the two rolls. (Figure 7.) The rolls are now completely covered. (Figure 8.) This completes the folds.

Now pick up the hanky roll, keeping it in the same position as it was on the table. Slip your thumbs into the slot. (Figure 9.) Holding the hanky firmly, begin rolling the hanky away from you much as you roll up a pair of socks. On the third roll, two little tails will pop out. (Figure 10.) Take one of these ends and, holding the "tail" so that the point is up, roll gently between the fingers until you have two tiny little rolls which you can tie in a knot to make into head and ears. Now the mouse is completed. (Figure 11.)

Lay the hanky mouse in the palm of your left hand with the

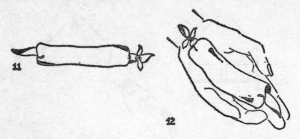

head pointing up the arm. Curve your fingers so that they are touching the roll. The tail hangs out over the fingers. (Figure 12.) Cover the mouse lightly with the right hand, making a stroking motion. As your hand moves from your wrist down toward your fingertips, make a quick motion with the fingers of the left hand. The mouse will be propelled up your arm. The trick is to cover any motion of the left hand with the right hand. The mouse will appear to be alive. The children will want to try the trick. If the mouse does not jump for them, explain that he is a shy mouse and doesn't jump for just anyone.

Salome the Dancer

Salome is a dancing hanky doll. Her talents lie particularly in the high-kicking department.

Take a woman's plain cotton or linen hanky. Tie a small knot in each of the two top corners. Then tie a knot in the center of the top hem. This forms Salome's head and two hands. (Figure 1.)

Now take hold of corner *A* in the left hand and corner *B* in the right hand and let the head and hands hang down toward the floor. Holding the corners tightly, spin the head and arms toward you several times until the hanky is rolled up tightly. (Figure 2.) The tight rolls are the legs. Now take hold of both legs with one hand and hold the head in the other hand. Pull so that the hanky is under tension. (Figure 3.) If you carefully let go of one leg and let it swing free, Salome will do a high kick. She may even spin around on one toe for you. (Figure 4.)

Repeat this verse as Salome performs:

> Salome was a dancer who really loved to kick.
> She kicked so high,
> She kicked the sky;
> That really is a trick.

Hanky Twins in a Hammock

Take a cotton or linen hanky with a plain edge. Lay it flat on a table as shown in figure 1. Fold the hanky across the center, bringing point A to point C. (Figure 2.) Now bring points D and B into center point X by rolling them in toward

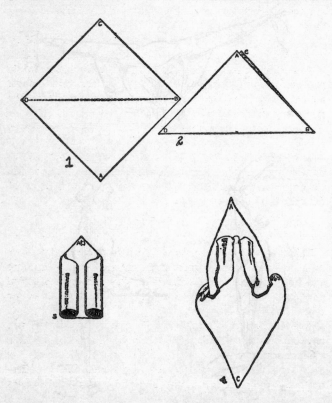

that point. (Figure 3.) Holding the rolls in position, take hold of point *A* in one hand and then separate point *C* and pull it gently downward to make the little hammock. (Figure 4.) The two rolls are the twins. Swing the hammock gently from side to side and have the children sing "Rockaby Baby" with you as you rock the twins.

PAPER-FOLDING TRICKS

Paper folding is almost a lost art. The folding tricks can be combined with a story so that a simple piece of paper becomes a magical thing. Paper folding takes time and patience to learn. It is not, however, difficult. Once the folds are learned they will never be forgotten. The best way to begin is to learn the first set of folds. Then go back to the beginning and do those all over again before going on to the next set of folds. If you continue to go back to the beginning each time while you are learning, you will be able to do the folds almost automatically. The story can be adapted to fit almost any group or any occasion.

The folds will be described first. Then the narrative that is possible will follow.

Take a piece of good bond paper 8½ by 11 inches. This is regular typing paper but the quality of the paper is important. Cut into an 8½-inch square. From this square a number of different things can be made.

Candy Dish

Take the square of paper and fold it from corner to corner on a diagonal. Make a good sharp crease. Now, open it up and fold diagonally across the other way and open up. You now have two diagonal creases that bisect each other in the center *E*. (Figure 1.)

1. Fold corners *A*, *B*, *C* and *D* into center point *E* and crease the folds carefully. (See figure 2.) You will now have a 6-inch square.

2. Turn the paper over so that the folded side is underneath and the plain side is up. (Figure 3.) Now fold corners

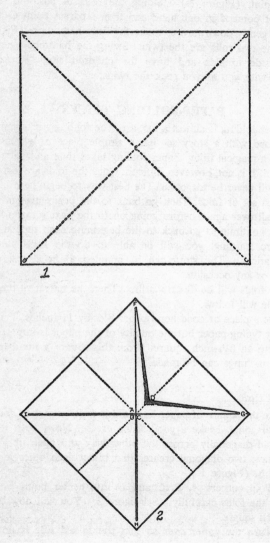

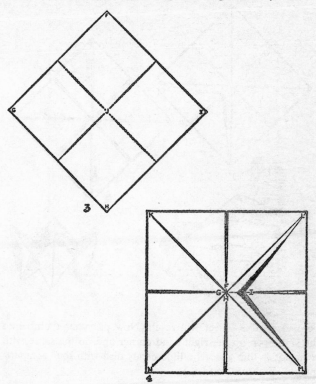

F, G, H and I of the square into the center J. You will now have a 4¼-inch square. (Figure 4.)

3. Turn the square over once more, so that the original corners A, B, C and D you folded in show, and fold the corners K, L, M and N into the center E. The square has been reduced to 3 inches. (Figure 5.) Turn this square over once more. (Figure 6.)

4. Hold the square in your hand so that your thumbs rest in the lower squares and your forefingers in the upper squares with the remaining fingers of each hand on the underside of the square. Now pinch the thumb and forefinger of one hand together. Do the same with the other hand. A four-

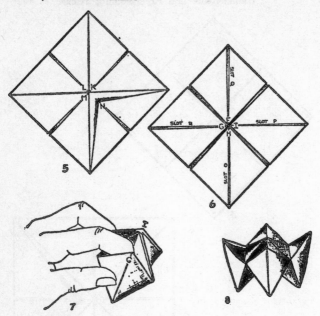

pointed starlike object will result. Now put your thumb into the slot, open up the right-hand corner and do the same with each slot so that you get a little candy dish with four compartments. (Figures 7 and 8.)

The Square Cake Dish

1. Flatten the candy dish so that it is again a 3-inch square with all the folds in it, as in figure 6. Hold it in the left hand with one point toward you and one away from you.

2. Put your finger in slot and pull corner *H* to the right until you have fold shown in figure 9. Do the same with each slot until you have what appears in figure 10.

3. Now on the reverse side pull out the points *K*, *L*, *M* and *N*, which are folded into the center, and use these as legs for the square cake plate. (Figure 11.) This is the square cake dish made especially for square cakes!

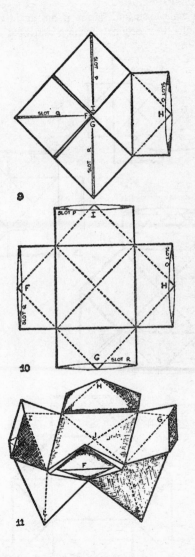

SLOT P
SLOT Q
SLOT O
SLOT R

9

SLOT P   I
SLOT O
F   H
SLOT Q
G   SLOT R

10

H
I   J   G
F

11

Turtle-Neck Sweater

Take the cake dish and flatten it out again by folding the legs back into their original position and hold it in your left

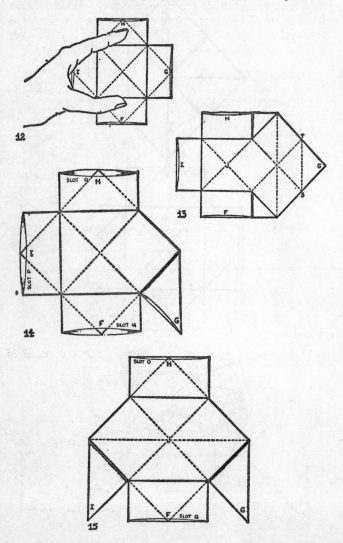

hand as shown in figure 12. Put your right index finger in the slot and pull gently until the paper opens out to what appears in figure 13. Pinch points *T* and *S* together to the back with thumb and forefinger so that they will fall into the folds. Point *G* will swing downward and you will have one sleeve of the sweater. (Figure 14.) Do the same on the left side for the sleeve. The sweater will look like figure 15.

Pair of Shorts

One needs shorts to wear with a turtle-neck sweater. These are simply made. Just fold *F* to *H* and you will have a pair of short pants. (Figure 16.)

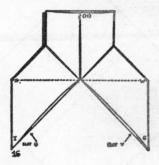

Steamboat

From the pair of shorts, we construct a steamboat. Hold

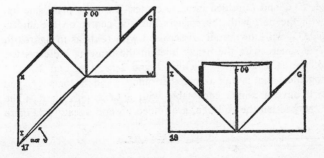

the shorts loosely in the left hand. Place the right thumb in slot *V* and push point *W* easily and gently downward with right forefinger until it falls into the old folds and looks like figure 17. Do the same on the left side and you have a steamboat. (Figure 18.)

Card Table with Tablecloth

Open up the piece of paper until you have the 5½-inch square. (See figure 3.) This is the square with the corners

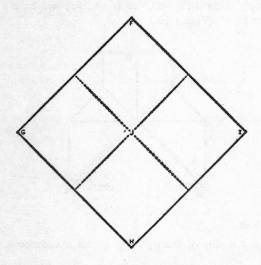

A, B, C and *D* folded into the center. Turn the plain side up, with the part with the corners into the center on the underside. It will now be all crisscrossed with folds as in figure 19. The square with the heavy lines in the drawing indicates top of the card table. By pinching 1 and 2 together and 3 and 4 together and 5 and 6 together and 7 and 8 together, you will have a 3-inch card table with a tablecloth on it. (The legs, you tell the children, are folded up underneath!) (Figure 20.)

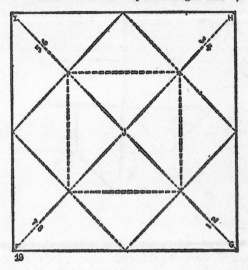

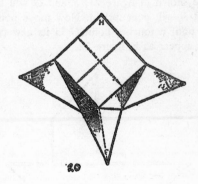

The Pinwheel

The pinwheel is made from the card table. Hold the card table with the plain side (figure 19) toward you. Take the lower right-hand corner and fold up. Fold the upper right-hand corner up, too. Turn both the corners on the left side down. Then turn the paper over. You will have a four-winged pinwheel. (Figure 21.)

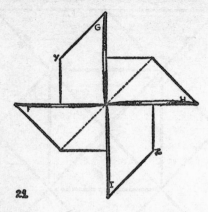

21

The Sailboat

The pinwheel moves easily into a sailboat. Fold point Y and point Z *back* toward each other gently along dotted diagonal line shown in figure 21. F and G will be on a line together and H will pop upright. Now move point I up and to the right until it touches point G in its new position. The sailboat will appear as in figure 22.

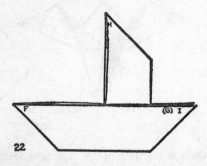

22

The Double Rowboat

From the sailboat position move point G around to the left until it touches point F. H will move down and touch point I. A double rowboat results. (Figure 23.) Hold between forefinger, which is in one boat, and thumb, which is in the other.

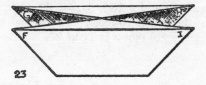

The Wallet

Reach inside the double rowboat and take hold of point *A* in the one boat. Pull this out and upward toward you until it opens up completely. It will look like figure 24. Fold points *B, F* and *I* into the center point (marked with a star) along the old folds. It will then look like figure 25. Now fold line 12 down toward line 34 so that point touches 3 and point 2

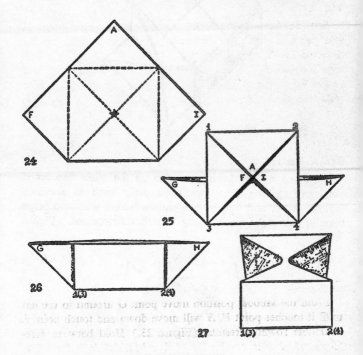

touches point 4. (Figure 26.) Repeat these steps with the other side of the double rowboat. You will end with a neat little wallet-type purse shown in figure 27.

Cap

Turn wallet upside down and pull flap 12 down to make visor of cap. Only a "square" could wear this cap (figure 28) but who doesn't have at least one friend who is a blockhead?

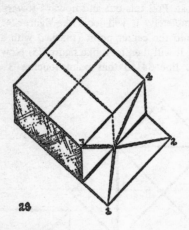

28

Bushel Basket

Turn cap upside down and open up the other flap, as if you were making a cap with two peaks such as Sherlock Holmes wore, and you have a square basket with two large handles just right for carrying square watermelons. (Figure 29.)

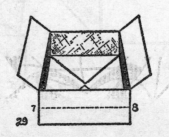

29

Picture Frame

Take the square bushel basket and fold along heavy dotted line 7, 8. Make a similar fold along each side of the square basket. You will have an accordion-pleat effect on each side. (Figure 30.) Now fold flap *A* under until it is flat against the bottom. Do the same with flap *B* and you have a picture frame as shown in figure 31.

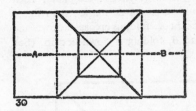

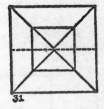

Chinese Junk

Open picture frame so that flaps *A* and *C* are in the position shown in figure 30. Fold the bottom of the frame back against the top, making the fold along the heavy dotted line shown in figure 30. Hold tightly between forefinger and thumb of left hand at point *Z* and pull out side flaps, which are the original points *A* and *C*, until they open out to points as in figure 32. Still holding tightly at point *Z*, gently pull right point upward.

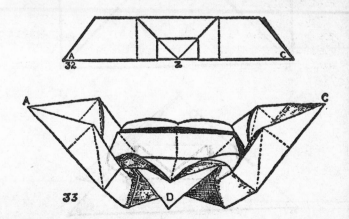

Do same with left point. You will have a Chinese junk. (Figure 33.)

The Beach Ball or Basketball

Take an 8¼-inch square of typing paper. Fold diagonally from corner to corner and crease. Make another diagonal fold across the other way so that the two diagonal folds cross. Make one horizontal fold across the center of the paper. Then open up the paper. It should have crease marks as in figure 34. Now bring point *D* to point *A*, folding crease *E* down and in. Do the same with *C* and *B*, folding *F* down and in. (See figure 35.)

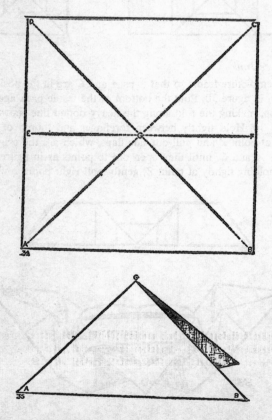

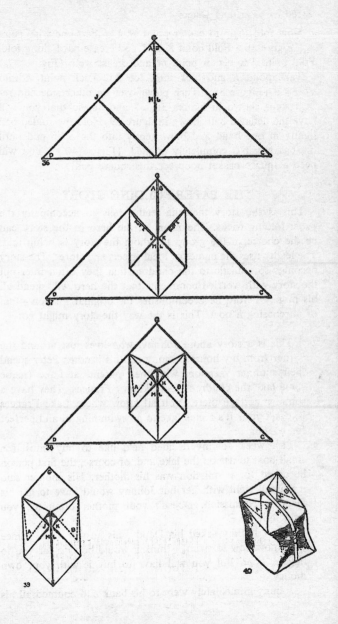

36

37

38

39

40

Now fold B up to center point G. Do the same with point A. (Figure 36.) Fold point K to L and crease hard along fold. Fold point J to center point M and crease well. (Figure 37.)

Take point B and tuck into slot #1. Tuck point A into slot #2. (Figure 38.) Turn paper over on other side and repeat steps shown in figures 36, 37 and 38, so that you will have the deflated ball shown in figure 39. Hold the folded ball lightly in one hand and blow gently into the open end until the basketball is completely inflated. (Figure 40.) (You will need a square basket hoop for this square ball!)

THE PAPER-FOLDING STORY

This is the story that the leader tells to accompany the paper-folding tricks. The name of the hero in the story can be the choice of the group to whom the story is being told. The leader uses the names of local streets and stores. The story becomes so realistic to the children that they often interrupt the story with worried comments that the hero will spend all his money before he accomplishes his original mission—that of purchasing a boat. This is the way the story might go:

This is a story about Johnny, who lives just around the corner from my house. Johnny and his brother Peter spend their summer vacations with their parents at Lake (name some lake the children would know) Frances. They have a summer cottage there. You all know where Lake Frances is, don't you? It's a nice lake to go swimming in and perfect for boating.

Last week Johnny decided he'd like to buy himself a small boat to use on the lake and, of course, the first person he asked for permission was his mother. His mother said it was all right with her but Johnny would have to get his Daddy's permission. Doesn't your mother often tell you that, too?

When Johnny asked his Daddy, his answer was: "Since you know how to swim, I think it would be safe for you to have a boat. But you will have to buy it with your own money."

Johnny immediately went to his bank and counted all his

money. He'd earned most of it cutting lawns, shoveling snow and running errands for his mother. The very next Saturday morning, Johnny took a (name a local bus) bus downtown and went to the X (name a local store) department store. On his way to the boat department, he passed a counter where glassware was sold. A piece on the counter caught his eye and he decided to buy it as a present for his mother. It was a beautiful green glass candy dish with four compartments. (Show the candy dish pictured in figure 8.) You see you can put nuts in this part and different kinds of candy in the other three parts.

Johnny decided this wasn't enough to buy his mother, who was always doing nice things for him, so he walked around and around the counter (continue folding until you have the cake dish) and he finally decided he'd buy a square cake dish he saw there. It would be perfect for a square birthday cake. He could almost see the candles on the cake. (Show square cake dish pictured in figure 11.)

As Johnny walked through the store he thought he ought to buy something for his Daddy. Just at that moment he was walking through the men's-wear department, and remembering that his Dad liked to wear sweaters he bought him a turtle-neck sweater. (See figure 15.) That didn't seem quite enough so he bought him a pair of shorts to wear with the sweater. (Figure 16.)

Feeling very happy about his purchases, Johnny went to the sporting-good department to find a boat. The only boat the store had left in stock was a steamboat. Johnny didn't want that kind of boat. (See figure 18.) It was too big and too expensive. He decided to go across the street to the Bay Company store. On his way out he saw a large crowd gathered around a counter. That could only mean a bargain! Johnny wriggled his way up to the counter to see what was being sold. It was a card table complete with tablecloth! (See figure 20.) It was just what the family needed so Johnny bought one. With the card table under one arm and his other purchases under the other, Johnny left the X department store and went out into the street. He crossed over to the Bay Company store and went in.

At the counter near the door he purchased a pinwheel for his bicycle. (Figure 21.) Upstairs in the boat department they had only sailboats (Figure 22) and double rowboats (Figure 23). Neither of these was what Johnny had in mind. There was nothing to do but try another store.

As Johnny walked up Main Street, a gust of wind blew his hat off and into the street. Before he could safely get to it a bus ran over it and smashed it flat. It was too dirty and too smashed to pick up, so Johnny sadly left it there and started up the street. You know the way you walk when you are feeling sad? With your head hanging down? That's the way Johnny was walking. Suddenly he kicked something on the sidewalk. It was a wallet. (See figure 27.) He looked inside and found the name and business address of the owner. The man's office was close by so Johnny immediately returned the billfold to the owner. The man was so happy he gave Johnny a ten-dollar reward. Johnny immediately went out and bought a new cap to replace the hat he'd lost. (Figure 28.) He also bought a square bushel basket to carry his packages in. (Figure 29.)

Johnny still didn't have his boat. He finally decided to try Green's sporting goods store. On the way he passed a ten-cent store. He remembered he needed a picture frame for a picture of his dog Buster. He bought a nice one. Buster would like that, he thought. (Figure 31.)

On his way to Green's he passed a theatrical agency. They might have just the boat he wanted. They had a boat, all right, but it was a Chinese junk. A junk would never do. (Figure 33.) Johnny went on to Green's. But they were sold out of boats! Poor Johnny! He decided to wait until another day when Daddy could come shopping with him. He hated to go home without anything for himself so he started around Green's looking here and there. He didn't want a bicycle. He already had one. (The leader stretches out this part of the story and lets the children try to guess what Johnny will eventually buy as the paper-folding of the ball takes a bit of time.) He passed by the ice skates and skis. He didn't want a kite. He finally decided to buy something he could use at the lake. What do you suppose it was?

(The children will guess anything from a bathing suit to a fishing rod. One may hit on a beach ball.) It was a beach ball that Johnny bought. But when you buy a beach ball how does it usually come? Flat? That's right. It has to be blown up. (Figures 39 and 40.) (Leader blows up ball and shows it to group and then tosses it into the audience.)

This stunt never fails to please a group no matter how often they see it. The story can be varied. Johnny may be going on a Christmas shopping expedition if the occasion is a Christmas party.

Chapter 12

Musical Games

A PARTY without music is only half a party. The guest to whom music does not appeal is the exception and most certainly not the rule. Musical games fit into almost every party. They can be used with large groups crowded into a small space. They can be used as table games at a banquet or family supper. They work with groups of mixed ages, adult groups and teenage groups. They are excellent activities for groups who can't be physically active but still like the fun of a game. Since musical games have versatility, they can be fitted into any theme or situation, whether it be a Christmas or St. Valentine's Day party, a mother-daughter or father-son banquet. They can be used at home parties, in church activities, with patients in a hospital ward and practically anywhere.

As in any contest-type game, we recommend the activity be a team game. Two heads are better than one, and several are better than two. Added to the fun of the game is the sharing of knowledge and the getting-better-acquainted aspect of the activity which is not possible when games are played with individuals competing against individuals. It is not important in these games to have teams of equal numbers. Where such an arrangement is impossible, as it is at banquets and in auditoriums, the teams are made up of groups small enough to be within hearing distance of a loud whisper. Where chairs can be moved into little circles, the teams can be of the same size.

Each team appoints a secretary or captain who writes down the answers as the decision of the group is reached. Group prizes such as a bag of wrapped candies or a sucker for each player are awarded the winners.

Musical games are good quieting-down activities to use near the end of a party. And since the players soon are humming along with the accompanist as they play the game, it is not difficult to go from this type of game into a community-sing program which always ends a party—may we say?—on a good note.

The games which follow are musical category games. A number of categories are covered to help you in planning several types of parties. It is fun to try to find a category which fits the group particularly. For example, use songs with numbers for an accountants' party, mother-daughter songs for a mother-daughter party or sports and date categories for teenagers. If you can't find the right category here, pick a suitable category and sit down with several good song collections and make your own list. You'll have the fun of inventing a new game and your group will enjoy playing it.

Mothers and Daughters

This game is appropriate at a mother-daughter party or dinner. Divide group into teams and give each team a pad and pencil. Have one player act as secretary. Have the secretary number the pad from one to ten down the left-hand side of the sheet. Announce that the pianist will play portions of songs, each of which will represent either a mother or daughter. The words or title will have the word "mother" or a girl's name in them. The team must give the classification as well as the name of each song. Finish the entire list and then allow teams to ask for repeats. Given below are songs which could be used for this game and the classifications which they represent.

Mother Songs	*Daughter Songs*
1. Just Before the Battle, Mother	1. Dinah
2. Mother Was a Lady	2. Juanita
3. Break the News to Mother	3. Bring a Torch, Jeanette, Isabella
4. I Want a Girl	4. Annie Laurie
5. M Is for Mother	5. Jeanie with the Light Brown Hair
6. Silent Night	6. Who is Sylvia?
7. Mother Machree	7. Darling Nelly Gray
8. Where is My Wandering Boy Tonight?	8. When You and I were Young, Maggie
9. Sometimes I Feel Like a	9. Oh! Susanna

Motherless Child
10. Ave Maria
11. Songs My Mother Taught Me
12. Missouri Waltz
13. Kentucky Babe
14. Summertime
15. Shortenin' Bread
16. Mighty Lak a Rose

10. Clementine
11. Charmaine
12. Daisy Bell
13. It Was Mary
14. Polly-Wolly Doodle
15. Sweet Genevieve
16. Ben Bolt

Fathers and Sons

Try this musical game at a father-son party or banquet.

Play as in Mothers and Daughters. Given below are lists of songs for each classification. The father songs mention father or dad. The son songs are those with boys' names in them.

Father Songs	Son Songs
1. I Want a Girl	1. Billy Boy
2. Yankee Doodle	2. John Peel
3. Summertime	3. Joshua Fit the Battle of Jericho
4. Sweet and Low	4. Little David, Play on Your Harp
5. America	5. Old Black Joe
6. Paw Paw Patch	6. Reuben and Rachel
	7. Ben Bolt
	8. When Johnny Comes Marching Home
	9. Annie Rooney (boy's name is Joe)
	10. Old Uncle Ned
	11. The First Noel
	12. Clancy Lowered the Boom

Father and Daughter

Play as above. Use father songs from Father and Son game and daughter songs from Mother and Daughter game. (See further instructions at beginning of this chapter.)

Method-of-Travel Song Game

For a *bon voyage* party, or for any party, this song game is especially apt. Divide group into teams and give each team a pad and pencil. One member of the team acts as secretary. Have the secretary number from one to fifteen down the left-hand side of pad. The pianist plays portions of melodies which indicate or name a method of travel or a conveyance of some type. Players on teams must give the name of the song as well as the type of conveyance. After all the tunes have been played, allow the teams time to ask for repeats before judging the answers.

Given below is a list of song titles and the conveyances they mention or represent.

Songs	Conveyance
1. Daisy Bell	Bicycle built for two
2. In My Merry Oldsmobile	Auto or, specifically, Oldsmobile
3. I've Been Working on the Railroad	Railroad
4. The Old Gray Mare	Horse
5. Camptown Races	Race horse
6. Oh! Susanna	Covered wagon
7. Sailing, Sailing	Clipper or sailing vessel
8. Donkey Riding	Riding a donkey engine
9. Jingle Bells	One-horse open sleigh
10. Moonlight Bay	Pleasure cruiser
11. Caisson Song	Ammunition wagon or caisson
12. Air Force Song	Fighter plane or bomber
13. Marching Through Georgia	Shank's ponies (walking on your own two feet)
14. Good News, Chariot's A-Coming	Chariot
15. On a Sunday Afternoon	Punt, rowboat or canoe
16. Good-by, My Lover, Good-by	Sailing boat
17. Erie Canal	Canal boat or barge
18. The Surrey with the Fringe on Top	Surrey

Musical Structures

Divide your group into teams and give each a pad and

pencil. Have teams select a secretary, who numbers pad from one to twelve down the left side of the paper. Instruct the teams that the pianist will play portions of songs. Each will imply or actually name a kind of structure. At the completion of the list, allow teams time to ask for repeats before judging the list.

Below is a list of songs and the structures implied or named in the songs or titles.

Songs	Structure
1. Bells of St. Mary's	Cathedral
2. Little Brown Church in the Vale	Church
3. Tavern in the Town	Tavern
4. Little Gray Home in the West	House
5. In a Cottage Small by a Waterfall	Cottage
6. In a Pawnshop	Pawnshop
7. Ten Little Indians	Wigwam
8. School Days	Schoolroom or schoolhouse
9. Take Me out to the Ball Game or a football song	Stadium
10. Three Blind Mice; Old MacDonald Had a Farm	Farmhouse
11. Silent Night; Away in a Manger	Stable
12. The Star-Spangled Banner	Fort
13. Old Kentucky Home	Cabin
14. Old Mill Stream; When You and I Were Young Maggie	Mill
15. Man On the Flying Trapeze	Circus tent
16. Tenting on the Old Camp-Ground	Tent
17. Penthouse Serenade	Penthouse
18. Old Folks at Home	Plantation

19. The Marines' Hymn	Halls of Montezuma (barracks)
20. Home Sweet Home	Palace
21. Three O'Clock in the Morning	Dance hall
22. On the Road to Mandalay	Pagoda or temple
23. Sweetheart of Sigma Chi	Fraternity house
24. Were You There?	Tomb
25. A Mighty Fortress	Fortress
26. Down in the Valley	Castle
27. Turkey in the Straw	Hen house or turkey house
28. Let the Rest of the World Go By	Nest

Musical Numbers

Play as game previously described. In this game, however, players attempt to determine the numbers mentioned or implied in the words or titles of the various songs played.

Songs with numbers in the titles or words are given below:

Songs	*Numbers*
1. Daisy Bell	"Bicycle built for *two*"
2. Three O'Clock in the Morning	Three
3. Take Me out to the Ball Game	One, two, three
4. Ten Little Indians	One through ten
5. Twelve Days of Christmas	One through twelve
6. My Little Margie	"There is really only *one*"
7. Fifteen Men on a Dead Man's Chest	Fifteen
8. The Erie Canal	"*Fifteen* miles on the Erie Canal"
9. Wonderful One	One
10. Grandfather's Clock	"It stood *ninety* years"
11. I'm Looking over a Four-Leaf Clover	Four
12. I've Got Sixpence	Six, four, two

13. Darktown Strutters' Ball	"Half-past *eight*"
14. Clementine	"And her shoes were number *nine*"
15. Ten Little Fingers and Ten Little Toes	Ten
16. Tea for Two	Two and three

Musical Number Variation

A variation of the game might be played in the following manner: Have the teams number their pads from one to ten down the left side of the paper. As a song is played they will write the title opposite the number on their pad which corresponds to the number in the song. Thus, "Three O'Clock in the Morning" would be written opposite three. "I'm Looking over a Four-Leaf Clover" would be written opposite four. There can be no duplicates so that there will be some hasty switching as a song which might fit into several different places is played. Warn the players that such will probably be the case.

Allow time for repeats of the songs at the end of the game before the judging. The pianist or leader must give each song a number as it is played since you will not play them in the proper order, obviously. We suggest that as a team decides where the song is to be placed on the list they write the number of the song after it so the song can be easily identified if the teams request that it be repeated. Only numbers one through ten or twelve can be used in this game. A list is given below for your convenience.

The Number	The Song
1. One	Wonderful One; Take Me out to the Ball Game
2. Two	Daisy Bell; Take Me out to the Ball Game; Tea for Two
3. Three	Three O'Clock in the Morning; We Three Kings; Tea for Two
4. Four	I'm Looking over a Four-Leaf Clover; I've Got Sixpence
5. Five	Ten Little Indians

6. Six   I've Got Sixpence
7. Seven   Twelve Days of Christmas
8. Eight   Darktown Strutters' Ball
9. Nine   Clementine
10. Ten   Ten Little Fingers and Ten Little Toes; Ten Little Indians
11. Eleven ⎫
12. Twelve ⎭ Twelve Days Of Christmas

Sports in Songs

Listed below are songs which name or suggest sports in the titles or in the words. Play portions of the song and have the teams guess which sports are named or suggested. There should be no two alike. Give teams a chance to ask for repeats on songs before judging the answers.

Songs	*Sports Suggested*
1. A-Hunting We Will Go; John Peel	Hunting
2. Daisy Bell	Bicycling
3. Skaters' Waltz	Skating
4. Take Me out to the Ball Game	Baseball
5. Ohio State Song, or any football song	Football
6. Row, Row, Row Your Boat	Rowing
7. Moonlight Bay; Sailing, Sailing	Sailing
8. Summertime	Fishing
9. In My Merry Oldsmobile	Driving
10. Camptown Races	Horse racing
11. Give Me My Boots and Saddle	Horseback riding
12. Jingle Bells	Sleigh riding
13. Song of the Hebrides (also called the Far Northland)	Hiking
14. The Keeper	Archery
15. Weggis Song	Mountain climbing
16. Johnny, Get Your Gun	Shooting
17. Tenting on the Old Camp-Ground	Camping
18. Tea for Two	Golfing

Dates in Songs

For the young people who are date conscious use this classification of songs. All the songs listed below suggest places to go and things to do on dates (as if they needed any suggestions). Divide group into teams and give each team paper and pencil. One player acts as secretary, numbering the sheet of paper from one to fifteen down the left edge of the paper. The pianist plays portions of tunes. There should be no duplicates. Permit the teams to ask for repeat plays of the numbers at the end of the game before judging the answers. Where no pianist or instrument is available, have the groups list songs that come under this category. Give a team prize for the best list. Limit the playing time to five minutes when playing the game without piano.

A list of songs suggesting places to have a date is given below.

Songs	*Suggested Places or Things to Do*
1. In the Good Old Summertime; While Strolling in the Park	Strolling in the park
2. Meet Me in St. Louis; Come to the Fair	Going to the fair
3. Jingle Bells	Sleigh riding
4. Skaters' Waltz	Ice or roller skating
5. Take Me out to the Ball Game	Baseball game
6. On, Wisconsin	Football game
7. Daisy Bell	Bicycling
8. In My Merry Oldsmobile	Driving
9. The Band Played On; Three o'Clock in the Morning	Dancing
10. After the Ball	Attending a ball
11. Row, Row, Row Your Boat; On a Sunday Afternoon	Boating
12. Sailing, Sailing	Sailing
13. The Animal Fair	Zoo or circus
14. Tea for Two	Afternoon tea date
15. Whiffenpoof Song; Tavern in the Town	Cocktail date

16. Bells of St. Mary's   Church
17. Turkey in the Straw   Square dance
18. Harvest Moon   You name it

Musical Style Show

In each of the following songs some particular costume or portion of costume is named or suggested. Divide group into teams and give each a pad and pencil. The pianist plays a portion of each tune. At the end of the list, give time to the teams to ask for repeats. If no musician is available, give the teams five minutes to list all the songs they can think of which name some piece of wearing apparel.

Songs	*Wearing Apparel Suggested or Named*
1. Old Gray Bonnet	Bonnet
2. Easter Parade	Easter bonnet and new Easter outfit
3. School Days	Calico
4. 'Round Her Neck She Wore a Yellow Ribbon	Ribbon
5. Alice-Blue Gown	Blue dress
6. Old Mill Stream	Gingham
7. Three Corners Has My Hat	Three-cornered hat
8. John Peel	Hunting coat
9. I Got Shoes	Shoes, robe
10. Won't You Sit Down, Lord	Clothing of white, blue, black and red
11. Bell-Bottom Trousers	Sailor's uniform
12. Golden Slippers	Golden shoes
13. Clementine	"Herring boxes without topses *sandals* were for Clementine"
14. Ten Little Indians	Feathers, beads

Birth-Month Songs

In a club or church group where all birthdays are celebrated at one big all-birthday party (see Chapter 2 for plans) this category is a good one. The pianist plays a song. The players, as they recognize which month is represented or actually named in the song, stand as their birth month is indicated. The rest of the group just sings or hums along and applauds the group which is standing.

Listed below are songs which indicate or actually name the months of the year.

Songs	Months Named or Represented
1. Harvest Moon	January, February, June and July are named in song. This could also represent October and November, both harvest months.
2. My Wild Irish Rose When Irish Eyes Are Smiling	March (St. Patrick's Day)
3. April Showers	April
4. Easter Parade	March or April
5. April Showers	May, April
6. Wedding March	June
7. Yankee-Doodle	July
8. In the Good Old Summertime	July, August
9. Take Me out to the Ball Game	April, May, June, July, August, September
10. Harvest Moon	October and November
11. School Days	September
12. Any Christmas carol	December
13. Over the River and Through the Woods	November

Naming the Baby

What could be more appropriate than songs with boys' and girls' names in them for a baby shower? Divide the group into small teams. Have the pianist play portions of a number of songs (ten to fifteen). If no piano or pianist is available, give teams five minutes to name as many songs as they can which have names in them.

A list is given below for your convenience. You will note that some are names of twins.

Song	Names
1. Jeanie with the Light Brown Hair	Jeanie
2. Old Black Joe	Joe
3. Annie Rooney	Annie and Joe
4. Reuben and Rachel	Reuben and Rachel
5. Annie Laurie	Annie or Laurie
6. Darling Nelly Gray	Nelly
7. Ben Bolt	Alice
8. Frankie and Johnny	Frankie and Johnny
9. Alice-Blue Gown	Alice
10. Lilac Time	Jeannine
11. Dinah	Dinah
12. Old Uncle Ned	Ned
13. Rosie O'Grady	Rosie
14. My Wild Irish Rose	Rose
15. Good King Wenceslas	Wenceslas
16. Li'l Liza Jane	Liza and Jane
17. Bring a Torch, Jeanette Isabella	Jeanette and Isabella
18. Santa Lucia	Lucia
19. Juanita	Juanita
20. When You and I Were Young, Maggie	Maggie
21. Sally in Our Alley	Sally
22. The Holly and the Ivy	Ivy
23. K-K-K-Katy	Katy
24. The First Noel	Noel
25. Little David, Play on Your Harp	David
26. Onward, Christian Soldiers	Christian
27. Joshua Fit the Battle of Jericho	Joshua
28. Clancy Lowered the Boom	Clancy
29. Hansel and Gretel	Hansel and Gretel
30. Hark, the Herald Angels Sing	Harold

Musical Colleges

Play as game previously described. Players attempt to name a college suggested or named in the song played. Songs with college or university names are listed below. Some of the songs merely give a location, and many possible names can be given for correct answers:

Songs	*Colleges Named or Suggested*
1. Moon over Miami	Miami University
2. On, Wisconsin	University of Wisconsin or any college or university in that state
3. The Last Time I saw Paris	Sorbonne
4. Oralee	West Point
5. Beautiful Ohio	Any of the many colleges in Ohio
6. On the Banks of the Wabash	Purdue, University of Indiana, etc.
7. California, Here I Come	Any California school
8. St. Louis Blues	Principia, University of St. Louis, etc.
9. Sidewalks of New York	New York University, City College of New York, etc.
10. Columbia, the Gem of the Ocean	Columbia University
11. Carolina Moon	Any college or university in North or South Carolina
12. The Eyes of Texas	Any Texas school
13. Oh! Susanna	Alabama or Louisiana schools
14. My Old Kentucky Home	Any Kentucky college or university
15. Any college alma mater	

Chapter 13

Paper-and-Pencil Games

ANY GAME is a tool for fun. The enjoyment of the group is primary, the game only a means to an objective. Paper-and-pencil games are more fun when played as team games. Team play takes the pressure off the individual, gets people better acquainted and adds to the enjoyment of all. When a number of players are thinking together, funny remarks and gay repartee are inevitable. When an individual plays alone he is so busy trying to find the answer, so he can make a good showing and not appear stupid, that he does not have time to enjoy himself. We recommend team play with paper-and-pencil games wherever this is possible. Teams may number from two to twelve players.

Mind Your P's and Q's

We all know about minding our P's and Q's but what can we do about other letters of the alphabet which sound like whole words? Divide group into teams and give each team captain a pad and pencil. Give the teams exactly five minutes to list all the words which sound like one letter of the alphabet. Proper names may be used. Teams must also give the word properly spelled opposite the word of one letter. For example *K* for Kay, *B* for bee, *C* for sea, *I* for eye, *U* for you.

Double P's and Q's

Play game as described above, but combine two or more letters of the alphabet to make words that are spelled much differently. A list below will give you ideas. (If you think these are stretches of the imagination wait until you see some of the answers your guests will give.)

II spells eyes	*KT* spells Katie
YY equal wise	*MT* spells empty

UU spells use

TT equals tease

EZ spells easy

EE equals ease

PU spells phew

NUE spells ennui

RT spells arty

TL spells teal

YR spells wire

XMN spells examine

XTC spells ecstasy

FE spells Effie

CT spells city

JL spells jail

BZ spells busy

LG spells algae

LE spells alley

NV spells envy

IC spells icy

KG spells cagey

LI spells ally

LN spells Ellen

LM spells alum

XII spells excise (X plus II's)

SA spells essay

IV spells ivy

DZ spells dizzy

DK spells decay

AT spells eighty

CQRT spells security

BD spells beady

ME spells Emmy

TDS spells tedious

NME spells enemy

TP spells teepee

VL spells veal

Variations of Double P's and Q's

Divide your group into teams of not more than five players. Give each a printed sheet like the one shown below. Give each team five minutes to try to fill in the list. Explain the game carefully and give some examples of correct answers. Before giving the starting signal, be sure that all players understand the game. This would be a good mixer or get-acquainted game.

Sample Sheet

Note to teams: Given below is a list of definitions. You can find words to match the definitions in the letters of the alphabet. For example, the answer to the question, "What part of the body is found in the alphabet?" could be *I* for "eye" or *II* for "eyes." The opposite of "hard" would be *EZ* (easy). Some answers can be given in single letters and some in double. The team giving the most correct answers and using the most letters wins. If you can give more than one answer to a question, by all means do so. Scoring will be on the basis of one point for each correct letter.

Definitions	*Words in the Letters of the Alphabet*
1. Girl's name	(KT, K, LN, FE)
2. Opposite of full	(MT—empty)
3. Bitter-tasting medicine	(LM—alum)
4. Vine	(IV—ivy)
5. Australian bird	(MU—emu)
6. Young beef	(VL—veal
7. A number	(AT—eighty)
8. Literary piece	(SA—essay)
9. Place of confinement	(JL—jail)
10. Drawn metal	(YR—wire)
11. To possess wisdom is to be	(YY—wise)
12. An abode	(TP—teepee)

Note: The answers would not be printed in the contest sheet. They are given here for the benefit of the reader. For other possible words and definitions see previously described game Double P's and Q's in this chapter.

Note: Additional suggestions follow:

1. An insect (*B* for bee)
2. Bird (*J* for jay)
3. Animal (*U* for ewe)
4. Long line (*Q* for queue)
5. Part of a house (*L* for ell)
6. Question (*Y* for why)
7. Vegetable (*P* for pea) or (*PP* for peas)
8. Beverage (*T* for tea)

Animal Babies

This is a good game to play at a baby shower. Divide group into small teams and give each team a pad and pencil. Have one member of the team number the pad from one to fifteen. The leader calls out the name of an animal. The teams try to name the term given to the young of that species. Or the teams may be given a printed list of animals which has been prepared beforehand. Give them five minutes to fill in the names of the young animals. A suggested list is given below:

Animal	Young
1. lion	1. cub
2. bear	2. cub
3. sheep	3. lamb
4. cod	4. codling
5. goose	5. gosling
6. swan	6. cygnet
7. elephant	7. calf
8. whale	8. calf
9. deer	9. fawn
10. swine	10. pig, shoat
11. mare	11. filly, foal
12. horse	12. foal
13. frog	13. polliwog, tadpole
14. duck	14. duckling
15. cat	15. kitten
16. dog	16. puppy
17. seal	17. calf
18. bull seal	18. bachelor

Variation: Another way to play the game is to provide teams with both lists and then have them try to match the proper terms.

Males and Females

Divide the group into small teams and give each paper and pencil. The leader calls out the name of an animal and the group attempts to name both the female and the male of that species. Or the leader might prepare lists to give each team. Teams in a limited period attempt to match the proper teams. A list is given below:

Male	Female
1. fox	1. Vixen
2. tiger	2. tigress
3. ram	3. ewe
4. stag	4. hind
5. stallion	5. mare
6. bull	6. cow
7. gander	7. goose

8. buck (deer, rabbit)	8. doe (deer, rabbit)
9. drake	9. duck
10. boar	10. sow
11. tomcat	11. she cat
12. dog	12. bitch
13. peacock	13. peahen
14. jackass	14. jenny

This game would be fun to use at a bride's shower.

Group Names

Play as in game described above. Players are asked to match group name with species. A list is given here:

Animals	*Group Names*
1. sheep	1. flock
2. whales	2. herd, school, gam
3. cattle	3. herd, drove
4. wolves	4. pack
5. fish	5. school, shoal, run
6. pheasants	6. nide
7. bees	7. swarm, hive, colony
8. geese	8. flock, gaggle, skein
9. ants	9. colony
10. quail	10. covey, bevy
11. porpoises	11. school
12. ducks	12. raft
13. pigs	13. drove
14. antelopes	14. herd
15. seals	15. pod, herd
16. monkeys	16. troop
17. horses	17. haras
18. worms	18. tangle
19. foxes	19. skulk
20. dogs	20. pack
21. lions	21. pride
22. snipe	22. wisp
23. leopards	23. leap
24. pups	24. litter
25. bears	25. sloth, sleuth

Animal Homes

Humans live in teepees, caves, houses, apartments, shacks and dozens of other types of shelters. Can the members of a team match up the correct shelter with the right animal? Play as in games described above. A list of animals and their shelters follows:

Animal	*Shelter*
1. dogs	1. kennel
2. chickens	2. coop
3. sheep	3. fold, pen
4. rabbits	4. hutch, warren, burrow
5. cows	5. cowyard, cow shed, byre, barn
6. pigeons	6. dovecot, columbary
7. pigs	7. sty
8. fish	8. aquarium
9. lions	9. den, lair
10. beavers	10. lodge
11. eagles	11. aerie
12. bees	12. hive
13. birds	13. nest

Baby's Arrival Time

At a baby shower divide the group into teams and give each a list similar to the one shown below except that the correct answers would not be listed opposite each other. It is the job of the team to match up the correct combinations.

Sample Game Sheet

We all know that the incubation or gestation period of a human baby is 9 months. Can you guess what it is for the animals listed below? The names of the animals are listed on one side and the correct answers on the other. Just fit the right answers to the names of the animals.

Animals	*Gestation Period*
1. elephant	1. 21 months
2. cow	2. 9½ months

3.	horse	3.	11 months
4.	sheep	4.	3 months
5.	dog	5.	2 months
6.	cat	6.	2 months
7.	rabbit	7.	1 month
8.	mouse	8.	19 days
9.	hen	9.	21 days
10.	goose	10.	26 days
11.	opossum	11.	13 days
12.	tiger	12.	3½ months
13.	chimpanzee	13.	7⅓ months
14.	zebra	14.	12 months
15.	giraffe	15.	14 months
16.	human	16.	280 days
17.	skunk	17.	63 days
18.	goat	18.	150 days
19.	fox	19.	51 days
20.	hog	20.	112 days

Life Spans

Divide your group into teams and give each a list like the one given below. Teams are to match up the correct expected life spans with the proper animal. The list given below is correctly matched. For the game it would be all mixed up.

	Expected Life Span		Animal
1.	152 years	1.	tortoise
2.	60 years	2.	elephant
3.	70 years	3.	man
4.	50 years	4.	parrot
5.	30 years	5.	chimpanzee
6.	28 years	6.	giraffe
7.	19 years	7.	tiger
8.	3 years, 3 months	8.	mouse
9.	24 hours	9.	mayfly
10.	26 years	10.	ostrich

Animal Sounds

Babies cry, gurgle, coo, whimper and make a dozen sounds. What sounds do the other animals make? Play as in game described above. A list of animals and sounds is given below. Make your own list of no more than fifteen for any one game. Mix up the answers and let the teams do the correct matching.

Animals	*Sounds*
1. alligators	1. bellow
2. turkeys	2. gobble
3. grouse	3. drum
4. horses	4. neigh, whinny, nicker
5. prairie chickens	5. boom
6. penguins	6. bray
7. marmots	7. whistle
8. cow moose	8. bawl
9. herons	9. squawk
10. bears	10. growl
11. elk	11. bugle
12. foxes	12. yap
13. chipmunks	13. chirr
14. squirrels	14. chatter, scold
15. wolves	15. howl (human variety: whistle)
16. elephants	16. trumpet
17. sheep	17. bleat
18. wild geese	18. honk
19. geese	19. gaggle, cackle, hiss
20. cocks	20. crow

PAPER-AND-PENCIL TREASURE HUNTS

Paper-and-pencil treasure hunts are good mixer activities. They help guests to become acquainted and provide an activity for the awkward moments before the party begins. They make excellent games to play while a group is waiting for dinner to be announced at company, club or church gatherings. They are flexible in their application as lists can be made up to fit each specific group. A number of different types are suggested below:

Autograph Hunt

Prepare a list like the one shown below. Have the list mimeographed and distributed to each guest. Guests must find a person whose name fits each category and get that person's autograph in the corresponding space. The first correct list handed in is awarded a prize.

Sample List

Listed below are clues which suggest first names. They do not necessarily apply to a specific individual but one whose name fits the clue. When you have found someone, have that person write his signature opposite the proper clue. When you have a complete list turn your paper in to the judges. Be sure to have your own name written in the proper space. Nicknames count.

Your name ....
Clues for names:

1. Someone whose first name rhymes with Ted. (Ed, Red, Ned, Jed) ....
2. Man's name that is something to be paid. (Bill) ......
3. Male species of the turkey family. (Tom)..........
4. A famous queen. (Anne, Elizabeth, Katherine)......
5. Name of a saint. (Anne, Francis, Joseph, Katherine) ....
6. A name that suggests a beach. (Sandy) ....
7. Name that rhymes with a part of the foot. (Joe, Neal, Joel) ....
8. A name that rhymes with duck. (Chuck) ....
9. A name that is also a city. (Hiram, Louis, Giles, Columbus) ....
10. A famous beauty. (Helen) ....
11. A name that rhymes with whim. (Tim, Jim, Slim) ....
12. A Shakespearean character. (Kate, Henry, Richard) ....
13. A Biblical name. (Amos, Ruth, Esther, John, James) ....

14. A double name such as Julianne. (Marianne, Annabel, Joanne) ....

15. A former president's name. (Remember this must be a first name.) (Lincoln, Harrison, Wilson, Arthur)
....

Note: Names given in parentheses are for the reader and would not be printed in the game sheets given to players.)

Church-Member Treasure Hunt

For a church conference where various churches are represented, a player might be given a list like the one below to fill in.

Sample List

Listed below are clues which suggest or name churches. Find a person who attends the named or suggested church. Have that person write his full signature and the name of his church opposite the proper clue. When you have a complete list, turn it in to the judges. Be sure your own name is on the list.

Your name..

Clues	Signatures and Church Names
1. Church name with a saint in it.	
2. Church that has a steeple.	
3. A new building in the past five years.	
4. A city's name in the church name.	
5. Has the word "first" in its name.	
6. Has the name of a street in its name.	
7. A name that has east, west, south or north in its name.	
8. A church whose name states that it is a community church.	
9. One whose name states its denomination.	
10. One whose name has the word "old" in it.	
11. Church with a disciple's name in it.	
12. Church that is built on a corner lot.	

Person Treasure Hunt

Give each guest a list like the one given below. He is instructed to find a person who fits the descriptive clue given in each instance. When he does, he is to get the person's signature and a bit of pertinent information. For example, if the clue is a person born out of the state, the player must have the person's signature and the name of the state where he was born. Make up a list as described in previous games. A suggested list of clues follows:

1. Someone born in this state (where party is being held).
....

2. Someone wearing bifocals. ....

3. Someone wearing two-tone shoes. ....

4. Someone wearing a fraternity or sorority pin. ....
....

5. Someone with blue eyes. ....

6. Someone wearing a lodge or fraternal-order ring or pin.
....

7. Someone with a monogrammed handkerchief. ....
....

8. Someone wearing a watch with diamonds in it. ......
....

9. Someone born in a foreign country. ....

10. A camera fiend. ....

11. A pipe smoker ....

12. Someone with a tattoo on his arm. ....

13. Someone who carries a lucky piece. ....

14. Someone carrying a pocket watch. ....

15. A graduate of one of the Big Ten (football) schools.
....

16. Someone who is a twin. ....

17. Someone whose grandmother is still living. ....
....

18. Someone who drives a Ford car. ....

19. Someone who works in a government job. ....

20. Someone born on a legal holiday, Christmas or New Year's Day. ....

Reunion Treasure Hunt

At a college, family or club reunion a list like the one given below would help guests to become reacquainted and caught up on the events of the past years.

Give each guest a list and have him find persons who fit the descriptive clues like those given below.

1. Someone married within the past year. ....
2. A parent of three or more children. ....
3. A grandparent for the first time within the past year. ....
4. Parent or grandparent of twins. ....
5. Someone married ten or more years. ....
6. Someone who traveled more than one hundred miles to the gathering. ....
7. Someone in business for himself. ....
8. Someone who flew to the gathering. ....
9. Someone who has traveled in Europe in the past five years. ....
10. Someone who celebrated a birthday within the past week or will in the next week. ....
11. Someone whose name is Smith. ....
12. Someone who lives on a farm. ....
13. Someone who moved into a new house within the past two years. ....
14. Someone who had a baby within the past year. ....
15. Someone who commutes by train to his or her work. ....
16. Someone who works for a newspaper. ....
17. Someone who is an officer in a club. ....
18. A World War II or Korean War veteran. ....
19. Someone who is a doctor of medicine. ....
20. Someone who holds a public office. ....

Mixed Mates

When a man and woman mate, their progeny are called children. See if your teams can match up the correct term with the proper animals when two different animals mate to produce a hybrid.

Animals Mating	*Hybrid Produced*
1. ass and mare	1. mule
2. swan and goose	2. swoose
3. zebra and mare	3. zebrula, zebroid
4. lion and tigress	4. liger
5. horse and cow	5. jumart
6. turkey and chicken	6. turken
7. bison and cattle	7. callalo
8. tiger and lioness	8. tigron

Chapter 14

Picnic Games and Contests

PLANNING THE PICNIC

GOOD PICNICS don't "just happen." They are the result of careful planning. Care should be exercised in the selection of the place. There should be ample space to take care of the particular group. The spot should be attractive and clean, equipped with picnic tables, fireplaces, toilet facilities, drinking fountains, playground area for the children, swimming facilities and ample play space for baseball games and picnic contests. There should be shaded areas for spectators and shelter in case of inclement weather.

In setting up the picnic program, consideration must be given to all persons who will attend and suitable games and contests planned for everyone.

The picnic games leader must have everything prepared in advance so that the program moves without undue delay between games. A contest area should be laid out in an open space that is relatively level and free from stones, broken glass or other debris. There should be a roped-off area beyond which spectators should not pass. Judges stationed at the starting and finish lines and along the course should be alert and conscientious. Nothing spoils a picnic program or makes for hard feelings faster than poor judging. Players don't mind losing if the winner wins fairly.

Prizes should be simple and inexpensive. There should be extra prizes in case of a close finish or a tie. Games should be selected that are as much fun for spectators as they are for the contestants.

Guessing contests, lucky-number drawings and other stunts help to make a picnic program interesting. Group activities such as dancing and community sings are essential in a good program.

If it is a basket picnic where guests bring their own food,

the sponsoring organization may wish to serve free ice cream,
lemonade and hot coffee or have them available for sale.

Each child present might be given a treasure poke filled
with candy bars, suckers, gum, balloons and cracker jacks and
some small toy such as a rubber ball or flying glider.

If the program is an all-day affair, it is wise to have recreation leaders on hand to direct the children in organized games,
especially if there is no playground or swimming facility available. A special quiet corner can be used for the nursery for
small children where, under leadership, they can color books,
hear stories and play simple games suited to their age group.
This will relieve the mothers and keep the children happy.

HINTS TO THE PICNIC GAMES LEADER

The better organized the picnic games program is, the
smoother it runs and the more enjoyable it is for all. The
leader must know the age range of the group attending and
should know approximately how many children are in each
age group so that the games program can be organized properly. Once all this information is known, the leader sets up a
program of games including a contest for each age group
and sometimes two or three contests for the age groups of
greater numbers. Thus, if you have ten 5-year-olds only one
contest would be planned for them, but if there are twenty-

Contest No.	Age	Sex	Contest	Props Needed	Prizes Needed
1.	5 and under	both	Scramble	peanuts, toys, candies, pennies, pencils, paper bags	0
2.	6–8	boys	Crab Race	none	1
3.	6–8	girls	Backward Walk	none	1
4.	9–12	boys	Stick Throw	12 sticks	2

five or thirty 6- to 9-year-olds, two or three contests might be
planned for this group. The leader, in compiling the list,
makes a chart which looks, in part, like that appearing above.

This is the operation chart from which the leader works. Once the entire program is set up, the leader assembles the properties and the prizes. Large shopping bags are lined up in a row and each is given a number. Into these bags go the properties needed for a particular contest. The prizes are also placed in these bags. At the picnic these bags are lined up in order on the field near the starting line and a custodian is appointed. As one contest ends the winners are taken to the custodian, who gives out the prizes and sees to it that the bag for the next contest is already on the starting line. In this manner, the games program proceeds without delay and interruptions.

Name Tag Drawing

At church, club or company picnics, name tags help people to get acquainted. Tags are particularly helpful in restoring lost children to their parents. As guests arrive they should check in at the headquarters table and get their name tags. These can also bear numbers which can be used later in a drawing.

Duplicate Number Tag Contest

Name tags are numbered. Two or three have duplicate numbers. Persons finding someone else with the same number are entitled to a prize.

Special Contests

Prizes may be awarded to any or all of the following:
1. Oldest person present.
2. Couple married longest.
3. Newest married couple.
4. Largest family present.
5. Youngest person present.
6. Person oldest in terms of service or membership.
7. Oldest twins present or any twins present.

If any of the above contests are to be held, the contests should be advertised on posters at the headquarters table. A person wishing to enter any contest fills out a card with his name and all necessary statistics and drops it in the box or jars provided for such a purpose. There should be a box or jar plainly labeled for each contest. Judges determine the winners and announce their names and award the prizes at a specified time when the greatest number of persons is gathered together in one place. This usually is mealtime.

Prizes for Special Contests and Drawings

If the picnic budget is limited, as is very often the case with church or club picnics, committee members might donate as prizes home-baked cakes or pies, baskets of produce from their gardens or potted plants which they have raised. Winners have choices of prizes, each winner making his selection before another winner is announced.

Guessing Contests

Set up a guessing-contest table with pads of paper, pencils tied to strings which are fastened to the table and boxes in which to place the guesses. Everyone gets a chance to participate. All a contestant has to do is write his name and his guess on a piece of paper and place it in the box provided. He repeats this procedure for every contest he enters, placing each guess in the correct box. Guesses for each contest are thus kept separated, making the judging easier. When the contests are carefully planned, the guessing object itself is the prize. Listed below are suggested contests in which the prize can be the object in question.

Ribbons and Bows

Fill a glass or plastic refrigerator jar or bottle, piggy bank or some other transparent and useful container with yards of vari-colored gift-wrap ribbons of different widths. Put in one or two little hair bows. Contestants try to guess the total number of inches of ribbon in the container. The guesses may be given in inches alone or yards and inches. Award the container and the contents to the winning guesser.

Tea and Teapot

Fill an attractive teapot with tea bags and loose tea. Be sure to fasten the lid with cellulose tape so that it will not be broken in the handling. Have contestants try to guess the total weight of pot and tea in ounces or in pounds and ounces. Winner gets the pot and the contents. For variation have contestants guess the number of tea bags in the teapot.

Cookie Jar

Fill an attractive jar with cookies. Guessers try to guess the exact number of cookies in the jar. Winner takes the jar and contents.

Watermelon Guess

With the point of a knife, scratch on the side of a melon: "Guess my weight and take me home." Contestants try to guess the weight of the melon. In case of a tie, cut the melon in half and give each winner a portion.

Melon Basket or Fruit Basket

Fill a small basket with honeydew melons and canteloupes, peaches, apples or other fruit in season. Contestants try to guess the total weight of basket and contents. Winner takes the basket and contents.

Peanut Bag

Fill a large transparent bag with peanuts in the shell. Guests try to guess the number of peanuts in the bag. Best guess wins the bag and contents.

Prize Ham or Sausage

Guests try to guess weight in pounds of a wrapped ham. Best guess wins the ham. A sausage can be used in place of the ham.

Smoker's Delight

Fill a transparent plastic box with loose cigarettes. Best guess wins the box and contents.

Candy Guess

Fill a refrigerator jar or glass casserole with all types of wrapped and unwrapped hard candies and chocolate bits. Winner gets the container and contents.

Sports Activities

Schedule a parents'-and-children's baseball game. Select two fathers as captains and have them choose up teams, with each choosing alternately an adult and a child until the team roster is filled. Extra players chosen as substitutes are given an opportunity to play a few innings. Set a definite time or inning limit to the game. Five innings or an hour is usually long enough.

Horseshoes

If the picnic area has horseshoe pits, be sure that equipment is available. Many of the older men will enjoy playing horseshoes.

Badminton

Put up badminton nets and provide paddles and outdoor shuttlecocks. This equipment will be kept busy throughout the day.

Volleyball

Mark off a volleyball court, put up a net and organize teams. This will provide fun for players and spectators alike.

SKILL GAMES

Set aside a portion of the picnic area for "Carnival Row." Set up six or more booths of skill games such as dart throw, baseball throw and others. See Chapter 5 for possible games.

Inexpensive prizes may be given to the high scorers. The challenge of such games will keep youngsters and adults busy and happy.

PICNIC GAMES

Picnic games are an important part of the program. Schedule a period for games when you expect the largest part of the crowd to be present. The middle of the afternoon is usually a good time. It should not be too soon after the meal hour.

The picnic games area should be roped off so that spectators cannot get in the way of the contestants. The games area should be clean and free from sharp stones, broken glass and sticks. It should be a level space of short cropped grass. If the games are to be run on a graveled or hard-topped surface, the games should be chosen with care to avoid scraped knees and other injuries.

GAMES FOR SMALL CHILDREN

Games for small children should be non-competitive. Every child should have a chance to win something. The games that follow are of the scramble or treasure-hunt type. The leader always holds back some of the treasure to give to the child who didn't find any so that each child goes away happy.

Treasure Scramble

Bring all the little children, five years and under, together in one spot. Give each child a paper bag in which to put his treasures. Keep the parents back and out of the way. Let the children stand in a circle at some distance from each other. After an explanation to the children, the treasures are scattered all over the ground. At the signal to begin, the children break and run to pick things up and put them in their bags. The leader keeps throwing new treasures here and there where the pickings are slim. The judges may aid the smallest children. Additional treasures are slipped into the bags of the smallest children so that they all have some loot.

The treasures to be scattered may be wrapped candies, balloons, wrapped suckers, peanuts in the shell, shiny new pennies, pencils, small plastic toys and boxes of crayons. An inflated balloon may also be given each child at the completion of this game.

Singing Games, Crafts and Stories

If there is a large number of small children at a picnic, it is wise to arrange to have a leader take these children off to a quiet spot and play singing games, tell stories and do simple craft projects with them for a period of an hour or so. This will give the children a fine time and will give relief to the parents who want to participate in games and activities.

PICNIC GAMES FOR BOYS AND GIRLS

Hunting Blind (Girls or Boys)

Have contestants form a large circle so that they are standing at least three feet apart. Give each a No. 10 paper bag to put over his head as a blind fold. At a signal all get down on their hands and knees, with heads toward the center of the ring. At the signal to begin, all begin feeling around with their hands as they crawl around trying to find a penny which the leader has dropped. If it is a large group, two or three pennies may be dropped and duplicate prizes given to each winner.

Penny Blind Hunt (Girls or Boys)

Blindfold all contestants with paper bags which they pull down over their faces. Line them all up on a starting line. Scatter pennies all over the field. Players keep all the pennies they find. The player with the most pennies and the one with the fewest win prizes. Peanuts or wrapped candies may be used instead of pennies.

Penny Blind Hunt Variation (Girls or Boys)

Play as described in game above but scatter a few nickels and dimes and one half dollar. There would not need to be a prize for this game. The money found is the prize.

Over and Under (Boys)

Line contestants up on starting line. About twenty feet away, stretch a wash line across the field. Have it held about two feet off the ground. At about twenty feet from this line stretch another about fifteen inches off the ground. The finish line should be about thirty feet beyond this second line. Players must run the course, jump over the first line, crawl under the second and continue on to the finish line. No player may hold the second line in his hand to raise it higher so that he can go under more easily.

Over and Over (Girls)

Play as in Over and Under described above except that the girls jump over both lines.

Hoop Di Doo (Boys)

Line contestants up on starting line. Have two fewer hoops than there are contestants scattered over the field. Boys must run to any hoop, pick it up and drop it over their heads. They then throw this hoop in any direction they wish. They must then find another hoop and step into it and pull it up over their heads. Now they are free to run to the finish line. Hoops will be flying in every direction in this free-for-all. The first contestant to complete the course wins the race. He must have gone through two hoops in the prescribed manner. This requires some close watching on the part of the judges.

Elimination Sit (Boys or Girls)

Give each contestant a large paper plate or a square piece of cardboard cut from a corrugated box. Players form a large circle and begin marching around at a signal from the leader with their paper seats held high over their heads. At the whistle, all put their paper seats on the ground and sit upon them as fast as they can. The last one down is eliminated. The players must be sitting on the paper and completely covering it. There will be a mad scramble and a lot of wiggling in the process of sitting properly on the paper seat. If the leader blows the whistle at short intervals occasionally, the scramble will be even funnier as the contestants will barely be back on their feet before it is time to sit down again. This game is fun to play and fun to watch. To make it funnier, require players to sit cross-legged with arms crossed on their chests. The last one to assume this position is eliminated.

Variation of Elimination Sit (Boys or Girls)

Put cardboard squares or paper plates on the ground in circle formation. Contestants form a circle on the inside of the paper seats. There are fewer paper seats than contestants.

Players march around on a signal and at a blast of the whistle they try to sit on one of the seats. Some one will always be eliminated. Take out some of the seats as the players are eliminated. To add to the fun, require contestants to be seated in a particular way; i.e., hands on top of heads, arms crossed on chests, legs crossed tailor-fashion, etc.

Backward Accuracy Toss (Boys or Girls)

Line up contestants on starting line. About twenty-five feet away, stretch another line. Contestants in turn toss a beanbag toward the finish line, trying to throw as close to the line as possible. This is difficult enough to do facing the line, but the contestants must stand with their backs to the line and must hold the beanbag with two hands while throwing. A throw over the line is out and eliminates the contestant. The closest throw in front of the line wins. For variation, a few soft-drink bottles may be lined up at intervals along the finish line. A throw accurate enough to hit a bottle wins a prize regardless of the position of the beanbag in relation to the line.

Rubber-Legged Race (Boys or Girls)

Have contestants line up on starting line. Have each choose a partner. Give each pair of contestants two rubber bands about one inch wide cut from an inner tube. Partners stand side by side with the right leg and foot of one player tight against the left leg and foot of the other. Players put one of the rubber bands around the instep and one at knee level so that their legs are held together at the foot and knee, thus giving the two players three legs with which to run. With arms around each other's waists or shoulders, the partners practice running. After the practice session the contestants are again lined up on the starting line. They are told that they must run to another line about fifty feet away, sit down on it, get up and then return to the starting line. The first couple across wins, providing they have followed all the rules. A broken rubber band eliminates the contestants. Or, if you wish, give each couple a "spare." In the case of a "blowout," the couple stops where it is on the field, puts on the spare and proceeds.

Change Tires Race (Boys or Girls)

Run this race as described above except at the halfway mark the players must take off the rubber bands, change position, put the rubber bands on and return to the starting line. Give each couple a spare so that they may continue in case one of the rubber bands breaks in the mad scramble to get them off and on again.

Pig-in-a-Poke Race (Boys and Girls)

Line up contestants on starting line and give each two large rubber bands cut from inner tubes. These must be bands cut on the diagonal of a tube. Players face each other and stand as close as possible. They put one band around both pairs of legs and pull it up to their knees. The other band stays around their ankles. Bound together at the feet and knees, they stand sidewise to the finish line about twenty-five to thirty feet away. They hold hands with each other and, at the signal, hop sideways to the finish line. They must hold hands while hopping. This will not be easy but it will be challenging to do and fun to watch.

Tug-and-Pull Race (Boys and Girls)

Line contestants up on starting line and have each choose a partner. Partners are to run to the finish line and back to the starting line with inside hands joined all the while they run. The trick is in the running. One starts out pulling the other behind him. When the leader blows the whistle, the one being pulled runs out in front and pulls his partner along behind him. At no time are the two partners to be alongside each other. One or the other is always in the lead, pulling the other along behind. There should be at least four changes in the race with each change signaled by the leader's whistle. Let the partners practice running in the prescribed manner so they understand what is expected of them.

Wheelbarrow Race (Boys)

This is always a popular picnic contest. Contestants choose partners and assume the wheelbarrow position. One player with his body parallel to the ground, face down, walks on his hands while being supported by his partner, who holds his feet off the ground and walks behind him. Players run to a line thirty feet distant, reverse positions and race back to the starting line.

Quoit Throw (Boys or Girls)

Line up contestants on starting line and have them choose partners. Give each pair a quoit made of heavy rope such as the kind that comes with a ring-toss game or one made of pieces of garden hose taped together at the ends so that it forms a large ring. Embroidery hoops taped together with electricians tape will be suitable. Half the contestants remain on the starting line while their partners move away from them about three feet and face them so that there are two lines of players. The quoits are held by the players standing on the starting line. At the signal to throw, they throw the quoit to their partners, who must catch it on the fly. Partners who miss are eliminated. When all quoits have been thrown, the leader gives a signal for the second line to step back three feet. Another signal to throw is given, the rings are thrown and the partners failing are eliminated. One line takes one step back away from the other. The signal is given for another throw. Unless the contest is conducted in this manner it is impossible to keep track of the throws and misses. After each throw the one line moves back. Play until all but one pair has been eliminated. A quoit may be caught in the hand or on the hand and allowed to slide up the arm.

Balloon Heads (Boys or Girls)

Line contestants up on starting line and have them choose partners. Give each pair a round balloon to inflate. When the balloon is inflated, tie the neck to hold in the air. Partners then face each other and stand so that they can hold the balloon between them with their foreheads. They must keep their hands on each other's shoulders at all times. At a signal to begin, they walk to the finish line in any way they wish so long as they keep the balloon in position while they walk. The first couple over the line, which is about fifty feet away, wins.

If the balloon gets away from the partners, they must stop where they are on the course and get the balloon into position before they can proceed.

Crab-Walk Race (Boys)

The crab walk is done in this manner: Boys sit on the ground with hands behind them. Using their hands and feet as legs, they raise themselves from a sitting position and try to

walk. If they walk feet first it is a regular crab walk. If they walk with their heads leading it is a backward crab walk. If they walk sideways it is a side crab walk. In any case, the crab walk makes a good race.

Blind Crab Walk (Boys)

Blindfold the boys with paper bags. Turn them with their backs to the finish line. At a signal, they begin crab walking to the finish line. This walk is difficult enough to do in a straight line when you can see, but it is even more difficult to do when blindfolded. Spectators cheer their favorites, who are going in every direction. Judges grab the first crab over the

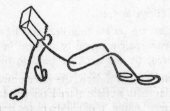

line but the leader lets the race continue for a few more minutes while crabs still scurry in every direction, not knowing the race is already over.

Tandem Crab Walk (Boys)

Line contestants up on the starting line and have each choose a partner. Have partners assume crab position, one partner with his head toward the finish line, one with his feet toward the finish line. One partner is in the lead, the other is behind him and has his feet as close to his partner's feet as possible. Have partners put a large rubber band, cut from an inner tube, around each pair of feet so that the crabs are hooked together tandem style, left foot to partner's right foot and vice versa. Allow partners to practice a tandem crab walk before beginning the race. Have the finish line only twenty-five feet away. Partners race to the finish line and without turning around, race back to the starting line. The tail of the crab is the head on the return trip.

Obstacle Crab Walk (Boys)

Have contestants assume front crab position (see directions in Crab Walk Race). Give each contestant a large rubber band cut from an inner tube to place around his ankles as a hobble. Contestants then have to walk with their hands and hop with their feet as they proceed along the course feet first.

Ducky Waddle (Boys or Girls)

Players line up on starting line and squat. They hold their ankles tightly with their hands and in this stooping position waddle toward the finish line *without letting go of their ankles*. Give contestants time to practice this walk so that they understand the rules.

Kangaroo Hop (Boys or Girls)

Contestants line up on starting line, heads toward finish line. In doing the kangaroo hop, the hands must be placed in front of the body and weight placed on the hands while the feet hop forward. Allow the children to practice this hop before starting the contest. The hop procedure must be used throughout the contest by the child or he is eliminated from the race.

Sidewise Kangaroo Hop (Boys or Girls)

Contestants line up on starting line with their left sides toward the finish line, which is about thirty-five feet away. The hop is done in this manner: Move hands to left side of body and then hop feet until they are even with the hands. There must be a change of weight from hands to feet on each hop. Let the children practice this hop until they understand how to do it. Eliminate any child who does not follow the rules during the contest.

Siamese Race (Boys or Girls)

Players choose partners. They stand back to back and lock arms together at the elbow. One player runs forward toward the finish line about twenty-five feet away, more or less dragging the player who is hooked on behind. In the running, if the player in front runs with his feet close together and the player behind with his feet wide apart it will be easier for both. At the finish line, without turning around the runners reverse direction so that the front player on the first lap is now running backward and the player who ran backward is now running forward. The contest ends on the starting line where it began. If the contestants fall or become unhooked they must hook up again before continuing along the course.

Sideways Siamese (Boys or Girls)

Play as above except that the contestants stand sidewise on the starting line and run in that position to the line and back.

PICNIC GAMES FOR MEN OR WOMEN

Stick Throw (Men)

Line up contestants on the starting line and have each choose a partner. The group is then organized into two lines, partner opposite partner, with the lines about three feet apart. Give all the players in one line foot-long pieces of broomsticks. At the signal to throw, players holding the sticks in both hands with palms up throw the sticks to their partners who must catch the sticks in both hands with palms up. A player failing to catch the stick eliminates himself and his partner. Both lines take one step backward away from each other and the players holding the sticks then throw on a signal from the leader. This process is repeated until all are eliminated except one pair.

Variation Stick Throw (Men)

Play as above but sticks must be thrown with both hands, palms down position, and must be caught in that same way. The partner catching will have to make a downward-snatch catch.

Vertical Club Throw (Men)

Play as in Stick Throw (see above) except that the stick is thrown with one hand in a vertical position, much as a baseball bat is thrown in choosing sides. It must be caught with one hand but not necessarily in a vertical position.

Broom Throw (Men)

Play as in Stick Throw, but give contestants child's-size brooms or regular full-size brooms. Since large groups would require many brooms, the game would have to be played off in heats with the finals being played off between heat winners.

Roll 'Em, Cowboy (For Men Who Smoke)

Line contestants up on a starting line. Give each a pack of roll-your-own tobacco and cigarette papers and a packet of book matches. At signal to begin, men open packs and attempt to roll a cigarette and get it lighted. The cigarette must be smokable. The first player to complete and light a roll-your-own wins. This is even funnier if the players wear gloves while playing.

Loaded Balloons (Men or Women)

This is cheaper, less messy and more fun than an egg throw. Fill round balloons with water and tie the necks to hold the water in. Have contestants choose partners and line up the contestants as in the Stick Throw previously described. If the balloon is dropped but does not break, the contestants are not eliminated. Only a broken balloon eliminates a couple. It is amazing to see how far a water-filled balloon can be thrown and how much punishment it will take before it will finally break, sprinkling the contestants and spectators alike.

Jet Launching (Women)

Give each contestant a large balloon. All balloons should be the same size and shape. Each player inflates the balloon to its maximum size and holds the air in by pinching the neck of the balloon. In turn, each contestant steps into the launching circle and launches his balloon into the air. The balloon will fly about crazily in the air until all the air is released. The balloon traveling the greatest distance from the circle wins a prize for the owner. To score this, as a balloon lands have the owner stand on that spot until another contestant's balloon travels farther and eliminates her. The last player standing on the field will be the winner. A tape line will be a good thing to have to determine distances in some instances. A variation is to give a prize to the contestant whose balloon comes nearest to a given target, such as a circle of rope placed on the ground.

What's a Minute? (Women)

Have women stand on starting line. When leader gives signal to begin, the women begin calculating the length of a minute. When a contestant thinks a minute is up, she steps backward one step from the starting line. The leader watches his watch and the contestants. The one who steps back at the second nearest the minute mark, wins. The leader must be careful not to give any indication when the time is drawing to a close, as contestants will be watching for a hint.

Volleyball Throw (Men or Women)

Have contestants sit on the ground with feet resting on the starting line. In turn, each contestant throws a volleyball or large rubber ball with both hands from a sitting position. The longest throw wins.

Variation Volleyball Throw (Men or Women)

From a sitting position, have contestants throw a volleyball or large rubber ball backward over their heads, using two hands for the throw. The longest throw wins.

Drink a Cup (Women, Men or Teenagers)

Give each contestant a paper cup partially filled with water. Contestants are to run to the finish line with the water-filled cups, turn and face starting line, kneel down, put the cups between their teeth and their hands behind their backs. They then lean back and drink the water, which they spill slowly into their mouths while holding the cup firmly in their teeth.

When their cups are empty, they are to run back to the finish line. First one over, wet or dry, wins!

COUPLE RACES FOR MEN AND WOMEN

Forehead Bottle Fill (Men and Women or Teenage Boys and Girls)

Have women select men partners. Give each woman a four-ounce paper cup. The men lie down on the ground with heads on the starting line and feet turned away from the finish line. At a center point about twenty feet from the women, who begin by standing next to their partners on the starting line and facing the finish line, place a bucket of water. Give each man a pop bottle which he balances on his forehead. He may use his hands to hold it there if necessary. At a signal to begin the women race to the bucket, fill their cups and rush back to their partners. They pour the contents

of the cup into the bottle and race back to the pail. The first woman to fill the bottle to the top wins for herself and her partner.

Immobile Tie (Men and Women)

Have each man choose a woman partner. Line men up on the starting line about five feet apart. Give each woman a fifty-foot ball of common string. Have men hold one end of the string in their teeth. At a signal to begin, women who are holding the ball of string begin winding string around men between the shoulders and the knees. The woman may run around the man or the man may turn in place. The first couple to use up the entire ball of string wins the contest.

Balloon Squeeze Break (Men, Women and Teenagers)

Have men choose women partners. Give each couple a

large balloon to inflate. When the balloon is inflated and tied to hold the air in, couples place the balloon between them at chest height. At a signal to begin, men and women hug each other and attempt to break the balloon. As soon as the balloon is broken they race to a line about thirty feet away. The first couple over wins. The larger the balloon, the funnier the game.

Swiggle Stick Contest (Men, Women and Teenagers)

See swiggle sticks described in Chapter 17. Give each couple a stick. When all are in place and everyone is ready give the signal to begin. The first couple to wind up and unwind its swiggle stick wins the contest.

Tooth No Nails (Men and Women)

Have each man choose a woman partner. Give each woman a pack of cigarettes. Men stand on the finish line with hands behind their backs. Women stand facing men, each holding an unopened pack of cigarettes in front of the men at shoulder height. At a signal to begin, the man begins to open the pack with his teeth, attempts to extract a cigarette from the pack and get one into his mouth in smoking fashion. The women are not permitted to do more than hold the pack. The first man to get a cigarette in that position wins. The couples keep the packs of cigarettes and the winning couple gets a prize in addition.

Open and Chew (Men and Women)

Have each woman choose a man partner and line up on the starting line. Women face men with hands behind their backs. Men hold unopened packages of gum at shoulder height toward the women. At a signal to begin, women attempt to open the package of gum with their teeth, extract a stick of gum, unwrap it and begin chewing it. The only help the men can give is to hold the pack firmly. As a stick is pulled out partially, the men hold the stick in place while the women attempt to unwrap one end and pull out the stick.

Bottle-Filling Race (Boys)

Line contestants up on starting line. Have players choose partners. Give each boy a pop bottle and a small paper cup (three- or four-ounce size). The boys put the bottles in their hip pockets. At a signal to begin, all contestants run to water-filled pails placed on the field, fill cups with water and then attempt to pour the water into the bottles in their partners' pocket. As both boys are trying to fill each other's bottles at the same time and in great haste, there will be considerable water spilled. The game is over when two partners can show two bottles brimming full.

Variation: Use this as a race for men and women. The women attempt to fill the bottle in the man's hip pocket. The man's job is only to furnish the pocket.

PICNIC GAMES FOR TEENAGE BOYS AND GIRLS

Balloon Stomp (Boys)

Give each contestant two small round balloons and two pieces of stout cord about two feet long. Boys inflate balloons, tie the necks securely and then tie one end of the string to the balloon and the other to an ankle. When all players are ready with a balloon tied to each ankle, have the boys form a circle holding hands. At the signal, boys break hands and begin stomping on the balloons of the other players, attempting to break them and at the same time attempting to protect their own from being broken. A player is eliminated when both his balloons are broken, no matter what the cause. Keep the play within a small area or the boys will chase each other over half the countryside. Allow time out for a minute or two as this is a very strenuous game. Play until two players are left and give each a prize.

Belt Balloon (Boys)

Play as above except that only one balloon is used and that is tied to the belt at the back. Keep the strings short so that the balloon is at waist height. Give each contestant a swatter made of rolled-up newspapers tied with a string or fastened with a rubber band. At a signal to begin, the boys attempt to break each other's balloons with the swatters. A broken balloon eliminates the player. Limit the play to a particular area. Play until all but two contestants have been eliminated and give each a prize.

Balloon Chin Carry (Boys and Girls)

Have boys select girl partners. Girls are lined up on the starting line facing their boy partners, who are on another line about twenty-five feet away. Girls are given a small round balloon which they inflate and tie to keep the air in. When all balloons are inflated, the girls place the balloons under their chins and press down with their chins so that the balloons are firmly held there without the use of hands. With the balloons in this position and with their hands clasped behind their backs, the girls, at the signal to begin, run to their boy partners. When they reach their boy partners, each balloon is transferred from under the chin of the girl to under the chin of the boy. This must be accomplished with no help from the hands, which both contestants must keep clasped behind their backs. When the boy has a firm grip on the balloon he races back to the finish line. First boy over wins for the couple, providing all rules have been observed. Should a balloon become loose while either contestant is racing or in the process of transferring from one to another, the balloon may be picked up and replaced in its proper position. The player, if running, must stop to do this and cannot proceed forward until the balloon is in place again.

Variation of Balloon Chin Carry (Boys and Girls)

Play as above with the same rules, but use long balloons instead of round ones. The effect is different.

Balloon Sit Upon (Boys and Girls)

Boys choose girl partners. Each couple is given a large round balloon to inflate. The balloon neck is tied to hold in the air. The boy is instructed to hold the balloon in one hand and his partner's hand in the other. In this position they run to another line about thirty feet away. The boy holds the balloon on the ground while the girl sits on it and attempts to break it. As soon as the balloon is broken, the boy pulls the girl to her feet and with hands joined they return to the starting line. The first couple over wins.

Cinderella and the Prince (Boys and Girls)

Have girls select boy partners. Girls sit down on the starting line and remove both shoes. Boys take shoes to another line thirty feet distant where all the shoes are mixed up in one pile. Then boys return to the starting line. At a signal to begin, all boys run to the pile of shoes, attempt to find their partner's shoes and return to the starting line where they must put the shoes on their girl partner's feet. To add to the confusion, the boy may toss shoes that do not belong to his partner in any direction. Shoes will be flying, girls will be shouting and boys will be hunting. The boys do all the work. The girls provide the shoes and feet and have only to sit and wait.

OTHER SUITABLE GAMES FOR TEENAGE BOYS

See also Quoit Throw, Stick Throw, Vertical Club Throw, Broom Throw, Loaded Balloons, Volleyball Throw, Drink a Cup, Rubber Legged Race and Wheelbarrow Race described in this chapter.

OTHER RACES FOR TEENAGE GIRLS

See also Jet Launching, Backward Accuracy Toss, Loaded Balloons and Drink a Cup described earlier in this chapter.

OTHER RACES FOR TEENAGE COUPLES

See also Open and Chew, Immobile Tie, Bottle Filling Race, Balloon Heads and Balloon Squeeze Break described in this chapter.

Chapter 15

Rhythmic Games and Stunts

RHYTHMIC activities have universal appeal. No person can be exposed to a rhythmic activity for long without responding. Watch a group of people listening to music. Heads will nod in time, feet will tap or hands will wave. The rhythmic beat of a drum gets toes to tapping and bodies to moving. It is literally impossible for spectators to remain bystanders. They soon become active and through participation experience a feeling of release and satisfaction.

Rhythmic activities are always good to include in any recreation program. Even the simplest ones are enjoyable. Some of the activities given here are simple and easy to master while others require skill learned only through practice. Even the practice sessions are fun in rhythms, however, and every hour of practice pays off in satisfaction and fun.

Song Rhythms

Play this game with a seated audience divided into team groups which are not necessarily equal in number. One group begins by beating out the rhythm of a well-known song by clapping its hands. The other groups try to guess the song. As soon as a group thinks it has the right answer, the members raise their hands. The first group begins again and the second attempts to clap along with it. If the answer is correct, the two groups will be clapping in the same rhythm. If no one can guess the tune, the team begins again and hums the melody while clapping. As soon as the other groups can, they join in humming and clapping out the rhythm. Each group has one opportunity to stump the other groups. Limit the selection of songs to a particular category, such as old-time songs, songs of the various military service and school songs.

Proverb Rhythms

Play as described above in Song Rhythms but have groups clap out proverbs.

Nursery-Rhyme Rhythms

Play as game described above but let teams clap out nursery rhymes. This gets easier the oftener you try it.

Fancy Clap

This is a good activity to use at a banquet or with a seated audience. The leader claps out the rhythm given below. After repeating it two or three times, the leader asks the group to join in the fun, warning them of the trick beat near the end of the clap. Try it several times until the group can do it in unison. The trick is to end at the same time.

Fancy Clap Rhythm Pattern

Chinese Toast

A Chinese Toast is the most fun when groups are seated at banquet tables and all of the dishes have not yet been cleared. The leader first demonstrates the toast. The group is then asked to clap out the rhythm first with their hands until they understand it. Once they have the rhythm, they stamp their feet in that rhythm once, slap their thighs in the same rhythm, clap their hands, then hit their palms on the table tops in the same rhythm. Then all stand, throw their hands into the air and yell, "Whee!" Now the real fun begins. The various persons responsible for the banquet are asked to stand while the group gives each a Chinese Toast. The rhythmic stamps and claps are preceded by these words spoken in unison by the group: "Let's give a Chinese Toast." The stamps and claps follow in rapid order. When a toast is for a specific person the group may so indicate by calling out that person's name in this manner: "To Mrs. Jones, let's give a Chinese Toast!" or "To the cooks, let's give a Chinese Toast."

CHINESE TOAST RHYTHM PATTERN

(Stamp feet)   (Slap thighs)
(Clap hands)   (Slap table)   Wheel

Hand-Clap Rhythms

This is an excellent stunt to use with large or small groups. Use it with groups seated in auditoriums or at banquet tables. Young and old will find it equally pleasurable.

Begin by clapping your hands in four-four rhythm. Beat out measure after measure of quarter notes. Have the groups join you until they are clapping in unison. Then change the quarter notes to half notes and beat out several measures of these. Now have the group clap through several measures of eighth notes. When the group recognizes the differences between the various notes, divide the group into three parts and assign the quarter notes to one group, the half notes to another and the eighth notes to the third. The leader now assumes the position of the director of an orchestra. Start off one group beating out its particular rhythm. By beating time with your forefinger and pointing at that group have them clap in time with you. Now point to another group and have that group clap in their rhythm. By pointing to one group and then to another (only the group being pointed at claps at that instant) an interesting rhythm pattern can be worked out. A number of suggested patterns are given below. After several patterns have been worked out, change the assign-

HAND-CLAP RHYTHM PATTERN I

ments of each group so each is clapping out a different beat. The eighth-note group will be glad to change to half notes to rest their hands and the half-note group will be eager for more activity.

HAND-CLAP RHYTHM PATTERN II

Ali Baba and the Forty Thieves

The group sits or stands in a circle. All chant together and repeat over and over: "Ali Baba and the forty thieves." When they have said the phrase once, the leader makes a repetitive motion with one or both hands or one or both feet, or some body motion in rhythm to the chant. He continues the same motion until the completion of the phrase, where-

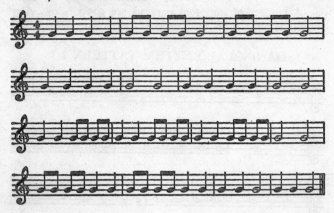

upon player #2 takes up the motion of the leader. The leader begins a new motion. At the completion of the phrase the second time, player #3 takes up the motion of player #2 and player #2 takes up the motion of the leader, who immediately begins another motion. The motions pass like waves around the circle. Actually each player is doing a different motion, each of which was started by the leader and passed from player to player. After a time, the leader ceases making motions but continues to chant. Gradually the motion around the circle ceases. The game ends as it began with all players standing or sitting motionless and chanting; that is, if the game hasn't broken up in laughter long before this.

Use this with large groups seated in an auditorium or stadium. Divide audience into sections and give each section a number. The leader starts the motions from the stage or center of the field. One section after another takes up the motions as they chant.

Suggested motions are clapping hands, slapping thighs, stamping feet, wiggling hands at temples, jumping motion, etc.

LUMMI STICKS (An American Indian Rhythm Game)

Lummi Sticks is a rhythmic activity credited to the Lummi Indians, a tribe who live on the Oregon coast. Other tribes seem to play a similar game, however. A Hopi Indian girl tells of learning it from her grandfather on the reservation.

The Maori people of New Zealand play a similar game, albeit their chant and stick patterns are different.

The Sticks

Experience has taught us that the best sticks are round, one inch in diameter and twelve or fourteen inches long. Sticks larger in diameter or of greater length are unwieldly. The sticks should be made from mop handles or dowel rods. Broomsticks are too soft and splinter readily, as does any soft wood. The sticks should be sanded until they are smooth and splinter free. If they are decorated with Indian designs, they must be shellacked or varnished. They may have small sleigh bells attached near the ends. These tend to get in the way, however. If the bell sound is desired during a demonstration, it is suggested that the players wear bracelets of sleigh bells which will give the desired sounds but will not interfere with the movement of the sticks.

Some groups have painted their sticks with fluorescent paint for demonstration purposes and have performed effectively under black light. For general purposes, however, smoothly sanded sticks twelve inches long and one inch in diameter are the best.

The Game of Lummi Sticks

The game is played with two or four players. The two-handed game only is described first. The four-handed game is described later in the chapter. Two players sit facing each other on the floor with legs crossed tailor fashion or with legs astride, whichever position is more comfortable for the individual player. Each player has a pair of Lummi Sticks. Whatever the length, the sticks of both players should be the same length.

The sticks are held lightly (not with a death grip) in the fingers, one in each hand at about the center, with the sticks vertical to the floor.

The sticks are manipulated in a number of different patterns. Each pattern is repeated as often as is necessary while the chant is sung through once. At the completion of the chant, the next pattern begins without a break. In case of a miss, the players try to recover the sticks as quickly as possible and to pick up the beat without a break. If a stick rolls out of reach, the pattern is broken and time out is called to permit a recovery. The pattern is begun again. There will be fewer and fewer misses as players become proficient. As the players increase in skill, they will want to speed up the rhythm a little, but the patterns are the prettiest and the most satisfying to perform at a moderate and steady pace.

LUMMI STICK CHANT

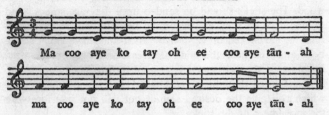

Ma coo aye ko tay oh ee coo aye tān - ah

ma coo aye ko tay oh ee coo aye tān - ah

Hilarity is a constant companion in Lummi Sticks, as unpredictable things happen particularly when beginners are involved. Black-and-blue shins are apt to be the order of the day in the beginning stages when flying sticks take their toll. Players who sit tailor fashion should take the precaution of covering their legs with blankets during early practice sessions until a degree of skill is achieved.

It is more difficult to give a written explanation of the game than to play it. The reader who takes the time to work out the patterns will be amply rewarded for his time by the hours of pleasure and enjoyment he will receive while playing this challenging Indian rhythm game. (All pattern titles are the author's.)

THE PATTERNS

A number of patterns are given here. It is to be remembered, however, that in any creative activity players will soon want to make up their own. This is to be encouraged.

Pease Porridge Hot

Pattern #1: Holding sticks lightly, with the fingers at the middle of the stick and with the sticks vertical to the floor, each player hits bottom ends on the floor, hits his own sticks together (slightly crossed), hits partner's right stick with his

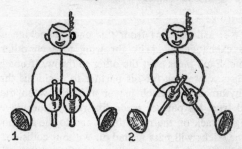

own right stick, hits ends on floor, hits own sticks together in crossed position, hits partner's left stick with own left stick. This is one complete pattern. Put simply, the pattern in time to the chant is:

Chant	Action
Ma	Hit ends on floor. (See figure 1.)
Coo	Hit own sticks together. (See figure 2.)
Aye	Hit partner's right stick with own right stick. (Figure 3.)
Ko	Hit ends on floor. (Figure 1.)
Tay	Hit own sticks together. (Figure 2.)
Oh	Hit partner's left stick. (Figure 4.)

This pattern fits four times to the music. (This is much like the Pease Porridge Hot game we play with our hands.)

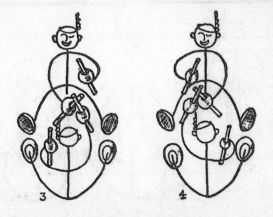

Single Throw

Pattern #2: All patterns from this one on include a throw. Partners exchange sticks by throwing to each other at the same time. Each must trust the other to throw. If one hesitates for an instant, waiting for his partner to begin his throw, the whole rhythm is lost. Each player must throw on the proper beat and trust his partner to do likewise. If the players keep to the right track on the right throw and to the left on the left throw, the sticks will pass in mid-air without collision. Players should practice throws and then try fitting them into the rhythm of the chant.

The sticks are held, as in pattern #1, lightly in the fingers at the center of the stick with the sticks vertical to the floor. The throw should be made with the stick in vertical position, much in the fashion boys use in throwing a baseball bat to each other in the choose-up stages of a game. The stick should be thrown high enough (no higher than shoulder level) to permit it to be caught before it hits the floor.

The second pattern is:

    Hit ends of sticks on floor. (Figure 1.)

    Hit own sticks together. (Hit sticks in parallel position vertical to the floor; do not cross on this hit.) (Figure 5.)

    Throw right stick to partner and catch the one he throws to you. (Figure 6.)

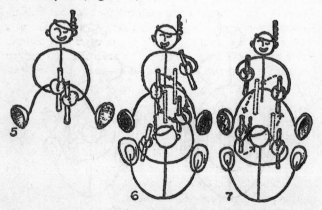

Hit ends of stick on floor.

Hit own sticks together.

Throw left stick to partner and catch stick he throws to you. (Figure 7.)

The whole pattern is done four times in rhythm to the chant.

The Two Throw

Pattern #3: This is the same as pattern #2 except the same stick is thrown twice in rapid succession. The complete pattern is:

Hit ends on floor (vertical position).

Hit own sticks together.

Throw right stick to partner and catch stick he throws to you.

Immediately throw right stick again and catch stick thrown to you.

Hit ends on floor (vertical position.)

Hit own sticks together.

Throw left stick to partner and catch stick he throws to you.

Immediately throw left stick again and catch stick thrown to you.

This pattern fits three times to the music.

The Double Throw

Pattern #4: You will note that each pattern becomes increasingly complicated, but since only one new trick is added at a time, the transition from the simple to the more difficult ones is easily made. The only difference between this and pattern #2 is that the right and left throws follow each other in rapid succession. The pattern is:

Hit ends of sticks on floor

Hit own sticks together.

Throw right stick to partner's left hand and catch stick he throws to you.

Immediately throw left stick to partner's left hand and catch stick he throws to you.

This pattern is repeated six times.

If, in throwing, the players use a little body English (slight lift to each shoulder) and keep their sticks to the right, their sticks will pass without colliding and an unbroken rhythm can be maintained.

Front Flip

Pattern #5: This is the same as pattern #4 except that a front flip is added to the pattern. The front flip is performed by holding the sticks lightly at one end with the other end tipped toward the floor away from the body. The tips are touched to the floor and then flipped a half turn toward the body and caught at the ends. Sliding the hands quickly to the center of the sticks, the player hits the ends of the sticks on the floor, with the sticks now in vertical position. Practice this flip until you have perfected it. It is a very satisfying maneuver. The rest of the pattern follows:

> Tip sticks away from you and hit ends on floor. (Figure 8.)
>
> Flip sticks toward you and catch (immediately slide hands to center of stick and turn sticks upright). (Figure 9.)
>
> Hit ends on floor (in vertical position).
>
> Hit own sticks together.
>
> Throw right to partner and catch stick he throws to you.

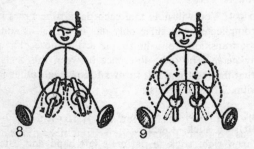

> Immediately throw left to partner and catch stick he throws to you.
>
> This pattern fits into the music four times.

Side Flips

Pattern #6: This pattern adds a side flip to pattern #5. Players hold sticks at sides of body with sticks tipped away from the body, hands at end of stick closest to body. The tipped ends are hit on the floor and the sticks are then flipped toward the body and caught at the opposite ends. Slide hands to center of stick and with sticks held in vertical position hit ends on floor. This is the side flip. The entire pattern is:

> Side flip and hit ends on floor vertical fashion. (Figure 10.)
> Front flip and hit ends on floor vertical fashion.
> Hit own sticks together.

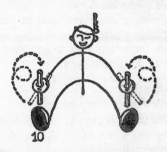

10

> Throw right stick to partner and catch his.
> Immediately throw left stick to partner and catch his.
> End with a front flip.
> This pattern fits twice into the music.

Front and Side Flip

Pattern #7: This combines a front and side flip. Do a front flip with the right stick and a side flip with the left stick at the same time. Hit ends on floor. Follow immediately with a side flip with the right stick and a front flip with the left stick. Hit ends on floor. Follow with a front flip with both sticks and hit ends on floor. The complete pattern is:

> Front flip with right stick, side flip with left stick. (Figure 11.)
> Hit ends of sticks on floor (still in those same positions).

Front flip with left stick, side flip with right stick.
(Figure 12.)

Hit ends on floor (sticks still in side and front positions).

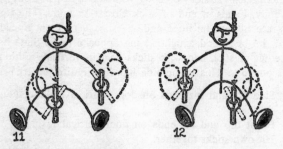

Hit ends of sticks on floor.

Throw right stick into right hand of partner and catch
stick he throws you.

Immediately throw left stick to left hand of partner and
catch stick he throws you.

Pattern is done twice to music.

Cross-Hands Side Flip

Pattern #8: Hold sticks at ends as for flip throw. Cross hands
in front of body and touch tip of right stick at left side and
tip of left stick at right side of body. Uncross hands and hit
right stick tip at right side of body and left stick tip at left
side of body. Flip sticks toward body and catch, but do not
hit ends on floor as in previous side flip. The entire pattern is:

Cross hands in front of body and hit ends on floor at
sides of body. (Figure 13.)

Uncross hands and hit tips again at sides of body.
(Figure 14.)

Do side flip but do not hit ends on floor after flip.

Do front flip.

Hit ends on floor (sticks in vertical position).

Hit sticks together.

Throw right stick to partner and catch stick he throws
to you.

Immediately throw left stick to partner and catch stick
he throws to you.

Flip sticks in front of body.
Hit ends on floor (vertical position).
This pattern fits only twice to the music.

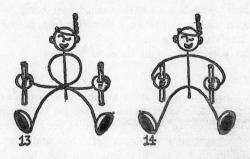

Squares to the Right

Pattern #9: This is not an easy one but it can be mastered. The "square throw" indicates the path the sticks follow as they move in this pattern. They actually travel around the sides of a square. To perform the "square throw," throw your right

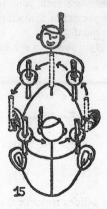

stick into your partner's left hand while throwing your left stick into your right hand and catch the stick your partner is throwing from his right hand into your left hand simultaneously. It sounds impossible, but it is easier to do than to describe. The entire pattern is:

Hit ends of sticks on floor (vertical position).

Hit own stick together.

Throw your right stick into your partner's left hand. (Figure 15.)

Throw your left stick into your right hand.

Catch stick your partner is throwing from his right hand into your left hand.

This pattern fits eight times to the music.

Squares to the Left

Pattern #10: This is the same as pattern #9 except that the sticks travel clockwise or to the left around the square. Thus you will be throwing your left stick into your partner's right hand, your right stick into your left hand and catching the stick your partner is throwing into your right hand from his left hand. The complete pattern is:

Hit ends of sticks on floor (vertical position).

Hit own sticks together.

Throw your left stick into your partner's right hand. (Figure 16.)

Throw your right stick into your left hand.

Catch stick your partner is throwing from his right hand into your left hand.

This pattern fits eight times to the music.

16

Alternate Right and Left Squares

Pattern #11: This pattern combines the right and left square throws in alternating fashion. The complete pattern is:

Hit ends of stick on floor (vertical position).
Hit own sticks together.
Square throw to right. (Figure 15.)
Hit ends of stick on floor.
Hit own sticks together.
Square throw to the left. (Figure 16.)
This pattern fits four times to the music.

Inside Outside Throws

Pattern #12: Hold sticks as in preceding patterns. The throw in this differs in that a player throws both sticks at the same time, one player's sticks taking the inside track with the partner's taking the outside track. The sticks travel in two parallel lines in an upright position. Players must decide who is to throw the inside track and who the outside track on the first turn. Thereafter, the players alternate inside and outside throws. Players sometimes have difficulty remembering which throw is coming up next. The easiest way is to watch the pair of sticks that goes down the inside track. No matter which player is throwing those sticks at the moment, that pair always travels the inside track and the other pair always travels the outside track. The pattern is:

Hit ends on the floor.
Hit own sticks together.
Player #1 throws both sticks down the inside track and catches player #2's sticks coming down the outside track. (Figure 17.)
Hit ends on floor.
Hit own sticks together.
Player #1 throws sticks down the outside track and catches player #2's sticks coming down the inside track. (Figure 18.)
(Note: Player #1 in figures 17 and 18 is facing the reader.)

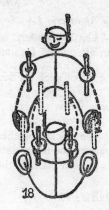

Rockaby Right and Left

Pattern #13: Hold sticks at one end, vertical position, hands close to the floor. Tilt sticks toward the left and touch tips to floor, tilt to right and touch to the floor. Keep fists close to floor during this motion. This is the "rockaby" motion. Put into the pattern it goes:

Tilt sticks to left and touch tips to floor. (Figure 19.)

Tilt sticks to right and touch tips to floor. (Figure 20.)

Hit ends on floor.

Hit own sticks together.

Throw right stick to partner's right hand and catch stick he throws to you.

Immediately throw left stick into partner's left hand and catch stick he throws to you.

This pattern fits four times to the music.

Rockaby Front and Back

Pattern #14: Hold sticks at one end, vertical position, hands close to floor. Tilt sticks toward partner and touch tips to floor, tilt sticks toward self and touch tips to floor. Keep fists close to floor during this motion. This the the "rockaby" front and back motion. The complete pattern is:

> Tilt sticks toward partner and touch tips to floor.
> Tilt sticks toward self and touch tips to floor.
> Hit ends on floor (vertical position, fists close to floor).
> Hit own sticks together.
> Throw right stick to partner's right hand and catch stick he throws.
> Immediately throw left stick to partner's left hand and catch stick he throws to you.
> This pattern fits four times into the music.

Triangle and Front Flip

Pattern #15: Hold sticks in center, vertical position, hands close together, fists touching. With hands close together, hit ends of sticks on floor in center front of body, hit both sticks at left front of body, hit both sticks at right front of body. This is the triangle. It is followed by a front flip and a double throw. (See directions for a front flip in pattern #5.) The whole pattern is:

> Hit stick ends on floor, vertical position, hands close together at center front. (Figure 21.)
> Hit sticks on floor, hands close together at left front. (Figure 22.)
> Hit sticks on floor, hands close together, at right front. (Figure 23.) (This is done in rapid succession.)
> Front flip.
> Hit ends on floor.
> Hit own sticks together.
> Throw right to partner's right hand and catch stick he throws you.
> Throw left to partner's left hand and catch stick he throws you.
> Front flip.

Hit ends on floor.

This pattern fits twice into the music.

21 22 23

The Three Flipper

Pattern #16: Hold both sticks at a diagonal position at left side of body and do a flip. Immediately perform another flip with both sticks at diagonal position at right side of body. Then do a front flip. (See pattern #5 for description of front flip.) The complete pattern is:

Side flip at left side of body (Both sticks on same side of body as in figure 24.)

Hit ends of stick on floor (still at left side).

Side flip at right side of body (both sticks on same side of body as in figure 25.)

Hit ends on floor (still at right side).

Front flip.

Hit ends on floor.

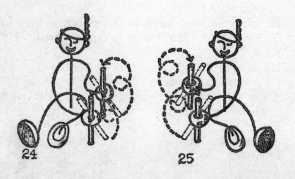

24 25

Throw right stick to partner's right hand and catch stick
he throws you.

Immediately throw left stick to partner's left hand and
catch stick he throws you.

This pattern fits twice to the music.

Four-Handed Lummi Sticks

When players have become skilled they will particularly
enjoy playing four-handed Lummi Sticks. The players sit
in a square, partners opposite each other. Many of the same
patterns used in the two-handed game can be done in the four-
handed game. There are others, of course, which can be done
only in the four-handed game. The trick in the four-handed
game is in the beginning. One set of partners begins the chant
and the pattern. The second set waits until the third beat before beginning. The first set has sung "makoo" before the
second set begins on the "aye." This puts the throws and hits
on the alternate beats so that sticks do not collide. All players
sing together, but the second set has the harder time as it
starts on the third beat and must therefore continue for two
beats at the end before starting the second pattern. In other
words, the second set is two beats behind on the movements
but sings the chant along with the first set.

FOUR-HANDED PATTERNS

Patterns #1, 2, 3, 4, 5, 6, 7, 8, 12, 15 and 16 can be done
in the four-handed game if the directions given above are
followed carefully.

In patterns 9, 10 and 11 (Squares to the Right, Squares to
the Left, Squares Right and Left), the sticks move around the
square from player to player, rather than across the square
from partner to partner; otherwise the patterns are the same.

Chapter 16

Singing Games and Dance Mixers

EVERYONE RESPONDS to music and rhythm. Both activities fill universal human needs. Singing games and dance mixers combine music and rhythm and thus become one of the most satisfying of the social and recreational activities.

Included in this chapter are singing games and dances for persons of all ages. Some are primarily children's activities while some may be used successfully with mixed groups of children and adults. At family parties in churches or business organizations where the age range may extend from three years to Grandma, the singing games can be used as party activities. If the adults can shed their dignity long enough to play the games with the children, the thrill the children will get from having their parents and grandparents playing with them will more than offset any feelings of embarrassment the adults may experience at first. Family play where all ages participate together is one of the most satisfying of human experiences.

No leader expects to conduct an entire program of activities scaled down to the youngest child present. After a short period of singing games in which all participate, the youngest children (under seven years of age) may then be separated from the group and taken off for a program of their own. The more difficult but still simple dance mixers are then introduced into the program. The wise leader works out a progression so that the dances gradually become more difficult and complicated. After three mixers selected on this basis, the group will be ready to go into square dancing. For example, the first dance mixer might use a swing and promenade, both of which are parts of any square dance. The next dance might introduce a grand right and left. When the group can perform this successfully a left allemande can be added. Once these square-dance techniques have been learned, the group is ready to go into a simple square dance.

The first half hour of mixers is a valuable one in many ways: It gets people acquainted by having the dancers constantly change partners. It gives the guests all the fun and satisfaction of dancing. It teaches one technique after another painlessly while the guests are dancing and having fun. Through a series of successful experiences, it gives the dancers more confidence in their ability and makes them ready to go on to something more difficult.

Once all these things have been accomplished, the party is well under way. The author has countless times taken a group (who would have been frightened to death to venture on the floor if a square dance were announced) and run them through a short period of dance mixers which employed square-dance techniques. Before the group realized what it was doing it was square dancing. Most of the dance mixers given here have been selected or invented with the above described technique in mind. The author is convinced anyone who can follow directions and can walk can square dance.

The music with simple accompaniment for the piano and chords for the accordionist or guitar player is given for every singing game and dance mixer.

SINGING GAMES

Looby Loo

This old English singing game is thought to date back to Druid customs where it was probably used as a dance in the worship of a deity. We like to tell the children it is the dance story of a child taking his Saturday-night bath in an old-fashioned washtub. He tests the temperature of the water with each hand, with each foot and then with his head. Satisfied, he finally jumps in for a quick bath, jumps out and shakes himself all over and his bath is over until the next Saturday night.

LOOBY LOO

Formation: Single circle facing in.

Words	Action
Here we go looby loo, Here we go looby la, Here we go looby loo,	Single circle formation, hands joined, walking to left.
All on a Saturday night.	Group reverses and circles right.
1. I put my left hand in,	Players put left hand into circle with elaborate motions.
I take my left hand out,	Each takes left hand out in same manner.
I give my left hand a shake, shake, shake,	Each shakes left hand vigorously three times.
And turn myself about!	Each turns himself about with little jumps.
Whee!	Facing into circle and jumps high in air, claps his hands high over his head and yells "Whee" in a loud voice.

Other Verses

2. I put my right hand in, etc.	
3. I put my left foot in, etc.	
4. I put my right foot in, etc.	
5. I put my big head in, etc.	
6. I put my big self in, etc.	Each jumps into circle, jumps out and shakes himself like a dog just out of water.

Hokey Pokey

The Hokey Pokey is very similar to Looby Loo with many additions. It is popular with teenage groups and adults as well as with children and family groups. Like Looby Loo, it has a "shake, shake, shake" and a "turn yourself about" part. For variations, we like to use a different action on the turn each time. Suggested turns are:

Words	Action
1. Duck-waddle turn.	(Players in stooping position on turn.)
2. Donkey-ears turn.	(Walking turn, with thumbs at temples and hands wiggling.)
3. One-foot-jump turn.	(Hop on one foot while turning.)
4. Hop turn.	(Hop on two feet on turn.)
5. Monkey turn.	(Assume walking position of ape and waddle from side to side on turn.)
6. Shake-and-wiggle turn.	(Walking turn with hands at shoulder height. Shake and wiggle hands vigorously.)
7. Skip turn.	(Turn with skipping step in place.)
8. Bobbing turn.	(Bob up and down on turn.)
9. Horse-riding turn.	(Hold imaginary reins in hands and ride galloping horse on turn.)
10. Spin around.	(Three fast turns in place.)
11. Clap hands.	(Plain turn, clap hands as you turn.)
12. Clap thigh.	(Knees slightly bent, hit hands on thighs as you turn.)

Formation: Single circle facing in.

Words	Action
1. Put your right hand in,	Put right hand in circle with exaggerated motion.
Take your right hand out,	Take right hand out.
Put your right hand in	Put right hand into circle again.
And you shake it all about,	Shake right hand vigorously.

HOKEY POKEY

Words	*Action*
And you do the hokey pokey	Players turn in place, hands over head, hands shaking furiously.
And you turn yourself about	
For that's what it's all about!	(Note: See above for variations on turns.)
Whee!	Players jump into air and yell "Whee!"

2. Put your left hand in, etc.
3. Put your right foot in, etc.
4. Put your left foot in, etc.
5. Put your right shoulder in, etc.
6. Put your left shoulder in, etc.
7. Put your right hip in, etc.
8. Put your left hip in, etc.
9. Put your front side in, etc.
10. Put your back side in, etc.
11. Put your whole self in, etc.

Words	Action
12. Now you kneel down	All players kneel facing into center.
And you kowtow,	With hands high over heads, players bow down low with hands touching floor.
Now you kneel down	Return to upright kneeling position.
And you kowtow,	Bowing motion.
And you kowtow, kow-tow,	Bowing motions in fast time.
Kowtow, kowtow,	
For that's what it's all about!	
Whee!	All collapse on floor as they yell "Whee!"

Note: This last verse is optional, of course. The children will love it. The old, decrepit and dignified adults may be satisfied to watch the younger dancers do this verse.

The Farmer in the Dell

One of the best-loved of the children's singing games.

Formation: Single circle, facing in, hands joined. One child (the *farmer*) is in the center.

Words	*Action*
1. The farmer in the dell,	Circle moves to the left, around the farmer in the center.
The farmer in the dell, Heigh ho, the derry-o, The farmer in the dell.	
2. The farmer takes a wife,	Farmer chooses a child from the circle and draws her into the circle.
The farmer takes a wife, Heigh ho, the derry-o, The farmer takes a wife, etc.	

THE FARMER IN THE DELL

The game continues in this fashion, with each newly chosen child picking another. See verses below:

Other Verses	Action
3. The wife takes a child, etc.	
4. The child takes the dog, etc.	
5. The dog takes the cat, etc.	
6. The cat takes the rat, etc.	
7. The rat takes the cheese, etc.	
8. The farmer goes home, etc.	The farmer leaves the group in the center and joins the circle.
9. The wife goes home, etc.	Wife leaves center and joins circle.
10. The child goes home, etc.	Each player leaves circle in turn as verses dictate.
11. The dog goes home, etc.	
12. The cat goes home, etc.	
13. The rat goes home, etc.	
14. The cheese stands alone, etc.	Circle moves in to cheese who stands alone. Children clap hands while singing last verse.

The Farmer Sows His Wheat

This game is sung to the same music as the Farmer in the Dell. See music for previous game. At the beginning, four children are chosen, one as the *farmer*, one as the *sun*, one as the *wind* and one as the *rain*. All the children take their places in the circle with hands joined with the exception of the *farmer* who stands near the inside edge of the circle. The *rain*, *sun* and *wind* step into the circle when their turns come and then step back into the circle when their turns are over.

This is as much a dramatic game as a rhythmic one. The four main "actors" make their parts as dramatic and convincing as possible as do the children in the circle itself, since they are actors, too.

This makes a particularly good game for demonstration purposes at special programs because it has much action.

Formation: Single circle facing in. Farmer in center.

Words	*Action*
1. The farmer sows his wheat, The farmer sows his wheat, Heigh ho, the derry-o, The farmer sows his wheat.	Group stands in circle formation facing center. *Farmer* skips around the circle making motions of sowing wheat. As *farmer* passes a child, the child stoops and remains in stooping position. As *farmer* ends his rounds, the entire circle is in stooping position.
2. The rain begins to fall, The rain begins to fall, Heigh ho, the derry-o, The rain begins to fall.	Child chosen as *rain* steps into the circle and skips around the circle making motions of falling rain over the heads of the stooping children. After the *rain* finishes going around the circle, he takes his place with the other children in stooping position.
3. The sun begins to shine, etc.	The child chosen as the *sun*, with arms forming large circle, skips around the circle and then takes her place with the other children who are still in stooping positions.
4. The wheat begins to grow, etc.	Children with hands raised above their shoulders, forefingers pointed upward, begin slowly rising to standing position, "growing" slowly until they

Words	Action
	reach full height with their hands extended high over their heads.
5. The wind begins to blow, etc.	The child chosen as *wind* skips around the circle making suitable motions with hands and body to represent the wind. The children in the circle, with hands high over their heads, sway from side to side, as if they were stalks of wheat swaying in the wind. After *wind* finishes her round, she joins the other children in the circle.
6. The farmer cuts his wheat, etc.	*Farmer* skips around the circle making cutting motions with hand at children's upraised arms. As *farmer* cuts at their arms the children allow their arms to fall at their sides.
7. He binds it into sheaves, etc.	*Farmer* skips around the circle and, with gentle pushes and little gathering motions, forms groups of three or four.
8. The sheaves begin to dance, etc.	The little groups join hands and skip merrily around in a little circle.

The main characters choose replacements and the game begins again. When a circle is large, sing some of the verses through twice to allow the farmer or the other characters to get all the way around the circle. This is often necessary in the "binding the sheaves" verse, as this takes more time than just skipping around the circle does. After a few times, the children learn to make their own sheaves and thus help the farmer.

Bluebird, Bluebird

This is another very popular children's singing game. The most difficult thing to do is to get it stopped. The children would go on forever, or at least until the entire circle has been brought into play. With a large group it is better, however, not to play the game until that point is reached. It is always better to stop any game when interest is high and go on to another; then the children will look forward to the time when they can play the game again and will never tire of it.

Formation: Single circle, facing in, hands joined and held high to make "windows." One child has been chosen to be *bluebird*. With a large group, two or three bluebirds may be used and each starts at a different place in the circle.

BLUEBIRD, BLUEBIRD

Words	*Action*
1. Bluebird, bluebird, in and out my window, Bluebird, bluebird, in and out my window, Bluebird, bluebird, in and out my window.	*Bluebird* moves in and out of the circle, under the raised arms of the children.
Oh, Johnny, I am tired.	All children raise hands high in air, in stretching and yawning motion. *Bluebird* has stopped and stands behind the child closest to him.
2. Take a little bird and tap him (or her) on the shoulder, Take a little bird and tap him on the shoulder, Take a little bird and tap him on the shoulder.	*Bluebird* stands behind a child. He puts one hand on each shoulder of the child before him. He raises his hands up and down, off and on the shoulders in time to the music. The other children are still in single circle facing in, clapping hands in time to the music.
Oh, Johnny, I am tired.	Yawning and stretching motion.

The entire game is repeated with the first *bluebird*, his hands on the shoulders of the second (or at waist if the second child is too tall) walking behind the newly chosen child. With each singing of the second verse a new child is added to the procession, until there is a long line going in and out the windows. With large groups, where more than one *bluebird* has been used, there will be two or three long "worms," as the children love to call them, weaving in and out under the arches formed by the children's arms.

Mazoo

This is a Southern singing game, popular with children wherever it is introduced.

Formation: Single circle, facing in, children holding hands around the circle, with hands high in the air making arches. One child is chosen to be *Mazoo*. In large groups, more than one Mazoo may be used.

MAZOO

Words	Action
1. Go in and out my window, Mazoo, Mazoo, Go in and out my window, Mazoo-zi-anna-zoo.	*Mazoo* weaves in and out the circle, walking under the arms of the children in the circle.
2. Now wash each tiny window, Mazoo, Mazoo, Now wash each tiny window, Mazoo-zi-anna-zoo.	*Mazoo* makes circular motion in front of the faces of the children as if washing windows. *Mazoo* washes as many windows as possible in the time the music allows.
3. Now let me see you shuffle, Mazoo, Mazoo, Now let me see you shuffle, Mazoo-zi-anna-zoo.	*Mazoo* does a little dance in the center of the circle, while the other children clap hands in rhythm.
4. Now choose a tiny partner, Mazoo, Mazoo, Now choose a tiny partner, Mazoo-zi-anna-zoo.	*Mazoo* selects a partner and the two join both hands and swing or skip around in place.

Note: To use as a mixer, omit the third verse and substitute instead the verse given below. After Mazoo chooses a partner, the two skip around the circle to the singing of this verse:

Now skip around the circle, Mazoo, Mazoo, Now skip around the circle, Mazoo-zi-anna-zoo.	The two children, holding hands in skating fashion, skip around the circle.

When the game begins again, the partners break up but remain in the circle and each begins weaving in and out. They both wash windows and choose new partners and skip with the new partners. Four children are in the center now. The number doubles with each repetition. Soon all the children are in the circle. Each then has a partner and you are ready for partner games.

All Around the Maypole

This is a popular game as it gives the children a chance to shine.

Formation: Single circle, hands joined, facing in, one child in the center as the maypole.

Words	Action
1. All around the maypole, tra la la, All around the maypole, tra la la, I like sugar and candy.	Children with hands joined in circle formation, facing in, walk to left around the *maypole* in the center.
2. Let me see you make a motion, tra la la, Let me see you make a motion, tra la la, I like sugar and candy.	Circle stops moving, children drop hands and clap in rhythm as child in center makes some repetitive motion such as arm swinging, jumping up and down, etc.
3. That's a very fine motion, etc.	Child in center continues making the motion and all the other children join in making the same motion.

ALL AROUND THE MAYPOLE

At the completion of the game, the child in center chooses a new maypole and then joins the other children in the circle. The game is repeated. Don't try to give every child a turn. When you start another game let the children who haven't had turns in previous games have the first turn in the new games.

When I Was a Schoolgirl

This is an acting-out singing game that is always fun to do. On the first part of each verse which names the occupation, the circle moves to the left with the children holding hands. At the words, "and this way went I," the circle stops moving and takes up the appropriate action of that verse.

Words	Action
1. Oh, when I was a schoolgirl,	Circle, facing in, hands joined, moving to left.

Words

A schoolgirl, a schoolgirl,
Oh, when I was a school-
girl,
Oh, *this way* went I.

Oh, this way went I, oh,
this way went I,
Oh, when I was a school-
girl,

Action

Circle stops, children drop
hands and turn and move
to right with dragging, re-
luctant feet and continue
in this fashion to the end
of this verse.

WHEN I WAS A SCHOOLGIRL

Words	Action
Oh, this way went I.	
2. Oh, when I was a teacher, etc.	Face into center and make scolding motions with forefinger.
3. Oh, when I was a lady, etc.	Walk haughtily around the circle, nose in air, hand on hip.
4. When I was a sailor, etc.	Face center of circle, pull ropes as if hoisting sails.
5. When I was a cobbler, etc.	Pound one fist on top of other as if pounding nails into shoes.
6. When I was a mover, etc.	Walk as if carrying heavy loads.
7. When I was a dancer, etc.	Imitate any type of dancing each child to his own liking.
8. When I was a cowboy, etc.	Legs bowed, motions of riding horse.
9. When my life was over, Was over, was over, When my life was over, How sorry was I, etc.	Dramatic motions of great sorrow.

Encourage the children to make up verses and appropriate actions.

The Muffin Man

Usually this game is played with a single-circle formation and one player in the center as *It*. The circle moves to the left singing the first verse. The circle stops moving on the second verse while the player in the center chooses a partner and skips around with her. The first player then joins the circle and the last player chosen stays in the circle to be *It* for the next game.

Variation: If you wish to have the children in couples at the end of the game, play the game differently. When players choose partners, both players stay in the circle; they break up when the game is repeated and each gets a new partner. This continues until all the children are in the center of the circle and none is left in the outside circle. Your group is then ready for a game in which partners are required.

THE MUFFIN MAN

Words	Action
Oh, have you seen the muffin man,	Single circle, holding hands, moving to the left around one or more players in the center who choose partners on the last line.
The muffin man, the muffin man?	
Oh, have you seen the muffin man	
Who lives in Drury Lane?	
Oh, yes, I've seen the muffin man,	Circle stops moving and faces in; players clap hands. Center players skip around the circle with partners. At end of verse, center players drop hands and look for new partners. (See explanation above for variations.)
The muffin man, the muffin man.	
Oh, yes, I've seen the muffin man	
Who lives in Drury Lane.	

The Mulberry Bush

This is another singing game which is filled with pantomime action, with each child giving his own action interpretation of the words. The children circle and "go round the mulberry bush" between each verse as music indicates.

Formation: Single circle.

THE MULBERRY BUSH

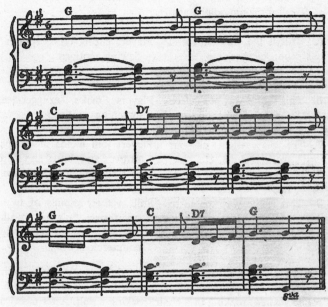

Words	*Action*
1. Here we go round the mulberry bush, The mulberry bush, the mulberry bush. Here we go round the mulberry bush So early in the morning.	Single circle, hands joined, circling to the left (walking, skipping). All children turn in place and clap hands.
2. This is the way we wash our clothes, etc., So early Monday morning.	Circle faces in, make motions of washing clothes on washboard.
3. This is the way we iron our clothes, etc.,	Motions of ironing.

Words	Action
So early Tuesday morning.	
4. This is the way we scrub our floors, etc., So early Wednesday morning.	Players on hands and knees. Scrubbing motions.
5. This is the way we mend our clothes, etc., So early Thursday morning.	Players sitting tailor fashion. Sewing motions.
6. This is the way we sweep the house, etc., So early Friday morning.	Players make exaggerated sweeping motions.
7. We play when all our work is done, etc., So early Saturday morning.	Players join hands in groups of twos and threes and skip around in their little circles.
8. This is the way we go to church, etc., So early Sunday morning.	Still in their groups of twos or threes, players walk solemnly around the circle counterclockwise.

Variation: This game can be adapted in many ways. Each verse may be built around such activities as riding a horse, roller skating, rocking in a chair, rocking a doll. After a series of such active verses, the game can end in a "resting verse" which leads nicely into a rest period.

I take my rest when my play is done, Play is done, play is done. I take my rest when my play is done So early in the morning.	Children all lie down in comfortable positions and lie as quietly as possible until leader gives signal to stretch and get up to play another game.

PARTNER DANCES

Hickory, Dickory, Dock

This is a children's singing game which is always popular

at family parties where children and parents play together. Formation: Double circle, partners facing each other, boys with backs to center.

HICKORY, DICKORY, DOCK

Words	Action
Hickory, dickory, dock, Tick, tock!	Partners facing, arms outstretched, with hands joined. Arms moving up and down with rocking motion. Hands on hips, stamp right foot, stamp left in

Words	Action
	time to music on "tick, tock."
The mouse ran up the clock,	Players with open hands (palms forward) held at temples to resemble ears, change places with partners with little running steps. Run in bent-over position.
Tick, tock!	Hands on hips, stamp right foot and then left.
The clock struck one,	Partners slap each other's right hands.
The mouse did run.	Players, hands to heads for ears, run back to place with little running steps in bent-over positions.
Hickory, dickory, dock,	Players facing, hands joined, arms outstretched, rocking motions with arms.
Tick, tock!	Hands on hips, stamp right foot and then left.

Play the game three times, each time more slowly than the last as if the clock were running down. After third time, make motions and sound of winding a clock and do the dance once more in very fast time.

Chimes of Dunkirk

This is a Danish dance of greeting which can be used as a mixer dance with adults' as well as children's groups. Partners are changed each time the dance is repeated.

Formation: Double circle with partners facing each other, men with their backs to center of the circle.

Call	Action
Bow to your partner, bow.	Partners bow and curtsy to each other.
Move to the right and bow.	Partners move to right, away from each other, and bow to new partner.

CHIMES OF DUNKIRK

Call	Action
Now turn your partner once around	New partners join both hands and turn once in a little circle and back to place.
And back to place.	
Now clap, clap, clap,	Partners, facing, clap their own hands three times in time to the music.
And stamp, stamp, stamp,	Stamp right foot, left foot and right foot in time to music.

| Now turn your partner once around | Partners join both hands, turn around once and come |
| And back to place. | back to place. |

The dance is then repeated several times, players dancing with a new partner each time.

Variation: To make this a talking mixer, change the words "clap, clap, clap" and "stamp, stamp, stamp" to "talk, talk, talk" and "talk, talk, talk." Urge players to introduce themselves and get in as many vital statistics as possible in the time allotted. Other variations might include slapping thighs instead of clapping hands, or clapping partner's left hand, then partner's right and then own hands, or slapping thighs, then slapping partner's right hand, then partner's left instead of the clapping and stamping described above. Players might also be asked to whistle instead of clapping or stamping.

Four-Times-Four Dance Mixer

This is a simple dance mixer which has four patterns of four counts each and gives a change of partner at the completion of each time through. It can be done to either the chorus of "Glow Worm," "I'm Looking over a Four-Leaf Clover" or any good marching tune such as "On, Wisconsin." The mixer is good for adult and teenage groups.

Formation: Double circle, with partners holding inside hands and moving counterclockwise around the circle with walking steps.

Music: "Camptown Races"

Call	Action
Forward four	Partners walk four steps forward, facing each other on the fourth step, men with backs to center of circle.
Back away four	Partners walk four steps backward away from each other.
Diagonal four	Dancers each move diagonally to the right, four steps toward a new partner.

CAMPTOWN RACES

Call	*Action*
Turn four	New partners join both hands and turn once around in four walking steps. (Partners may take dance position on turn. Partners stand side by side, right hips touching. Gentleman has right arm around lady's waist, holding her right

arm out at the side; lady
has left arm on gentleman's
shoulder.)

Yankee Doodle

This is a musical mixer which makes a good lead-up dance
to square dancing, as terms and techniques learned here are
also used in square dancing.

Formation: Couples (lady on the gentleman's right) standing
side by side, facing into the center of the circle, hands joined
all around the circle.

Calls	Action
(Verse Music)	
Everybody in four steps	Single circle, hands joined,
And everybody out.	moves into center three steps and back out again with walking steps.
Everybody in again	Repeat above action.
And everybody out.	
(Chorus Music)	
Ladies, in and out you go,	Ladies move into center and back out again.
	Gentlemen clap hands while standing in place.
Gents, in and out you go,	Gentlemen move into center and out again.
	Ladies clap hands while standing in place.
And swing your corner lady.	Gentleman swings left-hand lady.
(Verse Music)	
Swing your partner round and round,	Gentleman continues to swing his left-hand lady, who becomes his new partner.
Keep your partner busy;	
Swing your partner round and round	
But don't make her too dizzy.	
(Chorus Music)	
Promenade now two by two,	Gentleman promenades with corner lady, counterclock-
Promenade your partner new.	

YANKEE DOODLE

Calls	Action
Promenade now two by two Now make a single circle.	wise around the circle (walking steps, left hands joined in front, gentleman's right arm around the lady's shoulder, holding her right hand at her shoulder). On the call "make a single circle," couples face in quickly, join hands and make a circle.

Oh! Susanna

This is a good musical mixer that can also be used as a lead-up for a beginning group in square dancing since it teaches a grand right and left. When a group has mastered that, a left allemande can be added.

Formation: Couples in single circle, facing in, lady on the gent's right.

Calls	*Action*
(Verse Music)	
Ladies into center	From single circle, ladies

OH! SUSANNA

Calls	*Action*
And ladies out again.	walk four steps into center and walk out backward while gents clap hands in rhythm.
Gents into center And come back out again.	Gents walk into center in four steps. Walk out backward to place while ladies clap hands in rhythm.
(Verse Music Repeated) Right hand to your partner And a grand chain now you do. Count to five and keep that gal, For she's your partner new.	Partners face and take right hands, and begin a grand chain for five persons. Have group count aloud. Partner is number one. Gent turns fifth lady under her right arm and into promenade position.
(Chorus Music) Promenade your honey; Around the room you go. Keep your feet a-moving In any fancy step you know.	Partners promenade counterclockwise around the circle until the end of the chorus music, when the call "ladies into the center" comes again. Gent turns his lady from a promenade position and gently propels her into the center.

Note: If there is a mix-up on the grand chain, warn all dancers left without partners to step into the center of the circle where they can find a partner quickly and rejoin the promenading dancers. (If they step outside the circle, it is practically impossible to see the other "lost" dancers.) Assure the dancers left without partners that it is rarely the dancer who made the mistakes who is left without a partner so that no one need feel shame because he finds himself without a partner.

After a group has mastered the grand chain, add a left

allemande which precedes the grand chain. Since the left allemande is merely a windup beginning of the grand chain, dancers do not start to count until they begin the grand chain with their partners. With the allemande the call would be:

Calls	*Action*
(Verse Music)	
Ladies into the center	
And ladies out again.	
Gents into the center	
And come back out again.	
(Verse Music)	
It's left hand to your corner,	Dancers face their corners, take left hands and walk around their corners and back to their partners. Counting partners as "one" they grand chain to the fifth lady and promenade that new partner.
Around that gal you go,	
Back to your own with right hand out	
And a grand chain now you do.	
(Chorus Music)	
Promenade that lady.	
Around the room you go,	
Keep your feet a-moving	
In any fancy step you know.	

Ach Ja

This is an old German folk dance which never fails to please either a children's, teenage or adult group or one in which adults and children are mixed. Groups soon learn to call it the "bump dance."

Formation: Partners facing counterclockwise, promenade position.

Words	*Action*
(Verse)	
The father and the mother	Couples promenade.
To the little church go.	
Ach ja,	Partners bow deeply to each other.
Ach ja!	
	Partners turn backs to each

ACH JA

Words

Action

other and bow, managing
to bump each other as they
bow.

Couples promenade again.

They haven't any money
But they love each other so.
Ach ja,
Ach ja!

Partners bow to each other,
turn backs to each other
and bump.

(Chorus)

Words	Action
Tra la la,	Partners face each other (gents with backs to center of circle). With arms outstretched and hands joined at shoulder height they take one slow sliding step counterclockwise around the circle.
Tra la la,	Partners take another slow sliding step.
Tra la la la la la la, Tra la la, Tra la la, Tra la la la la la la la,	Partners take three fast sliding steps. Partners reverse direction and repeat two slow and three quick slides in opposite direction.
Ach ja,	Partners bow to each other.
Ach ja!	Partners move to the right, away from each other toward a new partner, and bow to new partner.

All Join Hands

This is a simple mixer which ends when everyone has a partner. It is a good mixer with which to begin a program. Suitable for all age groups and groups where children and adults are mixed.

Formation: Single circle holding hands, facing into center.

Calls	Action
Now we'll all join hands And circle around the ring,	Circle, with hands joined, moves to left. There may be one or more couples in the center, depending upon the size of the group.
While the couple (or couples) In the center do a right smart swing.	Center couples swing while circle moves around them.
Now we clap our hands	Circle stops moving, center

TURKEY IN THE STRAW

Calls	Action
And stamp our feet,	couple stops swinging. All players clap hands three times and stamp right foot,

Calls	Action
	then left and then right again.
And turn ourselves about;	All players turn around once in place.
And we smile real purty	Players in circle bend over,
Till somebody picks us out.	put hands on thighs and grin at players in center. Players in center each pick a new partner and take them back into the center. Number of couples in center doubles each time until all have partners.

Nellie Bly Mixer

This is a circle mixer for players who know a left allemande and simple do si do. It moves quickly, and since it is a singing call dance, the groups must execute all turns on the beat.

Formation: Single circle, couples standing side by side facing the center of the circle.

Music: "Nellie Bly"

Calls	Action
All join hands and circle left, Circle round the ring.	Circle, hands joined, moves to the left clockwise.
Stop right there, face your own,	Partners swing.
Give your gal a swing.	
Now swing with your corner,	Corners swing.
Go back and swing your own,	Partners swing.
Allemande left your corner gal,	Turn corners with the left hand.
Do si do your own.	Partners do si do.
Promenade your corner,	Men promenade with the
Promenade the hall,	corner girls.
Promenade that pretty little gal	Couples promenade until the call "all join hands" comes.
Until you hear the call.	They stop the promenade and face into the center

and all join hands to begin
the dance again.

NELLIE BLY

Good Night Ladies Mixer

This is a dance of greeting or farewell depending upon whether you sing "Good night, Ladies" or "Hello, Ladies." It is suitable for all age groups or for groups of adults and children mixed.

Formation: Double circle, partners facing each other, men with backs to the center of the circle.

GOOD NIGHT, LADIES

Words	Calls	Action
Good night, la-dies,	(Move to the right)	Partners shake hands as they sing and then move to the right to new partner.
Good night, la-dies,	(Move to the right)	Shake new partner's hand and move to right to new partner.
Good night, la-dies,	(Move to the right)	Shake new partner's hand and move to

Words	Calls	Action
		right to new partner.
We're going to leave you now.	(Move to the right)	Shake new partner's hand and take skating or promenade position.
Merrily we roll along, Roll along, roll along. Merrily we roll along O'er the dark blue sea.	(Promenade)	Dancers promenade or skip to this music. As dance begins again, shake hands with present partner on first "Good night, ladies" and move on to new partner.

Red River Valley Mixer

This is a mixer to the tune of "Red River Valley." It uses a grand chain, swing and promenade.

Formation: Couples in single-circle formation, lady standing to the gentleman's right.

Calls	Action
Now you all join hands in the valley And you circle to the left around the ring.	Circle moves to left with joined hands.
Stop where you are in the valley; Give your corner a whirly-twirly swing.	Gentlemen swing corner ladies.
Now come back to your gal in the valley; Take her right hand and start a grand chain. Count to five as you chain in the valley. Promenade with that new Red River gal.	Partners face and take right hands. Counting partner as number one, they grand chain for five persons and promenade with number five.
Promenade with this gal in the valley,	Promenade with new partner.

RED RIVER VALLEY

Calls	Action
Promenade with this partner so new,	
Promenade while you can in the valley	
For it's time now to bid her adieu.	Dancers form a single circle quickly to begin again on "all join hands."

Twos on Parade Mixer

Dancers must know a ladies' chain and do si do.

Formation: Couples are in sets of fours. Couples moving

THE GIRL I LEFT BEHIND ME

counterclockwise are know as couples #2; couples moving
clockwise are couples #1. To get dancers in sets of four,
have couples face one direction in promenade position. Num-

ber couples off by twos. Couples #1 will face about and face
couples #2. Each two couples are then in a set of four.
Music: "The Girl I Left Behind Me"

Calls	*Action*
The twos form an arch with a heigh di ho	Couple #2 forms arch by joining inside hands.
And the ones just dive right through,	Both couples move forward with couple #1 ducking under the arch formed by couple #2.
And you bow to the couple That you meet on the way With a "Howdy, how are you?"	Partners bow to new couple coming toward them.
Now all join hands and circle left, For that's the thing to do.	Two couples make a circle and move left once around and back to place.
Now circle back from whence you came;	Reverse direction and circle to right once around.
Your home's the place for you.	Back to original place in set.
With opposites do a do si do,	Corners or opposites do si do.
With partners do the same.	Partners do si do.
Now swing that gal, that corner gal,	Gents swing opposite ladies.
Then the one with which you came.	Partners swing their own ladies.
The ladies chain right over; It's an easy thing to do.	Ladies take right hands and cross the set, giving left hand to opposite gentlemen who turn them around by each putting right hand on the lady's back and pushing her gently forward around until she is facing the center of the set again.
Now chain right back to your own big man.	Ladies cross back, taking right hands as they cross

Calls	Action
He's waiting there for you.	and giving left hands to partners who turn their ladies back to place in the set.

The dance is repeated twelve or fifteen times, or until the couples who started out together meet again.

Turkey in the Straw Mixer

This mixer employs a left allemande, grand chain, promenade and a swing.

Formation: Couples in single circle with hands joined, the lady on the gentleman's right.

Calls	Action
Now you all join hands And you walk into the ring.	Circle with hands joined walks into the center of the ring.
You give a loud yell And you walk right out again.	Dancers give a loud yell and, still with hands joined, walk backward out of the center of the circle to their places.
Now swing with your partner As if you were alive.	Partners swing twice around.
Allemande with your corner And you grand chain five.	Give left hands to corners, walk around corners and come back to partner with right hand extended to begin a grand chain. Counting partner as number one, grand chain for five persons. Gentleman turns the number five lady under her arm into promenade position and begins a promenade.
Promenade, promenade,	New partners promenade un-

TURKEY IN THE STRAW

Calls	Action
Promenade with your partner so new.	til the end of the chorus music and then quickly form a single circle as the dance begins again with the first call.
Promenade, promenade, promenade	
As you used to do.	

Chapter 17

Tricks and Puzzlers

TRICKS AND puzzlers serve many purposes. They may be used as preparty activities that keep the early-arriving guest busy until the late-comers appear and the party program can begin. They serve as mixers and get-acquainted devices. Guests faced with what seems an unsolvable puzzle soon seek the aid and sympathy of another in the same fix.

Some of the tricks given here will help to fill in what might otherwise be a dull spot in a program. The puzzlers may be the trigger mechanisms which set off a whole chain of fun-producing events.

For more preparty and mixer activities, see also Mystery Treasure Hunt, Mystery Contests, Paper and Pencil Treasure Hunts, and Dance Mixers.

Buttonhole Gadgets

Prepare a number of buttonhole sticks in the following way: Cut some ⅜-inch strips into 5-inch lengths. Drill a hole about a half inch from one end. Thread a piece of strong string through the hole and tie the ends so that the string loop is just one quarter inch shorter than the stick. The sticks should be sanded down until they are smooth and splinter proof. A coat of shellac will improve the looks and keep the buttonhole sticks clean. (Meat skewers work very well if the points are dulled.) Now you are ready for some fun. As guests come in slip a buttonhole stick onto one of their button-holes on a sweater, vest or jacket. You slip them on so easily they all want to know what you expect them to do with the sticks. "Just take it off," you answer and the fun begins. They go on easily enough but they don't seem to come off. That's because you know the trick. Let the guests worry with them. If they get them off let them try putting them back on again.

The Trick: In putting on the buttonhole stick, put your left hand through the loop of string so that the loop lies across the top of your fingers. With your right hand through the loop take hold of the cloth around the buttonhole. With a sufficient amount of cloth in hand you can then poke the stick easily down through the buttonhole. With practice you can make this movement so quickly the trick is not perceptible. In removing the stick, work the stick so you can get your left hand into the loop; then gather enough cloth in your right hand so that you can slip the stick out backward.

Yoke Puzzle

Here's an old, old puzzle that always is fun to do. It's been said that it was once called the lovers' yoke. The young man or young lady gave the puzzle to the current sweetheart. If the sweetheart could solve it, it proved the intelligence of the prospect and aided the cause of the romance. While no promise is made here that it will help your romance, we know you'll have fun with it and can use it to make your parties more enjoyable for your guests.

Usually the puzzles are made of a piece of wood 5 inches long and about ½ inch wide. A ⅛-inch hole is drilled about ½ inch from each end and a ¼-inch hole is placed in the center. Take a piece of strong string about 12 inches long and fold it in half at the exact center. Slip the folded loop through the center hole and pull the ends through the loop. Place a bead or button on the end of the string and pull the right-hand string end through the right-hand end hole and tie a knot that won't slip through. Do the same with the left-hand string. You now have a puzzle with two loops, a bead on each loop. The trick is to get both the beads on the same loop without cutting the string or pulling an end loose in any way. Once you solve the puzzle you should not have any trouble getting the beads back in place again.

Solution: Pull the center loop down until you can slip the left bead through it, then pull the loop back through the center hole. If you work it correctly you will see how the bead can move along the string and onto the right-hand loop. Keep at it; you'll get it. The trick is in the center loop. Just don't let the string get twisted or tangled and it'll be easy as pie.

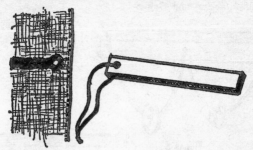

FIGURE 1

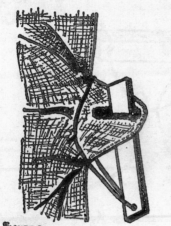

FIGURE 2

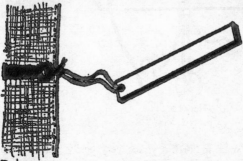

FIGURE 3

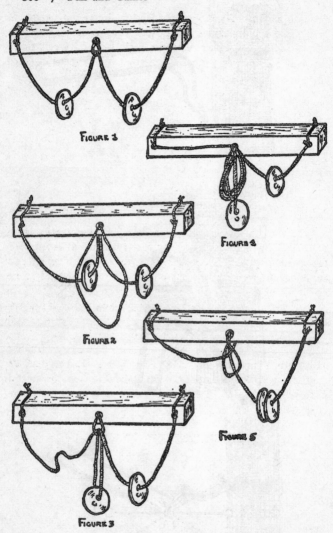

FIGURE 1

FIGURE 4

FIGURE 2

FIGURE 5

FIGURE 3

Wire Yoke

You can make the yokes very easily with stovepipe wire and a pair of pliers. Take a piece of wire about 8 inches long.

Fashion a loop at each end and one in the center. String as in directions given above except that you tie the ends of the strings in the end holes. You can make one in five minutes this way so you won't mind if the guests carry them away.

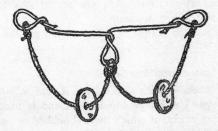

Spoke-and-Number Trick

This can be used as an individual puzzler or as a team activity. Give each team (six or fewer members) a sheet of cardboard on which five lines are drawn through a center hub so that you have a ten-spoke wheel. At the end of each spoke at the point of the hub draw a circle large enough to hold a playing piece. Give each team eleven playing pieces numbered from one to eleven. These can be pieces of cardboard, small wooden discs or bottle caps with the numbers written on with a china-marking pencil. The players attempt to place a number in each circle and one in the hub in such a manner as to make the totals of the three numbers in each spoke add up to eighteen. All pieces must be used and no numbers changed.

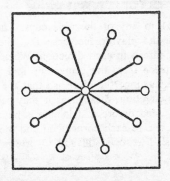

Note: The lines may be drawn on the floor with chalk. Give a team prize to the first group to turn in a correct answer. If the game goes too long without a winner, call time and proceed with the rest of the party but don't give out the solution. Later, after refreshments are served, the teams may want to go back to the puzzle.

Trick: It's easy as "fallin' off a log" if you put the six in the center.

Chinese Mathematical Puzzle

Take a muffin tin with nine cups in it. Use only the outside rows of cups. The center cup is dead and is used only for extra playing pieces, of which there should be at least twenty-six. Begin play with seven pieces in each corner cup and one in the middle ones. Each row then adds up to fifteen pieces. Players take turns alternately adding one playing piece (from

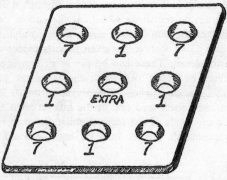

the center cup) to any of the nine cups. The other player must rearrange the playing pieces so that the totals of the cups remain at fifteen in each direction. When he is successful he adds a piece from the center cup and the first player must attempt to arrange the pieces so that the totals are still fifteen in each direction. Strange as it may seem, twenty-six pieces can be added before a stalemate is reached. The final arrangement is one in each corner cup and thirteen pieces in the center cups. The rows still add to fifteen each way but there are now fifty-six pieces on the board instead of the original thirty-two.

Mystery-Button Puzzle

Take a strip of soft leather or plastic upholstery material 6 inches in length and about 1½ inches wide. Make two 4-inch cuts down the length of the strip, beginning the cuts at about ½ inch from the top and ending them 1¼ inches from the bottom. Halfway between the end of the cuts and the bottom of the strip cut a hole about ½ inch in diameter. Cut a 6-inch piece of heavy string and put it over the cut center strips and bring the ends up through the hole. Tie a bead or button on each end of the string. The trick is to get the button string separated from the plastic strip without untying the buttons.

Solution: Grasp the center of the cut strip in your fingers and make a small fold. Slip the fold down through the hole far

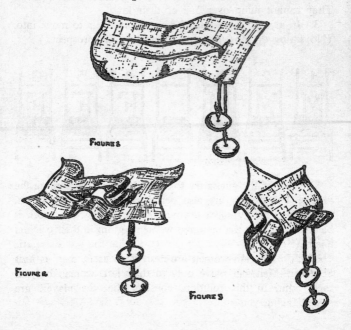

FIGURE 1

FIGURE 2

FIGURE 3

enough so that the string with the buttons can be pulled through the loop. Simple when you know how, what? But don't tell the secret to your guests. Just give them the assembled puzzle and let them figure it out. (You had to read a book to find out how it's done. Let them work it out for themselves!)

Move-and-Jump Puzzle

This is an old familiar coin or checker puzzle but playing it with people makes it an excellent parlor trick. Place seven chairs in a row. Seat three men on the chairs at one end and three women on the chairs at the other end. Leave the center chair vacant. The puzzle is to move the men down into the women's places and vice versa, following these rules:

1. Men and women can move in only one direction, not back and forth.

2. Each can move one chair or jump over an opposite. They cannot jump over one of their kind.

3. In a jump there must be an empty chair to move into. (No sitting on laps, however interesting the prospects.)

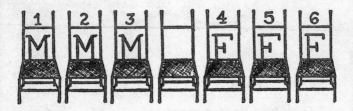

The rest of the guests try to solve the puzzle by calling the moves. The players are also permitted to make suggestions. When they finally solve the puzzle, see if they can work it backward so that the men and women end up in their original chairs.

(Note: In diagram women are designated as *F*, men as *M*.) Solution: Men can move only to their left, women only to their right. In this solution, consider that the players are seated facing you.

Moves:

> Man #3 moves into empty chair.
> Woman #4 jumps over man #3.
> Woman #5 moves into empty seat.
> Man #3 jumps over woman #5.
> Man #2 jumps over woman #4.
> Man #1 moves over.
> Woman #4 jumps over man #1.
> Woman #5 jumps over man #2.
> Woman #6 jumps over man #3.
> Man #3 moves over.
> Man #2 jumps over woman #6.
> Man #1 jumps over woman #5.
> Woman #5 moves over.
> Woman #6 jumps over man #1.
> Man #1 moves over and the puzzle is complete.

Variation of Move-and-Jump Puzzle

When a group solves the above, add two chairs to the row and a man and woman at each end, leaving the center seat vacant as in above. The puzzle is the same but a little more difficult. Number players from one to eight, leaving an empty chair between #4 and #5.

Solution:

> Man #4 moves over one chair.
> Woman #5 jumps over man #4.
> Woman #6 moves over.
> Man #4 jumps over woman #6.
> Man #3 jumps over woman #5.
> Man #2 moves over.
> Woman #5 jumps over man #2.
> Woman #6 jumps over man #3.
> Woman #7 jumps over man #4.
> Woman #8 moves over.
> Man #4 jumps over woman #8.
> Man #3 jumps over woman #7.
> Man #2 jumps over woman #6.
> Man #1 jumps over woman #5.

Woman #5 moves over.
Woman #6 jumps over man #1.
Woman #7 jumps over man #2.
Woman #8 jumps over man #3.
Man #3 moves over.
Man #2 jumps over woman #8.
Man #1 jumps over woman #7.
Woman #7 moves over.
Woman #8 jumps over man #1.
Man #1 moves over.

And the puzzle is solved!

Variation: If you don't have both sexes at the party, don't let that stop you from using this one. Have one team wear something that distinguishes it from the other or let one team sit with arms folded on chests or with hands clasped on top of heads.

Card or Coin Variation: To use as a table trick, use three red cards and three black cards but draw a diagram on the table so that the players can keep track of where the empty space is. Checkers of two colors or two kinds of coins can also be used for playing pieces.

Move-Two-Together Puzzle

Stand six players, three men and three women, in a row. The puzzle is to move two adjacent players at the same time without changing their order and in *three moves* end up with the six in a row but with the men and women alternating with no spaces left in between the players. Give each player a number to hold so that directions to move can be clearly given.

Solution: Number players from left to right in consecutive order.

Move 1 and 2 to the right of 6.
Move 6 and 1 to the right of 2.
Move 3 and 4 to the right of 5.

Rules: Adjacent players must be moved together and stand next to each other in their original order in each move; that is, they cannot move together and then do a fast switch. Have the two players to be moved hold inside hands so that they move properly.

Variation of Same Trick

Try this same puzzler with eight players and you'll find this a real "toughy." Stand the eight players in a row and number them from left to right. Give the players numbers to hold so that directions from the spectators can be given clearly and easily.

Solution:

Move 6 and 7 to the left of 1.

Move 3 and 4 to the right of 5.

Move 7 and 1 to the right of 2.

Move 4 and 8 to the left between 6 and 2.

Ten-to-Five Puzzle

Place ten chairs in a row, one alongside the other. Seat a player in each chair. The object is to end up with five couples sitting double on five chairs, but they must arrive there in a certain way. For a player to sit on another's lap, he must jump over two other players. Two players sitting on one chair count as two in a jump.

Solution: Numbering the chairs from left to right from one to ten, the jumps are as follows:

4 jumps to the left over 2 and 3 and sits on chair 1.

6 jumps to the right over 7 and 8 and sits on chair 9.

8 jumps to the left over 7 and 5 and sits on chair 3.

2 jumps to the right over 2 players on chair 3 and sits on chair 5.

10 jumps over players on chair 9 and sits on chair 7.

This leaves five chairs with two players and five empty chairs. If the players in this game prefer to continue to sit on one another's laps, who's to say "no"?

Magic Lift

One of the most baffling of parlor stunts is Magic Lift. Select a willing victim to sit on a straight chair. Four other players stand near the subject. Two stand on the left side, two on the right side. All are warned that this must be done in all seriousness and with deep concentration. The object is to show that with concentration and united effort, the seated person can be easily lifted into the air by the four players, who use only their fingers on the lift. The players who are to do the lifting clasp their hands, leaving only the two fore-fingers outstretched. At the signal to begin, all five, the four lifters and the seated player, count together: "One, two three." After each number is called there is a pause so that all take a deep breath together. After the third deep breath is taken, all hold their breath. The four lifters bend down. Two put their outstretched fingers under the knees of the seated person. The other two put their fingers under the armpits of the seated person. Still holding their breath, they lift. The seated person seems to float into the air. The person is placed back on the chair before all five expel their breath. The amazing thing is that if the same people try to lift the seated person without the breathing trick at the beginning, they cannot do it.

Players are cautioned not to expel breath or to laugh while the person is in midair or he comes down fast with a rude bump.

Balloon Shave

Hang inflated balloons on a long string so that they hang at about shoulder height of players who stand facing the balloons. Paint a face on each balloon with a felt marking pencil. Apply shaving soap to the balloon face with a brush or shaving lather from a pressurized can. Give contestants safety razors. At the signal to begin, players race to see which can shave the face the fastest. The balloons must be allowed to swing free and cannot be held by the players.

Variation: The balloon can be filled with water instead of air. We do not recommend playing either game in the living room!

The Unnecessary Covering

Get two volunteers (two men or two women but not one of each) from the group and ask them to sit on two chairs placed in the middle of the group. Leave plenty of space around the chairs. After the players are seated, cover them with a sheet. The players are instructed to remove any thing covering their bodies that is *not* necessary to decency and toss it out where the group may see. Belts, ties, shoes, socks and other pieces of wearing apparel will come flying out, accompanied by spicy comments, until the two players suddenly realize that the unnecessary covering is the sheet itself!

Use this trick only in a group where all are well acquainted and with volunteers only. This will be fun only if the two under the sheet are the type who appreciate a good joke on themselves and don't mind looking foolish in front of others.

Swiggle Sticks

Make a stick similar to the one shown in the diagram below. It can be constructed of white or yellow pine three-fourths of an inch thick. The cords (about fifty-four inches long) at the end are Venetian-blind cords. The ball is a small rubber sponge ball which can be purchased at a ten-cent store

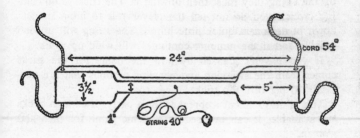

for five cents. Use a crochet hook and push it through the ball until the hook is visible. Hook a piece of crochet cotton into the hook and withdraw the crochet hook, pulling the string through the ball. Tie a button on one end of the cord and pull the cord through the ball until the button is resting against the ball. Make the crochet cotton about forty inches long. Thread it through the center hole in the Swiggle Stick and tie it so that the string is about a yard long.

Players take a partner. Each partner puts one end of the Swiggle Stick against his waist and ties the cord so that the stick is tight against his stomach. When the Swiggle Stick is in place, the partners place their hands on top of their heads and begin to sway in unison, attempting to wind the string with the ball on it around the stick. They may do this only

with swaying motions. When they have succeeded in winding up the string they must then unwind it. The trick to unwinding (which you do not tell the players) is to jump up and down in unison in quick little jumps. The string will unwind quickly and if the jumping continues will wind up again.

If you haven't guessed by now the name for the sticks comes from the swinging and wiggling motions that are necessary to perform the trick.

This is an excellent icebreaker for a party. If enough sticks are available, it can be used as a picnic game for men and women.

Chapter 18

Word Games and Stunts

WORD GAMES and stunts are enjoyed most by those who enjoy a battle of wits. Wherever possible, pit team against team rather than individual against individual. Use word games and stunts often. Make them a part of the quiet hour at camp or playground. Play them while traveling along the highway in an auto or while traveling by train or air. Slip them into party programs or introduce them into a social gathering at home. Players will find them stimulating and mirth-provoking.

THE PECULIAR LEADER GAMES

The leader begins the game by telling how peculiar he is. The players try to match the leader's odd ways by telling how queer they are. There is a trick to the game, and unless the players are peculiar in the same manner as the leader they are not admitted into the charmed circle of odd and peculiar people. There are many variations of oddities. A number are given below. Each type of peculiarity is one separate game and the leader plays until several of the players have caught on. He may change to another category, announcing that he is peculiar in another way. In any trick games, the secret is never given away (by the leader, at least). If the slow-to-catch-on-ers can worm the secret out of the good guessers, that is another matter.

The Peculiar Double Vowel and Consonants Game

The leader begins by saying: "I'm a peculiar person. I like coffee but I don't like tea. I like bubbles but I don't like baths. I like apples but I hate oranges. I like the moon but don't like the sun."

The players who think they have caught on give a sentence of their own. If they are correct they sit near the leader and

help him make up sentences. Eventually the players will catch
on that the leader likes words that have double consonants
or double vowels.

Some examples to start your mind buzzing are given below:

The Odd People Like:	They Do Not Like:
green	blue
yellow	orange
butterflies	moths
bees	flies
swimmers	waders
collars	ties
gee	gosh
slippers	shoes
noon	midnight
to toot a tooter	to blow a horn
bees that buzz	stinging insects
winners	losers
digging	spading
scallops	oysters
balls	bats
balloons	inflated bags
banners	flags
pools	lakes
doors	windows
glasses	spectacles
spoons	forks
cellophane	wax paper
celluloid	window panes
cellars	basements
Massachusetts	Maine
trees	plants
Mississippi	Louisiana
Pennsylvania	Ohio

The Peculiar Letters of the Alphabet

The leader with the peculiar tastes announces that he likes
pigtails but not queues (*Q's*), lakes but not seas (*C's*) and
milk but not tea (*T*). In each instance the thing he does not

like is a word which sounds like a single letter of the alphabet or, in some instances which sounds like two letters of the alphabet put together. Some examples are given below:

He Likes:	He Does Not Like:
butterflies	bees (*B's*)
beans	peas (*P's*)
ahs	ohs (*O's*)
smart people	people who are wise (*Y's*)
a life of work	a life of ease (*E's*)
me	you (*U*)
noses	eyes (*I's*)
haw	gee (*G*)
the river Styx	the river Dee (*D*)
what she is	what you are (*R*)
things that are difficult	things that are easy (*EZ*)
things made of rope	things made of wire (*YR*)
things that are full	things that are empty (*MT*)
people who win	people who excel (*XL*)
the smoothies	the cuties (*QT's*)

Spelling Relay

This game can be played with children of almost any age as well as adults. With small children it will be necessary to spell out the words, but the game will still be possible for them.

Divide group into two teams. Line them up in file fashion, one behind the other. About twenty feet in front of each put a table or chair on which a complete set of alphabet letters is placed. The letters should be printed on cards four inches by five inches or larger.

The leader announces the number of letters in the word to be spelled. If the word has five letters, the first five players in the line get ready. At the signal to go, they run to the cards, pick out the necessary letters and line up in the proper order holding the cards and facing their teammates. The first group to spell the word correctly wins a point for its team. This group then retires to the end of the line and the next players get ready.

The leader attempts to use words that have each letter used only once. The teams are warned if a word calls for the same letter in two places. The player holding that letter must wave it back and forth from one position to the other to show its proper place in the word. A list of words using each letter only once is given below for the leader's convenience:

word	blasphemy	orange
easy	baronet	dog
blue	bleach	mouse
speak	orchid	gainful
argue	project	furnish
carbon	respond	black
driftage	special	red
Gabriel	bachelor	cat
wonderful	bakery	builder
gravy	optical	guide

Choose-and-Spell Relay

Play the game as directed in Spelling Relay. The leader, however, instead of giving a word to spell, gives a classification. The team itself must decide which word it will spell before the members run up to collect the letters. For example, the leader will call out the classification of animal. Each team may choose a different animal to spell, choosing the shortest word they can think of to fit the classification. Some suggested classifications are given below for the leader's convenience:

animal	a girl's name	something sour
a president	a color	a farm animal
a city	something edible	a boy's name
a game	an object in the room	a fruit
an auto	a weapon	a beverage
a holiday	a tool	a piece of furniture
a state	something sweet	a river

Historic Twenty Questions

The leader thinks of the name of a famous person in history, living or dead. The players ask questions and try to establish the identity of the person within twenty questions. To keep an accurate score, any questioner should raise his hand and get permission to ask a question before he speaks. The leader keeps score on a blackboard or piece of paper, or the score is kept by one of the players.

Questions must be so phrased that the answer can be made with a "yes" or "no" answer. The player who makes the proper identification is leader for the next round.

Twenty-Questions Categories

The categories may be made on the basis of animal, mineral or vegetable. The leader need only announce into which classification his subject falls. The game is played as described above in Historic Twenty Questions.

Panel Twenty Questions

A panel of experts is selected. They sit at the front of the room facing the remainder of the group. The panel may select a subject among themselves and announce to the group whether it is animal, mineral or vegetable, or they may even state specifically that it is a famous person. Anyone in the group, upon receiving recognition from the panel, may ask a leading question of the panel. Any member of the panel may give the answer, which must be a "yes" or "no" answer, or the panel members may take regular turns in answering. The group attempts to guess the panel's subject in twenty questions.

Mystic Mind Reader

The leader works with an accomplice. The accomplice leaves the room while the group selects the name of a famous person, living or dead, within the hearing of the leader. The accomplice is called back into the room. The leader carries on a conversation with him that all the players hear. Somehow in the conversation, the necessary information is transmitted to the accomplice. He ventures a guess and comes up with the correct name. The group tries to guess how the trick is done. This game will keep a group going for hours.

In the method used, the actual name of the person is not transmitted. All clues given are words associated with that famous person. The accomplice tries to guess the name of the person through these words of association. For example, the name chosen is Gandhi. Association clues might be *India, dead, reformer*. As soon as the accomplice thinks he knows the correct name, he says the name aloud. He waits until he is fairly certain, however, before guessing. He may shake his head or look puzzled, indicating that he needs more clues to be certain.

The method of transmitting the clues is done in this manner: The leader takes the accomplice on a trip. The names of cities are used. The first letter in the name indicates the consonants. The vowels are given in a different manner. Each vowel is a number: *a* is one, *e* is two, *i* is three, *o* is four and *u* is five. As each word is spelled out, the end of the word is indicated by a change of method of transportation or announcement of a rest stop. Using the example of Gandhi and the association clues mentioned, the leader would take his accomplice on this trip to spell out the word India. "Let's take a trip. It will take us three days (the third vowel is *I*) to get ready. We'll travel first to New York (that gives the *n*). From there we'll go to Denver (that gives the *d*). We'll stay there three days (another *i*) and one (the last *a*) extra night. (Thus far we have spelled out *India*.) We'll take a plane (this indicates the end of one word and the beginning of another) and go on to Dallas (the *d* in the word *dead*), where we'll visit for two days and one night (the *e* and the *a*) and go back to Denver (the *d*). We'll drive (indicating the beginning of a new word) to Reno (the *r*) and stay for two days (the *e*) and go on to 'Frisco (the *f*). We'll take four (the *o*) days to see the sights and go back to Reno (the *r*) and go from there to Memphis (the *m*) to visit for two days (the *e*) and go on to Raleigh (the *r*). By this time, the accomplice should be able to say without hesitation that the person being identified is Gandhi. This is a game for adults who are well informed and like the challenge of a brain game.

Variations of Mystic Mind Reader

The vowel clues may be given in several ways. One couple played this game by using cities for consonants but using a clucking sound (such as the one used to urge on a horse) for the vowels. For the word "India" their routine would have sounded like this: "Cluck, cluck, cluck (in rapid succession), New York, Denver, cluck, cluck, cluck." With practice the clues can be given so rapidly that the heads of the players will be swimming. Another method of indicating vowels can be with the fingers. Mannerisms of rubbing the face are so common they are almost unnoticeable. The leader may rub his cheek with two fingers, or rub his nose or wipe his palm across his face, the number of fingers used indicating the vowel. Or all motions may be made with the right hand, which may be crossed over the left arm in a natural way but showing from one to five fingers. Another method is to hit the fist in the palm as if to help the thinking process. The number of hits determines which vowel is indicated. A combination of such clues will really stump the group.

Never tell the trick. Any of the smart persons who guess the method can be given opportunities to become the accomplices, but all are sworn to secrecy.

The Mystic Number Game

This will keep a group going for hours trying to guess how the trick is done. The leader and his accomplice print with a pen on their hands, unbeknown to the others, the numbers from one to sixteen in the order shown below or carry a small card in the palm of their hands. Or the numbers may be printed on a large card and placed on the floor for all the players to see. The accomplice leaves the room and the group selects a number. When the accomplice returns, the leader makes a simple statement to the accomplice, who, without hesitation, says the correct number.

The formula by which the accomplice operates is simple. The sixteen numbers are arranged in the manner shown below. They are mentally divided by the leader and his accomplice into four sections of four numbers each. Each individual section is again divided into four parts. Each set of four numbers is given a classification. The upper left section is *male*; the upper right, *female*; the lower left, *animal*; the lower right, *thing*. The correct classification is indicated by the leader by the use of a pronoun or noun in a sentence. Thus if the first noun in the sentence were a *thing*, the accomplice would know that the number was one of the four in the lower right-hand corner. He would not know which of the four numbers it was, however. To determine the specific number, the groups

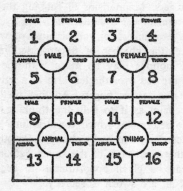

of four numbers are given classifications within their own sets. These are the same as the classification assigned to the larger groups and are in the same corresponding positions. The upper left number in any set of four numbers is *male;* the upper right number is *female;* the lower left number is *animal;* the lower right is *thing*. In giving the clue sentence, the leader uses two nouns, two pronouns or a combination of pronoun and thing, whichever is appropriate. For example, the number selected is eight. It is one of the upper right-hand set of numbers which is the female classification. The exact number is in the lower right corner which is the *thing* position. The clue sentence could be: "*She* sat on the *chair*" or "*Mary* kicked the *ball*." Or if the accomplice is a woman, the sentence might be: "*You* know the *answer*."

The leader and the accomplice should practice this stunt a bit. Their sentences can be most obscure and still give the clues.

When the players are getting warm to the trick, the accomplice and leader can change their clues by switching the classifications around. Playing cards may be used instead of numbers. The cards are placed in four rows of four cards and mentally divided into groups. The stunt works the same, except in this instance the group picks a card instead of a number and the card is identified by the accomplice.

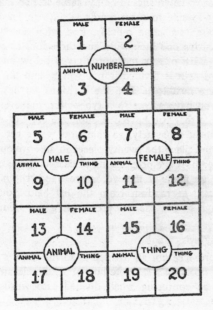

A fifth group of numbers may be added. This set might have a number as a clue with the numbers set up in this fashion and each set of four within a group still using the male, female, animal, thing classification. Thus, any sentence with a number would be in the first set of numbers.

Mystery Words

Divide groups into teams of not more than six players. Have each team gather around a card table or sit on the floor in small circles. Give each team an envelope containing twenty pieces of paper on which are written twenty words.

The words are the same for all teams. At the signal to begin, the teams attempt to use all twenty words and form them into ten complete words. This means that two words used correctly together will form another word. Some words may be used in several different ways, but unless they are used in a certain way there will be words left over and it will be impossible to complete ten words. The pieces of paper on which the words are written should be the same size so that they can be laid side-by-side to form words.

To prepare this game quickly, line off a sheet of typing paper into strips one inch wide and three-fourths of an inch long. Take a list of any ten words given below and put half of one word as it is divided in one square and the other half in the square next to it. Use the divisions as they are given below. If you have access to a typewriter, make enough carbon copies so that you have one duplicate copy of each team. Cut each sheet separately, so that you won't get the words mixed up, and place the twenty pieces in an envelope ready to hand to a team. If the proper kind of carbon is used, duplicate copies may be made if the words are handwritten. Any ten words selected at random from the list below ought to be tough enough to confuse any group for a few minutes.

Suggested Words

These words are not all divided as to the usual syllables or as to aid in pronouncing. Note how some simple and familiar words can be confusing when divided into words and not syllables.

cab - in	drag - on	bed - lam
cad - die	den - ounce	be - at
can - did	ear - nest	be - fore
but - ton	chap - lain	be - get
can - on	corn - ice	rat - her
am - ass	cot - ton	to - me
am - bush	hum - mock	ten - or
all - ow	man - age	men - ding
tar - tan	mass - age	bat - on

ten - don

tar - get

am - use

par - snip

par - son

arc - her

art - less

band - age

ban - tam

bar - gain

bar - on

car - mine

car - rot

cord - on

gas - ping

garb - age

lot - us

here - by

her - on

her - ring

flip - pant

imp - end

in - form

is - sue

off - ice

no - thing

may - or

bit - tern

be - low

be - long

and - iron

end - ow

leg - ate

lay - out

leg - end

less - on

care - less

dam - ask

fell - ow

far - thing

far - row

end - ear

cur - ate

cur - rant

us - age

win - some

wind - ow

yell - ow

what - not

imp - art

imp - lore

hit - her

mass - acre

four - some

fore - cast

for - tune

car - away

can - not

cap - able

pen - dent

plea - sure

end - anger

imp - act

be - am

be - get

bud - get

bob - bin

be - gun

back - lash

set - tee

ass - ail

plea - sing

pass - age

dig - it

ant - hem

feat - her

am - end

rot - ten

ear - ring

snows - hoe

am - our

par - able

par - don

read - just

ray - on

tan - gent

up - set

the - me

asp - halt

ring - let

buck - eye

or - deal

ow - let

us - her

mad - am

fat - her

Lucky Thirteen Guesses

A set of alphabet cards is required for this game. It may be played between two players or between two teams. The players in one team select a word. They pick out the letters in a word from the set of alphabet cards and place the letters, in the proper order, face down on the floor. The members of the other group, in turn, begin guessing the letters contained in the word. If a guess is correct the letter is turned face up. When a player guesses a letter that isn't in the word, a mark is scored against the team. One team attempts to turn all the letters up before it has thirteen points scored against it. To keep the proper score and at the same time show the guessing team which letters it has already eliminated, when a letter is guessed that is not in the word that letter is pulled out from the alphabet and placed where it can be seen. When the number of incorrect letters reaches thirteen, the round is over and a point is scored for the team which selected the word. That team gets another turn to make a new word. In other words, play does not go to the second team until it has correctly guessed a word. Play until one team has ten points.

Variation of Lucky Thirteen Guesses

Play as above with this difference. When a team selects a word, it announces a classification into which the word falls. For example, the team may select the name of a Biblical character, a tropical fruit or a baseball player. With that in mind, the other team goes to work trying to guess the word, guessing letter by letter as described above.

Words and Categories

Prepare a set of alphabet cards. Use standard three-by-five-inch filing cards. Print a letter of the alphabet on each card. On the reverse side of the card, on the lower edge, write a category. Turn the card around and write another category on the other edge. In this manner you will have some fifty categories that can be used. The leader gathers the players around him in a circle, with the leader being part of the circle so that he is facing all the players. Taking the cards which have been shuffled so that the letters are out of order, he announces a category and then turns the card over for all to see the letter. The first player to call out a word in the proper category that begins with the letter shown wins that card. At the end of the game, the player with the most cards is leader. The cards are shuffled again, and turned around so that the second set of categories is used in the next round. The procedure is repeated for each round.

A suggested list of categories follows:

boy's name

girl's name

cities

states

countries

rivers

movie star

something edible

nursery-rhyme character

Shakespearean character

fish

beverage

president

name of magazine

body of water

vegetable

fruit

vehicle

famous person in history

baseball player

writing implement

famous fictional detective

character in a song

automobile

grain

famous general

famous writer

major sport

insect

canal

famous inventor

capital city

famous battle

complimentary adjective

book title

song title

flower

bird

item found in grocery store

item found in drugstore

color

part of a house

weapon

tree

brand or trade-name

herb

type of airplane

famous painter

gem

famous street or boulevard

mineral

In writing the category on the back of the card, be sure that there is at least one possible answer for each category. In other words, for the letters *I*, *Z* and *Q* select categories with care so that some answer is possible for each category.

Index

A

C

Y

IF YOU ENJOYED READING THIS BOOK, YOU'LL BE INTERESTED IN THESE OTHER COLLIER BOOKS ON
Psychology

The titles listed here are available wherever good books are sold
COLLIER BOOKS, 111 Fourth Ave., New York 3, N.Y.